Title Page
Theme Song:
"In the Name of
Love," U2

1 0 0 1
ways to be
ROMANTIC
The #1 National Bestseller

Gregory J.P. Godek

SOURCEBOOKS CASABLANCA™
AN IMPRINT OF SOURCEBOOKS, INC.®
NAPERVILLE, ILLINOIS

Life is simply
too short not to
be romantic.

"Greg Godek should be nominated for the Nobel Peace Prize for teaching *1001 Ways To Be Romantic.*"
—*Boston Magazine*

All brand names and product names used in this book are trademarks, registered trademarks, or trade names of their respective holders. Sourcebooks, Inc., is not associated with any product or vendor in this book. Care has been taken to ensure the information in this book was accurate at the time of publication. Be advised that addresses, phone numbers, and web addresses may change and that companies may go out of business or change products or services.

Originally published in 1999 as *1001 Ways to be Romantic—Author's Annotated Edition.* This is a revised edition.

Published by Sourcebooks Casablanca, an imprint of Sourcebooks, Inc.
P.O. Box 4410, Naperville, Illinois 60567–4410
(630) 961–3900
Fax: (630) 961–2168
www.sourcebooks.com

ISBN-13: 978-1-4022-1004-4
ISBN-10: 1–4022-1004-3

Library of Congress Cataloging-in-Publication Data:
Godek, Gregory J.P.
1001 Ways to be Romantic/Gregory J.P. Godek—Authors Annotated Edition
    p. cm.
ISBN: 1-57071-481-9 (pbk: alk. Paper)
1. Courtship Miscellanea. 2. Dating (Social customs) Miscellanea. 3. Love Miscellanea.
    I. Title
HQ801.G554 1999 646.4'7—dc21 99-36946 CIP

Printed and bound in Canada
TR 10 9 8 7 6 5 4 3

"The book is a well-thumbed romantic Bible that I consult often."
—B. Wicker, Reader

Dedications

- To the romantics—who simply want *more.*

- To the cynics (the romantics of *tomorrow*).

- To those who want to fall in love again.

- To those who want to save romance from the scientists and psychologists—and put it back into the hands of the poets and dreamers and lovers.

- To my son, the future author, Thomas Valentine Godek.

- And to my bride, my best friend, my soul mate, Karyn Lynn Godek...(Who is more fun than you and me? *Nobody.*)

Dedication Page Theme Song:
"[This One Goes Out To] the One I Love," R.E.M.

"I like your book *1001 Ways To Be Romantic*! It will fill your brain with all kinds of wonderful romantic ideas. I like number 584!"
—Oprah Winfrey

Also by Greg Godek

- *10,000 Ways to Say I Love You*
- *Love Coupons*
- *I Love You Coupons*
- *Romantic Questions: 264 Outrageous, Sweet and Profound Questions*
- *Your Relationship Report Card*

"These books are worth memorizing."

—*Boston Herald*

Theme Song:

"Paperback Writer,"
The Beatles

Acknowledgments

- Deborah Werksman
- Bruce Jones
- Kate Broughton
- Dale Koppel
- Mary Ann Sabia
- Mary-Lynne Bohn
- Bonnie Robak
- John & Jean
- Warren & Judy
- Steven Jobs
- Lou Rizzo & UPS
- Sam & The Group
- Wolfgang Amadeus Mozart

Acknowledgments Page Theme Song:
"Thank You,"
Christina Aguilera

" *1001 Ways To Be Romantic.* That seems like an *awful* lot! I mean, guys, if the first *thousand* ideas don't work—what are the chances she's going to stick around when you say, 'Okay, just *one more*'?!"

—Jay Leno, *The Tonight Show*

Contents

Introduction I

Once Upon a Time 4
They Lived Happily
    Ever After 5

Little Things Mean a Lot 7
Bigger Is Better 8

Creative Gifts 9
Creative Gestures 10

Romance on a Budget.............12
Spare No Expense..................13

The Most Important Things
    I've Learned in Twenty
    Years of Teaching Romance....14
The Ten Commandments
    for Loving Couples..............15
Left-Brained* 16
Right-Brained* 17

Romance for Dummies 19
Romance for Smarties 20

What's Your Romantic "Style"?
    (Men) 21
What's Your Romantic "Style"?
    (Women) 22

Flowers 23
Chocolate 24
Jewelry 26
Perfume...............................27
Champagne...........................29
Lingerie 30
It's Not *What* You Do—...........31
—But *How* You Do It................33

To Do 34

I Do 35
Do's & Don'ts 37
Don'ts & Do's 39
Do 41
Don't 42

You Must Remember This 43
A Kiss Is Just a Kiss 45
A Sigh Is Just a Sigh 47
The Fundamental Things
    Apply..............................48
As Time Goes By 50
(Play It Again, Sam) 51

Love Notes (I) 52
Love Notes (II).....................53

Freshman Lessons 55
Sophomore Lessons 56
Junior Lessons 57
Senior Lessons......................58

Le Boudoir...........................59
La Cuisine............................61

Love Notes (III)....................62
Love Notes (IV) 63

"I Love You" 64
"Ai Shite Imasu" 66

Be Creative...........................67
Be Prepared 68

Always, Always, Always 70
Never, Never, *Never*................72
Gifts, Gifts, Gifts 73
Sex, Sex, Sex......................74

Love Notes (V) 76
Love Notes (VI)....................77

Lovesick............................78
Prescriptions for Love............79
Help for the Hopeless............80
Hope for the Helpless............82
Travel Tips........................83
A Suitcase Full of Romance....84
Fun & Games......................85
Weird & Wacky....................86
Cats & Dogs........................87
Satin & Lace.......................89
Strategies & Examples............90
Bed & Breakfasts..................92
Gifts & Presents...................94
Presents & Gifts...................96
Daily & Weekly....................97
Monthly & Yearly.................98
Yin & Yang........................99
Yang & Yin.......................100
Mozart............................101
Elvis...............................102
Lame Excuses (#'s 1-4)..........104
Lame Excuses (#'s 5-8)........105
Lame Excuses (#'s 9-12)........106
Lame Excuses (#'s 13-14)......107
For Men Only.....................108
For Women Only.................109
For Singles Only..................110
For Marrieds Only................111
A Month of Romance:
   Week 1........................113
A Month of Romance:
   Week 2........................114
A Month of Romance:
   Week 3........................116

A Month of Romance:
   Week 4........................117
The Golden Rules
   of Romance....................118
Rules Were Made to
   Be Broken.....................119
Be My Valentine!.................121
Kiss Me, You Fool!...............122
The Mathematics
   of Romance....................123
The Calculus of Love............125
Couplehood......................127
Parenthood.......................129
Erotica............................130
Exotica............................131
Creating an A+ Relationship..132
The Relationship
   Report Card...................135
Common Sense...................137
Uncommon Sense................138
It's the Thought That Counts....139
Actions Speak Louder Than
   Words.........................141
S.W.A.K..........................142
G.M.F.L..........................143
Can't Buy Me Love...............144
I Want to Hold Your Hand....146
Help!..............................147
All You Need Is Love............148
At Home..........................150
At Work..........................151
Sweet Stuff.......................152
Kid Stuff..........................153
Funny Stuff.......................154
Cool Stuff.........................155

Dirty Stuff..........................157

Sex! 158
Surprise! 159
Celebrate! 160
Outrageous!..........................162
Passionate!...........................163

Games People Play 164
Games Lovers Play 165

Off the Wall........................166
On the Wall.........................167

The Myths of Romance (I) 168
The Myths of Romance (II) 169

Men Are from Mars 170
Women Are from Venus 172
Men Are (Not)
    from Mars* 173
Women Are (Not)
    from Venus* 175

Tuning In 176
Fine Tuning.........................178

Starstruck!............................180
Lovestruck! 181

I'm in the Mood for Love 183
I'm in the Mood
    for Chocolate 184

The Gospel According
    to Godek 186

The Gospel According
    to Godek (Revisited)..........187

Getting Down To Business 188

Funny Business.....................189

Resources (I) 190
Resources (II) 192
Resources (III) 193
Resources (IV) 195

Slightly Outrageous 196
Quite Outrageous..................197
Slightly Naughty 198
Quite Naughty 200

Shopping for Dummies 201
Advanced Shopping
    Strategies 202

Words of Love/
    Shakespeare's 204
Words of Love/Poetic............206
Words of Love/Your Words......207
Words of Love/
    the Ancients 209

Memorize This List...............210
Memorize This List, Too 212

Togetherness 213
Twogetherness 215
Two....................................216
Two (II) 218

Gift Ideas (I) 237
Gift Ideas (II) 238

Gift Giving for Dummies 239
Gift Wrapping
    for Dummies 240

Television 241
Radio 242

1-800-ROMANCE 244
www.romance.com 245

Concepts (I) 246
Concepts (II) 248
Erotica (I) 250
Erotica (II) 251
Happy Birthday! (I) 253
Happy Birthday! (II) 254

Money Makes the
    World Go 'Round 256

Love Makes the
World Go 'Round 257

Do It Outside 258
Do It in Public 259

Just Do It! 260
Just a Little Bit Naughty 261

The Gift of Time 263
Time for Love 264

For Singles Only (I) 265
For Singles Only (II)............266

For Marrieds Only (I) 267
For Marrieds Only (II) 268

Merry Christmas 269
Happy Hanukkah 271
Happy Anniversary 272
Happy Birthday 273

Custom-Made 274
One-of-a-Kind...................275

Do-It-Yourself 276
Hide-and-Seek 277

Creativity Exercises 278
Exercising Your Creativity 279

Go Away! 281
Bon Voyage! 282

Cars 283
Sports 284

Dining In..........................285
Dining Out 286

By the Number 287
By the Book 288

Engaging Ideas 289
Will You Marry Me? 290

Marriage Matters 291
Monogamy—*Not Monotony*..........292

(More) Kid Stuff 294
(More) Funny Stuff 295

Bonus Pages: Beyond 1001

The 99 Best Love Songs of the
Twentieth (and Twenty-First)
Centuries (#'s 1-25) 220
The 99 Best Love Songs of the
Twentieth (and Twenty-First)
Centuries (#'s 26-50) 221
The 99 Best Love Songs of the
Twentieth (and Twenty-First)
Century (#'s 51-75) 222
The 99 Best Love Songs of the
Twentieth (and Twenty-First)
Century (#'s 76-99) 223

Songs to Help
Express Your Feelings 224

Best Love Song *Duets* 230
Best *Broadway* Love Songs..........232
Best Romantic Movies & Best
Romantic Movie Couples......233
Best Romantic Comedies 234
Great Date Movies 235
(More) Great Date Movies 236

(More) Cool Stuff 296

(More) Concepts 297

(More) Do-It-Yourself 298

(More) Custom-Made..........299

(More) Surprises 300

(More) Flowers 301

(More) Romance
    on a Budget 302

(More) Bubble Baths 303

Thinking of You 304

Think Different..................305

Choreography 306

Creativity 307

Cruisin' 309

Lovin' 310

Please, Mr. Postman.............311

You've Got Mail*.................312

Mindset of a Romantic.........313

Thinking Like a Romantic......314

Love Is............................316

"Love Is…" 317

The Way to a Man's Heart* 319

Recipes for Romance 320

Aphrodisiacs.....................321

(More) Recipes
    for Romance 323

Classic Romance.................324

Classical Romance...............325

Classic 326

Classy 327

Picture This 328

Picture Perfect....................329

Flower Power 331

More Power!* 332

Greg & Karyn 333

Heart & Soul......................334

Moon & Stars 336

Science Fiction 337

Wonderful Weekends...........339

Mark Your Calendar...........340

February 14th 342

Valentine's Day 343

For Lovers—of Books 344

Sex—by the Book 346

Married…with Children 347

Kid Stuff 348

Rituals of Romance 349

Romantic Rituals 350

Oldies but Goodies..............352

Oldies but Goodies: Movies ..354

Movie Madness 355

Mad About You 356

Great Escapes 357

Getting Away from It All 358

An Anniversary Gift List 360

A Romantic Basics Checklist ..361

Generating Ideas 362

Romantic Brainstorming 364

A Kick in the Pants.............365

Motivating Your Partner
    to Be More Romantic........366

Motivating the
    Romantically Impaired 367

Attitude Adjustment
    Section 368

License to Love 369

Baby, You Can
    Drive My Car 371

Little Love Stories (I) 372

Little Love Stories (II).........373

Notes from an
   A+ Relationship 374
Recipe for an
   A+ Relationship 376

Romance Across America 377
Romance Around the World ..379

The Right Stuff 381
The Write Stuff 382

Real Men *Are* Romantic 383
Real *Women*
   Are Romantic..................384

Guy Stuff 386
Gal Stuff 387

Characteristics of
   True Romantics 388
Characteristics of
   Crazy Romantics.............390

Speaking of Love 391
Speaking of Romance 392

What's in a Name? 394
The Meaning of a Name 395

And Now for Something
   Completely Different* 397
What Is Your Quest?...........398

Getting to Know You 400
Staying in Touch 401

Messages 402
Massages 404

ABC 405
XYZ 408
FYI 409

Gift Ideas 410
Coupon Ideas 411

How to Understand
   Each Other 412

How to Bed & Breakfast 414

Soundtrack to a Love Affair....415
Guidelines for a Love Affair ..417

Bubble Baths (I) 418
Bubble Baths (II) 419

A Touch of Class 420
A Touch 421

Work................................423
Play 424

Sex Tips for Gals 425
Sex Tips for Guys...............426

Romanti¢¢¢ Ideas...............426
Romantic Idea$$$ 427

Lawyers in Love 429
MBAs in Love 430

Hearts (#'s 1-75).................431

In My Humble Opinion 435
My Personal Favorites 436

Best of the Best 438
Best Brief Advice 439

Top 10 Reasons
   to Be Romantic 440
Top 45 Reasons
   to Be Romantic...............441

The End 442
The Beginning 443

Index 445

About the Author 451
Bye! ....Last Page

Introduction

Love may make the world go 'round, but it's *romantic* love that makes the ride worthwhile. We *need* love, but we *crave* romance (just like you *need* broccoli, but you *crave* chocolate!). It's romantic love that allows you to say *emphatically* "I'm *in* love with you," instead of merely, "I love you."

This book is about re-igniting passion and deepening intimacy. It is for young and old, singles and marrieds, men and women. It is for you if you want to turn your *relationship* into a *love affair*.

Why are so many marriages mediocre and boring? Not because they lack love, but because they lack romance. Love is lukewarm, comfortable—while romance is hot, exciting!
Everyone wants passion and romance in his or her life. But—

- Some people are uncertain how to create romance. This book shows you how.
- Some people are stuck in cultural stereotypes. This book helps you appreciate your partner as a unique and special individual.
- And some people have given up the search for romance out of frustration or cynicism. This book will re-inspire you.

"I respect and recommend Greg Godek's writings on love right along with William Shakespeare's."
—Margie LaPanja, Author of *The Goddess' Guide to Love*

Love in the twenty-first century is about practicing old-fashioned values with a modern twist. It is about honoring the timeless values of honesty, commitment, and caring, while expressing them creatively, uniquely, and passionately. And this is where romance comes in. Romance, you see, is the expression of love. Romance brings love *alive* in the world. Without romance, love is a sweet but empty concept.

I believe that expressing *love* is our purpose as human beings. Therefore, anything that helps you achieve this purpose is a *good thing*.

There are thousands, *millions* of ways of expressing love. These 1001 ideas are just the beginning.

Arlo & Janis © 1993. Reprinted by permission of Newspaper Enterprise Association, Inc.

"Greg Godek explains how to get the woo in wooing."

—*Cosmopolitan*

Once Upon a Time...

...two people fell in love. *Just like you.* They did all the classic romantic things. But the passion faded after a few months. Is this *inevitable*??

The "Classics" of romance are *fine* in the beginning. *Then* what??

1a He gave her a dozen roses *and* a box of chocolates on Valentine's Day.

1b She wrote him long, romantic love letters. He sent her greeting cards.

1c They talked and cooed on the phone. During work. And late at night.

1d He took her to see every romantic movie that year.

1e He gave her perfume. She gave him cologne.

1f They celebrated special occasions with a bottle of champagne.

1g She served dinner by candlelight. He served breakfast in bed.

Infatuation and what I call "Generic Romance" only go so far.

...They Lived Happily Ever After

Go beyond "Generic Romance." Couples with A+
Relationships* know the secret of creating unique and
personal ways to express their love.

---

*How would you grade your relationship?

A = Passionate, exciting, loving, fulfilling; not *perfect*—
but clearly excellent.

B = Very good, solid, better-than-most, consistent,
improving.

C = Average, acceptable, status quo, okay—but static, ho-hum,
sometimes *boring.*

D = Below average, unhappy, dismal; bad—but not hopeless.

F = Hopeless, depressing, dangerous; tried everything, it
didn't work.

---

2 Give your lover a dozen roses—and do it with a *creative twist.* Give
eleven red roses and *one* white rose. Attach a note that reads:

"In every bunch there's one who stands out—
and you are that one."

3 Sending a birthday card isn't just a good idea, it's an *obligatory* romantic gesture. But how about doing something *different* this year? On your lover's birthday, send a "thank you" card to his or her mother.

4 Gallantry never *really* goes out of style. So every once in a while kiss her hand with a *flourish*. Note: The *proper* way to kiss a woman's hand is to lower your lips to her hand. You *don't* raise her hand to your lips.

5 Thoughtfulness is merely the beginning! True romantics know how to go "above and beyond the call of duty": Following a bubble bath you've prepared for her, wrap her in a towel that *you've warmed up in the dryer.*

These are the secrets of turning your relationship into a love affair!

Little Things Mean a Lot

6 Gift wrap a wishbone in a jewelry box. Send it to her with a note that says, "I wish you were here."

7 Unplug the TV. Put a note on the screen saying, "Turn *me* on instead."

8 Go through revolving doors together.

Chapter
Theme Song:
"Love Don't Cost a Thing," Jennifer Lopez

9 Keep candles in the car. Eat dinner by candlelight the next time you go to McDonald's.

Pick wildflowers from a field or the side of the road.

10 Run your hands under hot water before joining your partner in bed(!)

11 Look—no, *gaze*—into each other's eyes more often.

12 Write him a little love note. Insert it into the book he's reading.

The relationship secret that's not really a secret: Express your love in lots of little ways.

Bigger Is Better

13 Go for it in a BIG way. Pull out *ALL* the stops. Don't tip-toe into being more romantic. Be outrageously romantic.

14 GIANT BANNERS are available from Supergram. The banners are printed on white or colored paper, and lamination is optional. The banners are about a foot tall, and tend to run from twelve feet long to thirty feet or more, depending on your message. Call 800-3-BANNER, or visit the website at www.supergram.net.

> Make a gesture that's as big as your heart.

15 Make a GIANT greeting card out of a big cardboard box.

16 Make a custom banner—a BIG banner—to welcome him home from a trip (or just to say "I love you!"). Use construction paper and crayons, or poster board and markers, or old sheets and spray paint.

17 Craig liked doing things in a *big* way. He was a dramatic and loud (though lovable) kind of guy. Mary, on the other hand, was proper and quiet (and just as lovable). Craig sometimes criticized Mary for not being expressive or outrageous enough. Until...one day when Craig returned home from a business trip and was greeted by Mary—and two hundred forty-three members of the local high school marching band on their front lawn. (Most people don't consider John Philip Sousa marches to be romantic—but *Craig* does!)

> You, too, can probably hire your local high school marching band for a relatively modest donation to its band fund!

Creative Gifts

18 Roses are fine—but a simple daisy can *really* communicate your feelings if you give it with flair. Pick a single daisy. Attach a note that says: *"She loves me—she loves me not."* (But don't leave anything to chance: Trim the daisy so there is an *odd* number of petals!)

19 You can create a theme gift-and-gesture by selecting the right love song:
• Get the song "I Dare You to Move," by Switchfoot—
  And rent the movie *A Walk to Remember*, featuring the song.
• Get the song "Northern Sky," by Nick Drake—
  And rent the movie *Serendipity*, featuring the song.
• Get the song "I Love You," by Sarah McLachlan—
  And rent the movie *Message in a Bottle*, featuring the song.

20 Here's how you can create a love note that *never comes to an end.* Structure a short love note or love poem so that it loops back on itself (where the last word leads back to the first word). Then write it on a Möbius strip.*
• First, cut a strip of paper about two inches wide and eighteen inches long.
• Now, compose your special love note. (See example on right.)

An "infinite" love note:
I love you,
And you love me;
This is as it ought to be.
Ask me why
And I'll reply—
I love you,
And you love me...

- Then write it on both sides of the strip of paper.
- Then twist one end of the paper strip 180 degrees and tape it to the other end.
- You've just created a Möbius strip.

• • •

*A Möbius strip is a curious geometric phenomenon through which you can literally turn a common two-sided piece of paper into *a surface with only one side*.

Get your honey: Two small gifts and one big one. Two red gifts and three green ones. One funny gift and two sweet ones.

Creative Gestures

21 Fake a power outage at home. (Loosen the fuses or throw the breaker switches.) With no TV to tempt you...with no computer to occupy you...with no furnace to heat you...you pretty much have *no choice* but to get out the candles, huddle around the fireplace and be romantic!

This is why the birth rate always rises nine months after every major power outage. True!

22 Being a liberated gal, the bride wanted to use a *hyphenated* last name when they got married. Being a romantic guy, the groom observed that the hyphen is *also* a minus sign. *Hmmm—what to do??* The creative couple now writes their name like this: Mr. & Mrs. J. Smith+Brown.

23 When she's traveling alone, arrange with an airline attendant to have a gift or flower delivered to her after the flight is airborne.

24 Her husband is a handyman. He loves to take things apart and put them back together again. She gave him a fancy DVD recorder for his birthday. Here's the creative twist: She took it apart and gave it to him wrapped in *sixteen* different boxes!

Copy a romantic poem onto fancy parchment paper. Roll it into a scroll, tie it with a red ribbon, and present it to your lover.

25 Play Trivial Pursuit. (In preparation for the game, create some *custom* cards that ask trivia questions about your relationship.)

Romance on a Budget

26a Write a love letter. Mail it. Cost: 41¢.*

26b Pick flowers from the side of the road. Cost: Zero.

26c Watching falling stars together. Cost: Nada.

26d Walk hand-in-hand together. Cost: Nothing.

You can be romantic on a budget without being "cheap."

26e Memorize her favorite poem or passage from a book—and recite it during lovemaking. Cost: Zilch.

26f Kiss for five full minutes. Cost: Absolutely free.

26g Go to vacation spots *off-season*. Cost: 20 percent to 50 percent less than usual.

• • •

*Postal rates subject to the whims of the U.S. government.

Frugal travel tip: When the U.S. dollar is strong compared with foreign currency, travel abroad. When the U.S. dollar is weak, travel within the country.

Spare No Expense

27a The best way to spend the *most* money for the *smallest* gift is to buy *diamonds*.

27b The best way to spend the *most* money for *food* is to dine at a *five-star restaurant*.

27c The best way to spend the *most* money for *lingerie* is to buy an outfit from La Perla.

27d The best way to spend the *most* money to *fly* is to travel first class.

Play Monopoly together. Use real money!

La Perla has three shops in New York, Miami, and Los Angeles. Call 212-459-2775, or visit the website at www.laperla.com.

27e The best way to spend the *most* money on *men's clothing* is to have a suit *custom-made*.

27f The best way to spend the *most* money on *women's clothing* is to buy her *haute couture*.

27g The best way to spend the *most* money on a *hotel room* is to reserve the *honeymoon suite*.

"True love is eternal, infinite, and always like itself. It is equal and pure, without violent demonstrations: it is seen with white hairs and is always young in the heart."
—Honore de Balzac

The Most Important Things I've Learned in Twenty Years of Teaching Romance

28

- *How* is more important than *why*.
- Gender stereotyping blinds you to your partner's uniqueness.
- The speed of love is 1.7 mph.
- Everybody wants an A+ Relationship.
- Love has no reason. It never needs to be explained or defended.
- "Good chemistry" has nothing to do with compatibility.
- You can't keep the infatuation—but you can keep the passion.
- The process *must* be respected. (There ain't no shortcuts.)
- Everyone is an amateur when it comes to matters of the heart.
- The metaphors of love you use create your reality.
- Romantics are happier than most people.
- "Communication" is, maybe, 10 percent of an A+ Relationship. Creating a loving long-term relationship is the most difficult, time-consuming, and complicated challenge you will face in your entire life. Also the most rewarding.
- The passion is more important than the happy ending. Life is too short not to be romantic.

"Love, like a river, will cut a new path whenever it meets an obstacle."
—Crystal Middlemas

Life is too short *not* to be romantic.

The Ten Commandments
for Loving Couples

29

1. Thou shalt give 100 percent.
2. Thou shalt treat your partner as the unique individual he or she truly is.
3. Thou shalt stay connected through word and deed.
4. Thou shalt accept change and support growth in yourself and your mate.
5. Thou shalt live your love.
6. Thou shalt share: the love and fear, the work and play.
7. Thou shalt listen, listen, listen.
8. Thou shalt honor the subtle wisdom of the heart and listen to the powerful insights of the mind.
9. Thou shalt not be a jerk or a nag.
10. Thou shalt integrate the *purity* of spiritual love with the *passion* of physical love and the *power* of emotional love.

If love is really your top priority, then you never really "sacrifice" for it.

"There is nothing holier in this life of ours than the first consciousness of love, the first fluttering of its silken wings."
—Henry Wadsworth Longfellow

*Left-Brained**

30 For those of you who like to analyze and compute things:

- Spend 10% more time together.
- Generate 33% more laughter in your life together.
- Focus 100% of your attention when listening to him or her.
- Create a 10% increase in the amount of fun you have together.
- Give up 10% of your hobby time, and give it to your partner.
- Reduce your complaining by 50%.
- Reduce your criticizing by 62%.
- Say "I love you" 300% more often.
- Spend 10% as much time kissing as you spend watching TV every day.
- Be 25% more creative in your relationship.
- Be 10% more thoughtful/considerate.
- If you're talkative by nature, talk 20% less, and listen 20% more.
- If you're quiet by nature, open up and talk 20% more.

> *Left-Brained people tend to be logical and practical. They *think* first and *feel* second.

B.C. © 1978. By permission of Johnny Hart and Creators Syndicate, Inc.

31 Analyze the number of your sexual encounters as a function of the frequency of your romantic gestures. Is there a correlation? (Hmm...There just *might* be a lesson here!)

Right-Brained*

32 Characteristics of True Romantics:
- Taps into his or her creativity regularly.
- Is just a little bit "naughty."
- Takes love seriously—
- But has a great sense of humor.
- Makes his or her intimate love relationship a top priority. Makes romantic gestures without ulterior motives.
- Is flexible.
- Celebrates sexuality.
- Appreciates his or her partner's uniqueness.
- Celebrates both the masculine and the feminine.
- Is a pretty good mind-reader.
- Sees the world in a slightly offbeat way.
- Maintains a deep, spiritual connection with his or her partner.
- Is spontaneous.
- Defines him or herself as a "lover"—regardless of other roles.
- Remembers important dates and anniversaries.
- Continuously learns and grows.

> *Right-Brained people tend to be creative and spontaneous. They *feel* first and *think* second.

- Is in touch with his or her feelings.
- Pursues new and different experiences.
- Gives of himself or herself without expectations.
- Does lots of little things.
- Gives without being asked.

33 One morning, for no particular reason, Susan quietly slipped out of bed, tiptoed to the stereo, selected "Fanfare for the Common Man" (by Aaron Copeland), cranked the volume *all the way up*, started the music, and gleefully leaped on a very surprised (but delighted) Michael.

Additional music that gives the same effect:
- "The William Tell Overture," Gioacchino Rossini
- "The 1812 Overture," Peter Ilych Tchaikovsky

Who are the better romantics: right-brainers or left-brainers? Everyone *thinks* it's the right-brained, creative types by a long shot. But a great many left-brainers are tremendously romantic. It's just that the right-brainers are louder and more spontaneous about it. But those logical types are great planners of surprises and great at noticing little but important things about their partners.

Romance for Dummies

34 Practice "Even-Day/Odd-Day" Romance: On *even* days it's *your* turn to be romantic, and on *odd* days it's your *partner's* turn.

> Variation on a theme: "Flip-a-Coin" Romance

35 No time—or too lazy—to wrap those gifts? Buy fancy bags and pre-decorated boxes for gift-wrapping presents.

36 Ask her best girlfriend—or her mother—for help. Ask her to go shopping with you (secretly!). Tell her you want to spend *one afternoon* shopping for a *year's worth of gifts* for your partner. Establish a budget, let her think about it for a week, then go shopping together.

37 Place a *standing order* with a local florist. Give him your anniversary date, her birth date, and instruct him to send flowers *automatically* on those dates. Also on

> (Shhh! Keep this one under your hat!)

Valentine's Day, and (if it's appropriate) on Mother's Day, and—just to be safe—have him send a bouquet once a month. Give the florist your charge card number and have him bill you automatically. This technique is for the forever-forgetful and the terminally unorganized! I know that the true romantics out there will be *aghast* at this suggestion, but hey, sometimes the end justifies the means.

> "For it was not into my ear you whispered, but into my heart. It was not my lips you kissed, but my soul."
> —Judy Garland

Romance for Smarties

Efbs mpwfs:
J mpwf zpv, J bepsf zpv,
J offe zpv, J xbou zpv,
Mpwf boe ljttft,
Nf

38 Write a love letter in *code*. Give your lover a challenge:
- Try a message in Morse Code (See the message at left.)
- Next is a simple code, created by shifting all of the letters in the alphabet one place to the right (A becomes B; B becomes C, etc.).

39 Visit a museum. Visit an art gallery. Walk a formal garden. Attend a symphony. Attend an opera.

40 $(\sqrt{144} \times 3) + (8/\pi \times \pi/2)$
Attend a lecture. Take a class together at a local college. Expanding your horizons can deepen your relationship.

Note: Operas aren't as painful as you may assume they are. So give one a try!

What's Your Romantic "Style"? (Men)

41 Which person or character most closely matches your or your lover's style of romance? Identifying the similarities and differences can help you become more aware of your own strengths and weaknesses, and can help you express love in ways that your partner appreciates most.

- The *Romeo* Type: Passionate and impetuous
- The *Fred Astaire* Type: Sophisticated and elegant
- The *Humphrey Bogart* Type: Tough guy with a heart of gold
- The *Jimmy Stewart* Type: The boy next door
- The *James Bond* Type: The playboy heartbreaker
- The *Indiana Jones* Type: Adventurous and charmingly bumbling
- The *Rhett Butler* Type: Arrogant but charming
- The *Don Quixote* Type: Irrepressible and outrageous
- The *Don Juan* Type: Seductive and charming
- The *Cyrano de Bergerac* Type: Witty and literary
- The *Paul Newman* Type: Rugged and quiet
- The *James Dean* Type: The rebel and bad boy
- The *Sean Connery* Type: Dashing and experienced
- The *Vincent van Gogh* Type: Artistic and moody
- The *Lord Byron* Type: Poet and dreamer
- The *Frank Sinatra* Type: Tough but suave
- The *James T. Kirk* Type: The adventurous seducer
- The *Clark Gable* Type: Smooth and smart

> You romantic devil, you!

What's Your Romantic "Style"? (Women)

42 Okay ladies, it's *your* turn. What's your romantic style? (Guys: What is your gal's romantic style?)

- The *Scarlett O'Hara* Type: Feisty and dramatic
- The *Meg Ryan* Type: The girl next door, sweet and adorable
- The *Juliet* Type: Passionate and impetuous
- The *Jane Eyre* Type: Romantic and idealistic
- The *Marilyn Monroe* Type: Sultry and seductive
- The *Billie Holiday* Type: Artistic and loyal to a fault
- The *Jane Seymour* Type: Classic and elegant
- The *Elizabeth Barrett Browning* Type: Poetic and artistic
- The *Cher* Type: Exotic and creative
- The *Mae West* Type: Sassy and bold
- The *Ingrid Bergman* Type: Smooth and intriguing
  - The *Madonna* Type: Bold and fun
    - The *Greta Garbo* Type: Sensual and enigmatic

Is your romantic style subtle or obvious?

"Men always want to be a woman's first love—women like to be a man's last romance."
—Oscar Wilde

Flowers

43 "A flower a day keeps the divorce lawyer away." (Overheard one evening in the Romance Class.)

44 Did you know...that different color roses have different meanings?
- Red roses = LOVE & PASSION
- Pink Roses = A *Romantic* Friendship
- Yellow Roses = Friendship & Respect
- White Roses = Purity & Adoration

You single folks should pay *special* attention to this. Early in a relationship is often too soon to send *red* roses. If you're not absolutely *certain* that you're both madly, passionately, crazy in love—*don't* give *red* roses! Send pink or yellow.

Chapter Theme Song: "This Flower," Kasey Chambers

Fabulous gift idea

For flower-lovers, nature-lovers and art-lovers alike: Get your partner a beautiful botanical illustration that's personalized with your message or quote in calligraphy. Visit www.heartstringsdesigns.com.

45 Place a single flower under the windshield wiper of his car.

46
- 1-800-FLOWERS, www.1800flowers.com
- 1-800-580-2913, www. proflowers.com
- 1-800-SEND-FTD, www.ftd.com

It's hard to go wrong with flowers!

Chocolate

47 Reliable sources report that chocolate just may *really* be an aphrodisiac. (Great news for chocoholics!) Chocolate contains large amounts of phenylethylamine, a chemical that also is naturally produced by the body when one is experiencing feelings of love.

48 *Long-stem chocolate roses!* Have a dozen shipped to your sweetie. Call Lyla's Chocolates at 415-383-8887.

English: "Excuse me, where is the nearest chocolate?"

French: "Excusez-moi, où est le chocolat le plus proche?"

German: "Entschuldigen Sie bitte, wo ist die nächste Schokolade?"

49 (Inspired by *Willy Wonka and the Chocolate Factory*.) Create a custom contest just for your favorite chocoholic. Make a series of *Golden Tickets* to insert in chocolate bar wrappers. Make the tickets redeemable for romantic gifts and gestures. If you use your imagination, this *one* idea could supply the two of you with romantic fun for *years* to come.

"What's important in life?" When you poll people, you pretty much get these answers—in this order: 1) Love, 2) Sex, 3) Money, 4) Chocolate

50

- Ghirardelli Chocolates: 800-877-9338, www.ghirardelli.com
- See's Candies: 800-347-7337, www.sees.com
- Godiva Chocolatier: 800-9-GODIVA, www.godiva.com
- Hershey: 800-437-7439, www.hersheypa.com
- Harry & David: 800-547-3033, www.harryanddavid.com
- Gevalia: 800-GEVALIA, www.gevalia.com

Jewelry

51 Get her a diamond cut into a heart shape. (It's not the most *brilliant* cut—but it is the most *meaningful.*)

52
- Hide a diamond ring in a cake.
- Bury a necklace in a pie.
- Drape a pearl necklace around her teddy bear's neck.

Note: Talk to your local jeweler before cooking or baking jewelry or hiding gems in your food. Why? Because pearls dissolve in champagne and rubies crack when heated!

When it comes to jewelry, bigger is *not* better—*better* is better! In other words, quality is what counts.

53 Here are the twelve birthstones—and their symbolic meanings.

Accompany the jewelry gift with a poem about the symbolic meaning of his or her birthstone:
- January: *Garnet*—faith & constancy
- February: *Amethyst*—happiness & sincerity
- March: *Aquamarine*—courage & hope
- April: *Diamond*—innocence & joy

Buying fine jewelry is unlike any other purchase. It's an investment in a gift that should last many lifetimes! Learn more by contacting the Jewelry Information Center at www.jic.org.

- May: *Emerald*—peace & tranquility
- June: *Pearl*—purity & wisdom
- July: *Ruby*—nobility & passion
- August: *Sardonyx*—joy & power
- September: *Sapphire*—truth & hope
- October: *Opal*—tender love & confidence
- November: *Topaz*—fidelity & friendship
- December: *Turquoise*—success & understanding

Songs to accompany your jewelry gifts:

"Turquoise," Vast
"Diamonds and Pearls," Prince
"Emerald," Thin Lizzy
"Fields of Gold," Sting
"Pearl," Sade
"Sapphire," The Clash
"Ruby Red," Jann Arden
"Diamonds are a Girl's Best Friend," Marilyn Monroe

Perfume

54 There probably would be no such thing as perfume if it weren't for the concept of romantic love. Think about it. We'd still have champagne, chocolate, flowers, and jewelry. But there would simply be no reason for perfume to exist if it weren't for love. So one could say that:

Perfume = Romance

Perfume may be the essence of romance. Romantic love distilled into a bottle. Interesting, huh?

55 You *could* have a special perfume custom-made for your one-of-a-kind woman! Match the fragrance to her personality: Is she light and breezy, or sophisticated and alluring, or sexy and sensual?
• Caswell-Massey, 518 Lexington Avenue, New York City, New York 10017; 212-755-2254 or 800-326-0500, or visit www.caswellmassey.com.

56 Get the whole "family of products" in the fragrance of her favorite perfume (bath powder, soaps, cremes, candles, etc.).

57 Well *of course* you should get perfume for her that she simply loves. *And* a scent that reflects her personality. And a scent that *you* like!

Send her a message or create a theme gift through the *name* of a perfume:

Allure
Attraction
Chance
Cool Water
Destiny
Eternity
Glamorous
Glow
Intuition
Impulse
Obsession
Paris
Serenity
Passion
Pleasures
Tabu
White Diamonds

Champagne

58 Romantic arithmetic: Champagne = Celebration.

59 Buy a case of champagne. Label each of the twelve bottles:

1. His birthday
2. Her birthday
3. For a midnight snack
4. Anniversary (of meeting)
5. Anniversary (of marrying)
6. For a picnic
7. Before making love
8. Celebrate a milestone at work
9. Christmas/Hanukkah/holiday
10. The first day of spring
11. The first snowfall
12. For making up after a fight

Chapter Theme Song:
"Champagne High,"
Sister Hazel

60 Buy wine and champagne *by the case.* You'll typically get a 20 percent discount off the per-bottle price. You'll save money, and always have a bottle on hand for those "Spontaneous Celebrations."

61 Always have a bottle of Dom Perignon on hand. (For those extra-special occasions.)

62 Always have several bottles of Korbel on hand. (For those spontaneous little celebrations.)

You do, of course, have two crystal champagne flutes with your initials on them. Don't you?!

Lingerie

6 3 The topic of lingerie is the one place where love, sex, and romance all come together. This is why the topic is so enticing, so sexy, so sensitive.
- Gals: Guys really, really, really, really, *really* love gals in lingerie.
- Guys: Approach this topic *sensitively.*

6 4
- Gals: When in doubt, wear a garter belt and stockings.
- Guys: When in doubt, more foreplay.

6 5 Go through her Victoria's Secret catalog and rate the items one through ten. Write your ratings in the margins.

6 6 Guys: Spread out on the bed the lingerie outfit you'd like her to wear.

6 7 I've been asked by several men in the Romance Class to convey this message to the ladies: "Nothing completes a great lingerie outfit like a pair of great high heels."

Special note to gals who have health concerns about high heels: "You don't need to be on your feet for more than a minute or two."

When you're in Los Angeles, California:

Visit the Lingerie Museum, featuring items from Mae West, Zsa Zsa Gabor and Madonna, plus four decades of lingerie history. At Frederick's of Hollywood, 6608 Hollywood Boulevard, in Hollywood. Call 323-466-8506.

Lingerie Coupon

Nighties! Teddies! Garter Belts!

This coupon is good for a
$100 shopping spree.

Shoppers must be at
least 18 years of age.

It's Not What You Do—

68 Don't just walk into the house tonight the way you always do. Pause on the porch; ring the doorbell; and greet her with one red rose and a bottle of champagne.

69 *Never* give a gift or present without wrapping it. Get extra-nice wrapping paper and fancy bows. If you truly have two left thumbs, get the store to do your gift-wrapping for you.

70 One woman in the Romance Class told us that her husband always manages to incorporate her favorite teddy bear into his many gift presentations.

- He's given her diamond earrings by putting them on the bear's ears.
- He's strung pearls around the bear's neck.
- He's packed the bear inside boxes along with other gifts.
- He's put funny notes in the bear's paw.

71 Not that it really matters, but I was just wondering...

- Why do we have birthday cakes and wedding cakes, but no anniversary cakes or Valentine's cakes?
- Why do we have Christmas tree ornaments, but no special ornaments with which to celebrate other special occasions?
- Why is Columbus Day a national holiday, but Valentine's Day *isn't*?
- Why is it crude to tell jokes that characterize races and religions in stereotyped ways, but it's acceptable to be a "gender bigot" and stereotype men and women?

Do it with style
Do it with flair.
Do it with attention
to detail.
Do it with a flourish.

—But How You Do It

72 Want to jazz up the presentation of a special meal? Buy a little hunk of dry ice from a local ice house. Put it in a bowl of water and place it on your serving tray. You'll create wondrous, billowing white clouds!

73 Strings of pearls have been known to appear inside real oyster shells at fancy restaurants.

> How about presenting a gift of pearls to the tune of "A String of Pearls," by Glenn Miller?

74 And many diamond rings seem to find their way to the bottom of a glass of champagne.

75 Okay, let's say you've decided to give her the complete collection of The Moody Blues' (her all-time favorite group) albums. Let's now give this gift a creative twist. Instead of simply wrapping the CDs and handing them to her, do this:

- Remove the CDs from their cases.
- Hide the CDs around the house.
- Gift-wrap all the CD cases separately.
- Attach a note to each gift...
- Each note gives clues to the location of the CD...
- And each note's clues are based on each album's title.
  - *Days of Future Passed* is hidden in a photo album.
  - *To Our Children's Children's Children* is in the kids' toy box.
  - *On the Threshold of a Dream* is hidden in your bedroom.
  - *Long Distance Voyager* is hidden along with airline tickets to Tahiti.

> Best love songs by The Moody Blues:
>
> "Nights in White Satin"
> "Watching and Waiting"
> "Want to Be With You"
> "So Deep Within You"
> "In My World"

To Do

76 Write "Romantic Reminders" on your "To Do" list at work. (What's the use of being a great success in the business world if you're a miserable failure in your personal life?) Romantic Reminders will remind you that there's another part of your life that's quite important.

A great book: *To-Do Lists of the Dead,* by Jonathan Katz

77

- A do-it-yourself romantic Saturday afternoon: 2 bicycles, 5 hours, 1 bottle of wine.
- A do-it-yourself romantic date: 2 movie tickets, 1 Tub-o'-Popcorn, 2 Cokes.
- A do-it-yourself romantic picnic: 1 loaf of bread, 1 hunk of cheese, 1 bottle of wine.
- A do-it-yourself romantic Sunday afternoon: 1 canoe, 1 lazy day, 2 starstruck lovers.

78 Pay close attention to the subtle signals, the non-verbal clues, the body language and tone of voice that your lover uses.

79 *Anticipate* your partner.
- Is he stressed at work? Would he like a back rub or time alone?
- Does she need a dinner out or a movie in?
- Does he need extra sleep or a surprise lovemaking session?
- Take extra good care of her during the most difficult days of her menstrual cycle.

If *some* form of romance is not on your To Do list, you may want to re-evaluate your priorities.

I Do

80 Special musical selections for a "Wedding Day Playlist" for your iPod, for you to share with your bride or groom on your wedding day:

- "Life Is Wonderful," by Jason Mraz, on the album *Mr. A-Z*
- "Untitled," by Teitur, on the album *Poetry and Aeroplanes*
- "You Are So Beautiful (To Me)", by Joe Cocker, on the album *I Can Stand a Little Rain*
- "Truly," by Lionel Richie, on the album *Lionel Richie*
- "With You I'm Born Again," by Billy Preston & Syreeta, on the album *Late at Night*
- "Reflections in a Summer Pond," by Paul Winter, on the album *Sun Singer*
- "Overjoyed," by Christine Kane, on the album *Right Outta Nowhere*

Chapter Theme Song:
"I Do (Cherish You)," 98 Degrees

81 For those of you who do not want a traditional wedding ceremony:

• Get married on *skis*—at Heavenly Resort, in Lake Tahoe, California. Call 800-HEAVENLY; or visit www.skiheavenly.com.

Get married *underwater*—at the Amoray Dive Resort in Key Largo, Florida. Call 800-4AMORAY, or visit www.amoray.com.

• Tie the knot on a *beach*—on the tropical island of Fiji. Call 800-YEA-FIJI; or visit www.bulafiji.com.

• Create a truly *fairy-tale wedding*—at Walt Disney World, in Orlando, Florida. Call 407-828-3400; or visit www.disneyweddings.com

82 Plan ahead—*way* ahead! Get a friend to buy fifty of the top magazines and newspapers that are on the newsstand on your wedding day. (Everything from *The New York Times* to *The New Yorker*; *Cosmo* and *Playboy*; *TV Guide* and *Time*; *Harper's* and *Highlights for Children*; *Sports Illustrated* and *The National Enquirer*.)

Pack them safely away (in a dark, dry, cool place) and present them to your partner—*on your twenty-fifth wedding anniversary!*

Do's & Don'ts

83

■ Don't buy roses for Valentine's Day—
❏ Do buy flowers that begin with the first letter of her name.

• • •

■ Don't go to the beach on crowded weekends—
❏ Do go mid-week.

• • •

■ Don't go to popular vacation spots during their busy seasons—
❏ Do go right before or after the busy season.

• • •

■ Don't turn yourself into a martyr—
❏ Do make some sacrifices for each other

• • •

■ Don't read the newspaper at the breakfast table—
❏ Do talk with one another over breakfast.

• • •

■ Don't give him a birthday present—
❏ Do give him seven gifts, one for each day of his birthday week.

• • •

■ Don't leave lovemaking until just before sleeping—
❏ Do schedule more time for foreplay.

• • •

■ Don't make love the same way every time—
❏ Do eliminate distractions for two to three hours.

- Don't rush through lovemaking—
- Do slow down! You'll both enjoy yourselves, and each other, more.

• • •

- Don't: Negotiate—as if your relationship were a business deal—
- Do: Learn the gentle art of loving compromise.

• • •

- Don't try to change your partner—
- Do accept him or her for the special, unique person he or she is.

• • •

- Don't act your age—
- Do wacky things; express your quirkiness; be creative.

■ *Don't* wait.
❏ *Do* be romantic.

(I mean now— *right now!* Put down this book and go do something romantic!)

Don'ts & Do's

84 Don't try to have a *"perfect" relationship*. There's no such thing. Expecting one will only paralyze you. Once you eliminate the goal of perfection, nothing can hold you back! You'll lose your fear of "doing it right." You'll lose your fear of taking risks. And people who take risks, who live life creatively and sponta-neously, live more fun-filled, passionate lives.

Chapter Theme Songs (and good advice):

"Don't Change," Everclear

"Don't Stay Home" and "Don't Dwell," 311

"Don't Leave Me Alone," Extreme

"Don't Mess with My Love," M2M

"Don't Walk Away," MXPX

"Don't Stop Dancing," Creed

"Don't Shut Me Out," Keith Urban

"Don't Let Me Down," No Doubt

85

■ Don't buy gifts at the last minute. (You probably won't find a great gift, and you probably will pay top dollar.)

❏ Do plan ahead. (Less stress for you, more joy for your partner, less effect on your wallet.)

86 *Don't relate to your lover as a stereotype.* He's an individual, not a statistic. And she's a unique person, not "just like all women." Today's tabloid topics, talk-show trends, and sex surveys have only limited relevance to you and your lover and your relationship. Take it all with a large grain of salt. *You'll never lose by treating your partner as a unique and special person.*

More Chapter Theme Songs (and good advice):

"Don't Be Stupid (You Know I Love You)," Shania Twain

"Don't Make Me Love You," Christina Aguilera

"Don't Forget About Us," Mariah Carey

"Don't Stop the Love," 98 Degrees

"Don't Push Love Away," The Juliana Theory

Do

87

- *Go out of your way for him or her.* Being romantic only when it's convenient is like giving flowers on Valentine's Day—it's expected and, frankly, it's no big deal!
- *Always* pick him or her up at the airport after a trip—no matter what time the flight arrives
- Offer to stop at the store on the way home from work.
- Take care of the kids when it's not "your turn."

88

Decide to fall in love all over again. That's it—just *decide.* You don't need to read books that analyze your relationship. You don't need therapy. You just need to *decide.*

Just think of the great opportunity you have: The less romantic you've been, the more dramatic the change will be! I've had guys in the Romance Class simply *make up their minds* to be more romantic. They've reported that this simple decision led to falling in love with their wives all over again.

Overwhelm him/her!
Honor him/her!
Woo him/her!
Date him/her!
Stimulate him/her!
Nurture him/her!
Understand him/her!
Support him/her!
Calm him/her!
Surprise him/her!
Delight him/her!

89

Accompany each other to doctor appointments. Going along for routine check-ups gives you opportunities for quickie coffee dates. And accompanying him or her when there are difficult problems allows you to provide emotional support.

90 *Listen!* Listen with your ears, mind, and heart. Listen for the meaning behind his actions. Listen for the message behind her words.

Don't

91

- Don't gloat when you're right.
- Don't sulk when you don't get your way.
- Don't worry—be happy.
- Don't try to pack too much into the weekend.
- Don't over-schedule your vacations.
- Don't make the same mistake twice.
- Don't undermine your partner's authority with your kids.
- Don't reveal the ending of a movie!
- Don't spend your "Prime Time" watching TV.
- Don't drink and drive—not ever.
- Don't stop.
- Don't be a "cover-stealer" in bed.
- Don't interrupt when he or she is talking.
- Don't wait—express your love right now.
- Don't hold grudges.
- Don't take one another for granted.
- Don't go a single day without saying, "I love you."
- Don't let your mind wander during conversations.

Chapter Theme Song:
"Don't Save it All for Christmas Day,"
Celine Dion

- Don't wait for your partner to read your mind.
- Don't just sign "Love" on your Valentine's Day card; be eloquent.
- Don't be so judgmental.
- Don't wait until the last minute to make Valentine's Day dinner reservations.
- Don't even try to leave the house during a blizzard. Snuggle together for a romantic day off.

"Spoil your husband, but don't spoil your children."
—Louise Seier Giddings Currey

You Must Remember This

92 Remember: Romance isn't barter!

You'll lose every time if you use romantic gestures to barter for favors or forgiveness. The following "unspoken agreements" may have had some validity in the past, but they don't cut it anymore: "I'll take you to a movie and dinner if you'll sleep with me," "I'll cook dinner for you if you'll let me nag you," "I'll give you flowers if you'll forgive me for being a jerk."

Romance is the expression of your love for that special person. It's not a bargaining chip. If you use it as one, you cheapen the gesture, devalue your relationship, and up the ante for the next round of bartering.

You must remember— her birthday! Or your name is "Mud," bud!

93

- Start saving mementos of your life together. Create a "Memories Box."
- Save movie stubs, theater programs, and restaurant receipts.
- Save sand and seashells from your beach vacations.
- Save labels from wine bottles and corks from champagne bottles.
- Save restaurant menus and placemats.
- Save maps from your road trips.
- Save plane tickets, movie tickets, event tickets, theater tickets, etc.
- Use these mementos to create a unique gift for a special anniversary. Make a collage, a scroll, a memory box, or a scrapbook.

You must remember—your *anniversary!* Why not take a personal holiday?

You must remember—*Valentine's Day!* C'mon, spring for flowers *and* chocolates!

A Kiss Is Just a Kiss

94

- Give her one Hershey's Kiss.
- Give her one *thousand* Hershey's Kisses.
- Remove all the little paper strips (that say "Kisses" on them) from a couple hundred Hershey's Kisses. Fill a little jewelry box with them. Wrap 'em up and present them to her.
- Write a clever certificate explaining that the little paper slips are coupons redeemable for one kiss each.

FYI—33,000,000 Hershey's Kisses are made daily.

95

Best movie kisses:

- *The Notebook:* When rain-drenched Noah and Allie can no longer deny their feelings and kiss in the rain.
- *Spider-Man:* Mary Jane uncovers Spidey's mouth from beneath his mask and kisses him while he hangs upside-down.
- *Gone with the Wind:* When Rhett steals a major kiss from Scarlett while he's helping her escape as Atlanta burns.

FYI—For love letters and emails:

X's symbolize kisses; O's symbolize hugs.

Use capital X's for smooches; lower case x's for pecks.

Use capital O's for bear hugs; lower case o's for squeezes.

96 Best songs about kissing:
- "Kiss Me," Sixpence None the Richer
- "Hold Me, Thrill Me, Kiss Me, Kill Me," U2
- "A Kiss to Build a Dream On," Louis Armstrong
- "Kissing You," Des'ree
- "Kiss Me Goodbye," Petula Clark
- "Let's Just Kiss," Harry Connick Jr.
- "The Kiss," The Cure
- "This Kiss," Faith Hill
- "Haul Off and Kiss Me," Caroline Aiken
- "A Little Kiss Each Morning," Rudy Valee
- "Put That Kiss Back Where You Found It," Benny Goodman

FYI—Thirty-four facial muscles are used when you kiss.

A Sigh Is Just a Sigh

97 Spread rose petals all over the bedroom.

98 Do you think you're the only one who writes "mushy," exuberant poetry? Well, think again…

Miss you, miss you, miss you;
Everything I do
Echoes with the laughter
And the voice of You.
You're on every corner,
Every turn and twist,
Every old familiar spot
Whispers how you're missed.

Oh, I miss you, miss you!
God! I miss you, Girl!
There's a strange, sad silence
'Mid the busy whirl,
Just as tho' the ordinary
Daily things I do
Wait with me, expectant
For a word from You.

—David Cory, Selections from *Miss You*

99 A well-crafted love letter will bring a sigh to your lover. Love letters also make treasured keep-sakes. But many people tell me they feel uncomfortable or silly when attempting to write a real love letter. Some think it's not cool to express their true/passionate/insecure feelings.

Write a "five-minute love poem." Set this book down—right now!—and spend the next five minutes writing a quick love poem. (Do this once a day for a week and you'll get pretty good at it!)

Maybe you'd feel more comfortable if you could only see some-one else's love letters, huh? How about a selection from an unabashed love letter from Napoleon Bonaparte to Josephine De Beauharnais:

"I wake filled with thoughts of you. Your portrait and the intoxicating evening which we spent yesterday have left my senses in turmoil. Sweet, incomparable Josephine, what a strange effect you have on my heart!"

The Fundamental Things Apply

100 Romantics have their priorities straight.

What are your priorities? What I mean is, what are your *true* priorities? In other words, *how do you spend your time?* How you spend your time reflects your true priorities. (Most people *claim* that home and family are most important to them, but their *actions* don't reflect this.)

Living a life full of love is about getting your *actions* into alignment with your *beliefs*.

"The secret to having a good marriage is to understand that marriage must be total, it must be permanent, and it must be equal."

—Frank Pittman

- Make an honest appraisal of how you spend your time. Make a chart of how you spend an average week. You'll probably make some interesting discoveries!
- Say to her, "Let's plan a special outing: A lunch-date, dinner-date, movie—whatever. You choose the time and place, and I'll be there—*regardless of my previous plans*." This shows that she has top priority—over work, friends, hobbies, etc.
- You sometimes work overtime at work, right? Why not occasionally work "overtime" on your relationship?

IOI Romantics know that love is a *process*.
While on the one hand romantics tend to live in the moment, we also expect to be around for awhile—so we don't fret too much about today's problems. We know that love, like life, is a *process*. Things change. Things grow. There is a future coming our way, and it's probably going to be pretty good!

> You might also want to read a book called *Love—The Course They Forgot To Teach You In School*, by some guy named Godek.

Adjust your daily schedule *in some small way* to advance the *process* of love in your life.

Read a book to increase your understanding of the *process* of love. I suggest *Love & Respect: The Love She Most Desires, The Respect He Desperately Needs*, by Emerson Eggerichs.

As Time Goes By

102 Love is timeless—and to *prove* it, cover up all the clocks in your house for the entire weekend. (Remember that one of the best things about being on vacation is the freedom from schedules and clocks and appointments. You can create a mini-vacation by freeing yourself from the tyranny of the clock for 48 hours.)

Chapter Theme Song: "Only Time," Enya

103 Get her a wristwatch. Inscribe it with: *I always have time for you.*

104 Get a little bottle. (Maybe an antique bottle or quirky jar.) Fill it with sand. Cork it. Label it: "Extra Time." Give it to your partner.

Inspired by Jim Croce's song "Time in a Bottle."

105 He gave her a simple little music box that plays "As Time Goes By." In the card he wrote: *"As times goes by* I love you more and more."

106 You say you need *more time* in order to be more romantic? So *create* more time! The strategies for how to do so are in a great little book called *No Time for Sex: Finding the Time You Need for Getting the Love You Want,* by David and Claudia Arp.

(Play It Again, Sam)

107a Multiple viewings of your lover's favorite movie.

107b Multiple honeymoons. (Not for newlyweds only!)

107c Multiple orgasms(!)

108 Renew your wedding vows. You could create a private little ceremony for just the two of you. Or you could restage an entire formal wedding!

Chapter Theme Songs:
"Let's Do It Again," TLC
"Again," John Legend

109 Revisit the place where you proposed marriage. Take along a bottle of champagne. Toast your good fortune in having found each other.

110
* Re-enact your first date.
* Relive your first *night* together.

111 When's the last time you sat on his lap and "made-out" like you did in high school??

Familiar gestures— performed with a creative twist—are hallmarks of people with A+ relationships.

Love Notes (I)

112 Write "*I love you*" on the bathroom mirror with a piece of soap.

Yes, the writer has to clean the mirror.

113
* Write her a love letter or poem on one sheet of paper. Glue it to thin cardboard; cut it up into puzzle-shaped pieces; then mail all the pieces to her.
* Or, mail one puzzle piece per day!

114 Write "I love you" on every page of a pack of Post-It Notes. Stick 'em *all over* the house!

115
* Write little love notes on the eggs in the refrigerator.
* Draw funny faces on the eggs in the refrigerator.

116 Cut out interesting/suggestive/unusual/funny headlines from the daily newspapers. When you've collected about twenty-five of them, simply dump them in an envelope and mail them to your lover.

117 Write a short note to your lover that's spread out over several postcards. Write a short phrase on each postcard, then mail one at a time. You'll build anticipation for the romantic conclusion on the final postcard. (Maybe deliver that last one *in person*.)

Love Notes (II)

118 Do you remember "passing notes" in school? Do you remember how to fold them up so they tuck into a neat little square? *If not, find a teenager to advise you.*

119 Put notes on various household products:
- Joy dishwashing liquid: "Every day with you is a Joy."
- Cheerios: "Just knowing you love me cheers me up!"
- Old Spice cologne: "You spice up my life!"
- Ritz Crackers: "Let's 'Put On The Ritz' tonight! Let's go dancing!"
- A roll of Lifesavers: "You're a lifesaver!"
- Caress soap: "This is what I'm going to do to you tonight."

120
- Mail her a pack of matches. Attach a note: "I'm *hot* for you."
- Mail him a pair of oven mitts. Attach a note: "I'm *hot* for you."
- Mail her a bottle of Tabasco sauce. Attach a note: "I'm *hot* for you."
- Mail him a pair of your sexiest panties. The note: "I'm *hot* for you."

Chapter Theme Song:
"Love Letters,"
Diana Krall

Don't sign your love letters: "You're one-in-a-million." (That would mean that there are *six thousand* of her in the world.)

121 Send an old-fashioned telegram. Call Western Union at 800-325-6000 or visit www.westernunion.com.

122 Write funny love notes on a roll of toilet paper.

Write notes on balloons with markers.

Trace your initials in the dust on the coffee table.

Write funny notes in the margins of her *Cosmopolitan* magazine.

Write sexy notes in the margins of his *Playboy* magazine.

Jot love notes in his appointment calendar.

Write romantic reminders on her To Do List.

Freshman Lessons

123 Romance is a *state of mind*. If you have the right mindset, you can make cleaning the bathroom romantic. If you have the *wrong* mindset, you can turn a moonlit stroll on the beach into a miserable experience.

Chapter Theme Song:
"I've Got a Lot to Learn,"
Brooks & Dunn

124 Romance is a *state of being*. It's about taking action on your feelings. It's a recognition that love in the *abstract* has no real meaning at all! Romance is best defined as "love-in-action." Love is the *feeling*—romance is the action. Got it?? Romance often *starts* as a "state of mind," but it must move beyond mere thoughts and intentions, and be communicated to your lover—through words, gifts, presents, gestures, touches, looks—through *action*.

125 Romance is about the *little things*. It's much more about the small gestures—the little ways of making daily life with your lover a bit more special—than it is about extravagant, expensive gestures.

126 There are two kinds of romance: 1) Obligatory, and 2) Optional. *Obligatory* romance is required by law. Look, if you forget to send roses on Valentine's Day, you'd simply better not show up at home! But *optional* romance is really more romantic. It's more genuine. It's making the romantic gesture *when you're not required to*. It's arriving home on a Tuesday after work with a bottle of champagne—just because! It's massages and messages. It's cards and candles and songs and...

Freshman Orientation: Start with the basics, be yourself, take it one step at a time.

Sophomore Lessons

127 Move beyond what I call "Generic Romance."

Generic Romance is the stuff that our culture has *defined* as "romantic": Chocolate, champagne, dinners, diamonds, movies, roses, lingerie, perfume, flowers, cards, and candy. *Yes,* this stuff is romantic—yes, I give roses to my wife Karyn sometimes—but it's only a *start,* it's just skimming the surface.

If you expect your relationship to survive (much less *thrive*) for fifty years or more, you must move waaay beyond Generic Romance.

Chapter Theme Song:
"You Learn," Alanis Morissette

128 Timing is *everything.*
• Pulling surprises requires a superb sense of timing.
• Belated birthday cards ought to be outlawed.
• Chocolate is romantic—*but not if she's on a diet.*
• Stick to small romantic gestures when he's totally preoccupied with a big work project. (Save the biggies until he can appreciate them.)

129 Flirt with her at a party, as if you were both single.
• Freshmen level: Flirt just a little. Wink. Compliment her.
• Sophomore level: Act out a complete "pick-up" fantasy, without any of the other guests being aware of what you're doing.
• Junior level: Continue the fantasy as you return home!
• Senior level: Act out the complete "pick-up" fantasy at the party—and sneak off to an empty room, porch, or closet, and make mad, passionate love!

Are you ready to move beyond Generic Romance?

Junior Lessons

130 Turn common, everyday events into "little celebrations"—opportunities to express your love for your partner. We're not talking *passion* here, but *affection*. (*We'll get to passion elsewhere!*...) A tiny bit of forethought can turn the ordinary into the special. Eat dinner by candlelight. Tie a ribbon around a cup of bedtime tea. Pop your own popcorn while watching a video at home. Turn his birth*day* into a birthday *month*! Give her a bottle of champagne as a "thank you" for doing the grocery shopping. Leave a greeting card on his car seat when he's about to run errands for you.

> Chapter
> Theme Song:
> "You're Learning,"
> Emmylou Harris

131 Recognize that *one* mode of expression isn't enough.
   We all have natural patterns that we follow; behaviors that are easy, natural, habitual; modes of expression that we fall into without even thinking about it. And these modes of expression are not particularly gender-based (even though pop psychology claims otherwise). Do you *talk* about your feelings—or do you *act* on your feelings? Are you quick and spontaneous—or slow and methodical? Do you process information primarily through your head—or through your heart? Do you express yourself directly—or subtly?

There's no "right" and "wrong" here—simply "your" way and your partner's way. So the first lesson is to accept that your partner has a variety of *different* ways of expressing his or her feelings. Honor and respect these differences, and I *promise* that this alone will greatly improve your relationship!

The second lesson is to recognize your own modes of communication. Your easiest path to better communication will be through your natural channels. (See the index entry for *The Acorn Principle*.)

> "Love is the triumph of imagination over intelligence."
> —H.L. Mencken

Senior Lessons

132

- Senior Biology: When it comes to sex and sexuality, men and women are *different!*
- Senior Psychology: But when it comes to emotions and love, men and women are much more *alike* than we are *different*.

Wow! The things you learn when you read the real psychological literature, instead of relying on pop psychology!

133 *You can be yourself and it works!* It's astonishing to me that so many people think that "being romantic" somehow means something *other* than "being yourself."

Men don't *really* expect women to be playmates, and women don't *really* expect men to be Harlequin heroes. What we all really want is the spark, the magic, the thrill of love: the experience we all had at the *beginning* of our relationships. This experience can be recreated through romance—that is, through the creative expression of your feelings. You never need to be someone you aren't, but you *do* need to stay in touch with your feelings, and then act on them.

134 Start with any basic romantic concept, then *give it a twist*—build on it, expand it, exaggerate it, use your creativity, put your personal stamp on it—and you'll create an *endless* supply of new romantic ideas.

Le Boudoir

135 The bedroom is your private, romantic hideaway. Don't turn it into an all-purpose room.
- Get rid of that TV!
- No bright lights!
- No exercise equipment.
- Keep flowers on the nightstand.
- Always have candles handy.
- Massage oil is a must.

136 Don't simply have breakfast in bed—make it an *elegant feast*. Whip up something special: Blueberry pancakes? Cinnamon toast? Fresh-squeezed orange juice? French-roast coffee?

Serve on your good china and best crystal. Add lots of candles. And flowers, too.

137 "Breakfast in bed is 'nice'—but rather *common*, don't you think?" said one couple in the Romance Class. "We think the class would be interested in one of our favorite pastimes: *Dinner* in bed!"

138
• Canopy beds: Most Romantic Kind of Bed/Feminine Category
• Brass beds: Most Romantic Kind of Bed/Masculine Category

Chapter Theme Song:
"Here in My Room,"
Incubus

After she's asleep, quietly place a greeting card in front of her alarm clock. In the morning before she arises, ask her what time it is.

The True Test of Love & Tolerance: Letting her warm her cold feet on you in bed.

La Cuisine

139 Get to know the owner, manager or *maître d'* at your favorite restaurant. Become a "regular" and you'll get the best tables, best service, and best wines, plus inside tips on what's *really* best on the menu tonight.

140 "The Great Search for the Most Romantic Restaurant in Town." Create a list of candidates garnered from restaurant reviews and tips from your friends. Visit a different restaurant each week. Rate them according to your own personal standards.

> Chapter
> **Theme Song:**
> "Hungry,"
> Eric Clapton

141 Does your partner have a favorite meal that he or she *always* orders when dining out? If so, write-up a "custom description" of the meal and secretly tape it into his or her menu. ("Pasta Prima Patricia." "Beefy Bob Wellington." "Eggs à la Lisa.")

142 Have lunch or dinner in an *unusual* place. Museums have quirky cafés. Airports have restaurants with great views. All-night diners are cool places to hang out.

143 Get up extra early on a weekday and go *out* for breakfast with your lover. It's a great way to start the day in a totally different way.

Love Notes (III)

144 Write one love letter on twenty-five different index cards. Hide these all over the house. Finding all of them will be the *first* challenge. Putting them in order will be the *second* challenge.

145 Let comic strips speak for you. Tape them to the refrigerator. Hide them in her purse. Hide them in his briefcase. Pack them in her suitcase.
- Blondie and Dagwood's marriage issues
- Cathy's dating dilemmas
- Charlie Brown's unrequited love
- Rose and Jimbo's ongoing romance
- Brenda Starr's wry observations about love
- Dilbert's disastrous attempts at dating

146 If you're not much of a writer, create an *audio* love letter. Sit down with a digital voice recorder and just talk to her for ten minutes. Then upload the sound file to your computer and e-mail it to her.

Write a love letter—but write it in *reversed letters,* so your lover has to hold it up to a mirror to read it.

147 Add flair to your love notes and envelopes with festive, wacky, or personalized rubber stamps. (You can even have a photograph made into a rubber stamp!) Call Creative Mode at 608-838-8011; or write to 2934 County Road MN, Stoughton, Wisconsin 53589; or visit www.creativemode.com.

Love Notes (IV)

148 Finding special meaning in various items is a romantically useful habit to develop. Here are a few album titles that might inspire you.

Attach an appropriate note to the CD and give it to your lover. Or create a musical "Love Coupon" with a theme that matches the title of the CD.

- *Come Away with Me,* Norah Jones
- *Love Scenes,* Diana Krall
- *August,* Eric Clapton
- *Greatest Hits,* Mariah Carey
- *Desire,* Bob Dylan
- *Fantasy,* Carole King
- *Lovers Rock,* Sade
- *You Sing to Me,* Marc Antony
- *In the Dark,* The Grateful Dead
- *Keith Urban,* Keith Urban
- *No Name Face,* Lifehouse
- *You Light Up My Life,* Leann Rimes
- *Still Crazy After All These Years,* Paul Simon
- *Savage Garden,* Savage Garden
- *No Angel,* Dido
- *Romance (Music for Piano),* on the Narada Label
- *Beauty of Love,* Shardad

What albums in *your* collection have especially meaningful titles?

Personal recommendation:

Aaron Skyy's new CD, *Skyy's the Limit.*

Includes some great romantic R&B songs like "Love Letter" and "Can't Stop Lovin' You," as well as the hit, "The One."

- *My Heart,* Martina McBride
- *No Ordinary Love,* Sade
- *Let's Talk About Love,* Celine Dion
- *Fields of Gold,* Sting
- *Dressed to Kill,* Kiss
- *Heart to Heart,* David Sanborn
- *Let's Live for Today,* The Grass Roots
- *You Got What It Takes,* The Dave Clark Five
- *Dirty Mind,* Prince
- *Love to Love You Baby,* Donna Summer
- *Please Love Me Forever,* Bobby Vinton

"I Love You"

149 "*I love you.*" The all-purpose, over-used phrase...that we never tire of hearing. Say it. Say it often. Say it with *feeling.* Mean it.

150 Upside-down stamps on envelopes mean "I love you."

This tradition was started during World War I as soldiers and their gals wrote love letters back and forth, including this "love code."

151 You could learn how to say "I love you" using sign language. These two books will show you how:

- *The Joy of Signing,* by Lottie Riekoff
- *A Basic Course in American Sign Language,* by Tom Humphries

If you get more ambitious, you could move beyond a simple "I love you" and learn how to have silent and intimate conversations of love with one another across crowded rooms.

152 Call her from work for no other reason than to tell her, "I love you."

Chapter Theme Songs:

"I Love You," Climax Blues Band

"I Love You," Faith Hill

"I Love You," Donna Summer

"I Love You," Sarah McLachlan

"I Love You," Celine Dion

"I Love You," Mary J. Blige

"Ai Shite Imasu"

153

1. English: "I love you"
2. Apache: "Shi ingôlth-a"
3. Arabic: "'Ahebbek"
4. Armenian: "Sírem zk´ez"
5. Aztec: "Nimitzlaco'tla"
6. Bengali: "Ami tomake bhalo basi"
7. Bulgarian: "Obícom te"
8. Burmese: "Chítte"
9. Cambodian: "Khñoms(r)alañ 'neak"
10. Cantonese: "Kgoh òi nei"
11. Cherokee: "Kykéyu"
12. Cheyenne: "Ne-méhotatse"
13. Chinese: "Wo ài nei"
14. Czech: "Miluji vás"
15. Danish: "Eg elskar dig"
16. Dutch: "It hous van jou"
17. Egyptian: "Anna bahebek"
18. Eskimo: "Nagligivaget"
19. Finnish: "Mínä rákistan sínua"
20. French: "Je t'aime"
21. Gaelic (Irish): "Mo ghradh thú"
22. German: "Ich liebe dich"
23. Greek: "Sàs agapo"
24. Romany: "Mándi komova toot"
25. Hawaiian: "Aloha wau ia oe"
26. Hebrew: "Aní ohev otakh"
27. Hindi: "Mayn toojh ko pyár karta hun"
28. Hungarian: "Szeretlék"
29. Icelandic: "Eg elska pig"
30. Indonesian: "Saja tjinta padamu"
31. Irish: "Thaim in grabh leat"
32. Italian: "Ti amo"
33. Japanese: "Ai shite imasu"
34. Korean: "Na nun tangsh-inul sarang hamnida"
35. Kurdish: "Asektem"
36. Latin: "Ego te amo"
37. Mandarin: "Wo ài ni"
38. Mohawk: "Konoronhkwa"
39. Norwegian: "Jeg elsker deg"
40. Persian: "Aseketem"
41. Polish: "Ja cie kocham"
42. Portugese: "Eu te amo"
43. Russian: "Ya lyablyu tyebya"
44. Samoan: "O te alofa ya te oe"
45. Sanskrit: "Aham twan sne-ham karomi"

46. Sioux: "Techi ´hila"
47. Somali: "Wankudja'alahai"
48. Spanish: "Te amo"
49. Swahili: "Mimi naku-penda"
50. Swedish: "Jag älskar dig"
51. Taiwanese: "Ngùa ai dì"
52. Thai: "Pom rak khun"
53. Tibetan: "Khyod-la cags-so"
54. Turkish: "Seni severim"
55. Ukrainian: "Ya vas kikháyu"
56. Vietnamese: "Anh yëu em"
57. Welsh: "Rwy'n dy garu di"
58. Yiddish: "Ich libe dich"
59. Yugoslavian: "Ja te volim"
60. Zulu: "Ngi ya thandela wena"

Be Creative

154 Create a "Romantic Ideas Jar."

- Write a hundred romantic ideas on separate slips of paper. Fill a jar with them. Once a week, one of you picks an idea at random and has to implement it within the next week. Take turns being the chooser.
- Or, number slips of paper one through 1001. Pick a number, then refer to the corresponding number in this book. (For this activity, you may want to skip the chapter "Spare No Expense"!)
- Or, number slips of paper one through 10,000(!)—and use the Romantic Idea Jar to choose items from my book, *10,000 Ways To Say I Love You*.

Everyone has tremendous creative potential inside. You just need to tap into it!

155 Is she a crossword fanatic? Create a *custom* crossword puzzle for her. Make the clues reminiscent of your relationship and life together; include private jokes, funny phrases, and names of favorite songs. (And maybe some suggestive stuff! Hmmm?!)

For a *real* surprise: Carefully glue her custom crossword puzzle over the top of the Sunday *New York Times'* crossword puzzle—and wait for her to discover it!

156 Remove the mechanism from a musical card and attach it to the bottom of a dinner plate or to the inside of a heart-shaped box of chocolates.

Be Prepared

157 Be prepared—for *anything*! Create a "Gift Closet." Gather gifts ahead of time; buy things on sale; order quantities of items and get discounts; buy things during end-of-season sales; pick up presents on a whim. Then warehouse them and save them for later!

- Never again will you have to rush around at the last minute looking for an anniversary gift.
- You'll have more fun giving gifts and presents.
- Your partner will appreciate it.
- You'll save money!
- You'll be prepared to surprise her whenever the inspiration strikes you.

If you live in a *very small* house or apartment, create a "Gift Drawer" or store a "Gift Box" under your bed.

158 Be prepared for spontaneous romantic escapes! Have "His" and "Hers" overnight bags packed at all times. Keep under the bed or in the car trunk.

Seems like a paradox, but it's not: "Preparing for spontaneity!"

159 Be prepared for shopping! Know *all* of your partner's sizes! You should be able to buy *any* item of clothing for him or her, and have it fit 80 percent of the time.

- Could you buy her *any* item of lingerie? A coat? A sweater?
- Could you buy him a pair of shoes? A pair of gloves? A *hat*?

Be prepared—
always have on hand:

A bottle of champagne
A romantic greeting card
A sexy greeting card
Love Stamps
A local/regional "Calendar of Events"
A few candles
Scented bubble bath
A fun little "Trinket Gift"
A little extra cash
A CD of romantic music
A bottle of massage oil

Always, Always, Always

160 Always, always, *always* stay in touch with the special, memorable, unique ways that the two of you have *fun* together.
- What's the most fun you've ever had with your clothes on? Well, do it again!
- What's the most fun you've ever had with your clothes off? *Well?!*

161
- Learn your partner's "hot buttons"— and vow to never hit them.
- Learn your partner's pet peeves—and avoid them.
- Learn your partner's "blind spots"—and help him or her cope.
- Learn your partner's "soft spots"—and indulge them.
- Learn what turns your partner off—and avoid those behaviors.
- Learn what turns your partner on—and practice, practice, *practice*!

Chapter
Theme Songs:
"Always," Bon Jovi
"Always," U2
"Always," Blink 182

When's the last time you really *played* together?

162 Always remember that there are many—thousands, *millions!*—of ways of expressing love. And remember that your partner has the right to express his or her love in ways that may not be what you want or expect. When you insist that romance take a *particular* form, this reflects your rigidity or insecurity.

You do, of course, have the right to have *some* of the romance come to you in the form you desire. But don't expect your partner to read your mind! If you want something in your life, you must take responsibility for mani-festing it. You might simply talk with your partner about your wants and needs. Some people recognize subtle hints while others need lists and reminders.

If you work *with* your partner's personality instead of *against* it, your relationship will be much happier.

Books to enhance the *fun* in your life:

Play Therapy with Adults, by Charles E. Schaefer

Play Therapy: The Art of Relationship, by Garry L. Landreth

Beyond Love and Work: Why Adults Need to Play, by Lenore Terr

Never, Never, Never

163 When you're talking with your lover on the phone, never, never, *never* interrupt your conversation to answer another call via Call Waiting. Let your answering service pick up that incoming call! A+ Couples know it's important to give one another their undivided, focused attention.

164

* Never, never, *never* wallpaper together.
* Never, never, *never* disrespect her.
* Never, never, *never* embarrass him in public.
* Never, never, *never* give checks as gifts.
* Never, never, *never* nag.
  * Never, never, *never* forget your partner's birthday.
    * Never, never, *never* throw out something that belongs to him or her.
      * Never, never, *never* betray a confidence.
      * Never, never, *never* refer to your wife as "My Old Lady."
      * Never, never, *never* give her practical gifts.
      * Never, never, *never* say, "Yes, dear," just to appease her.
    * Never, never, *never* joke about her PMS.
    * Never, never, *never* withhold sex to punish him.
  * Never, never, *never* give her the "silent treatment."
* Never, never, *never* return his car with an empty gas tank.
* Never, never, *never* say "What's for dinner?" before saying "I love you."

Never, never, *never* say, "I told you so."

Gifts, Gifts, Gifts

165 The Forty-Six Kinds of Gifts

1. The Surprise Gift
2. The Trinket Gift
3. The "Just what I always wanted" Gift
4. The Classically Romantic Gift
5. The Perfume Gift
6. The Sexy Gift
7. The "Oh, you shouldn't have!—But I love it!" Gift
8. The Obligatory Gift
9. The Optional Gift
10. The Kooky Gift
11. The Keepsake Gift
12. The "How did you find it?!" Gift
13. The Homemade Gift
14. The Unbelievably Expensive Gift
15. The Gag Gift
16. The Gift that Keeps on Giving
17. The One Gigantic Item Gift
18. Theme Gifts
19. Personalized Gifts
20. The Gift of Travel
21. The Gift of Food
22. The Gift in His or Her Favorite Color
23. The Meaningful Gift
24. The Funny Gift
25. The Practical Gift
26. The Frivolous Gift
27. The First-Class Gift
28. The Custom Romance Certificate Gift
29. The Gift-Within-a-Gift-Within-a-Gift Gift
30. The Beautifully Wrapped Gift
31. Birthday Gifts
32. Anniversary Gifts
33. The Gift of Time
34. The Gift of Cash
35. The Gift Certificate
36. The Gift of Yourself
37. The Cheap Gift

38. The Charming Gift
39. The Gift of Flowers
40. The Gift for No Particular Reason
41. The Family Heirloom Gift
42. The Gift of Art
43. The Decadent Gift
44. The Gift of Chocolate
45. The Gift Cruise
46. The Gift in a Teeny, Tiny Package

This list may inspire your thinking, give you a creative kick, or simply serve as a reminder.

Sex, Sex, Sex

166 Here's something that may surprise you: "The Torah obligates a man to pleasure his wife so that she reaches sexual climax before [he does]." This practical/sexual/spiritual advice is from the amazing book *Kosher Sex: A Recipe for Passion and Intimacy*, by Rabbi Shmuley Boteach.

167

• Time yourselves: How *fast* can you make love??
• Time yourselves: How *long* can you make sex last??

Chapter Theme Song: "SexyBack," Justin Timberlake

168
- Increase the frequency of your lovemaking by 33%.
- Increase the time you spend on foreplay by 150%.
- Increase the quality of your lovemaking by 21%.
- Be 15% less inhibited in your lovemaking.

169 Learn to program your TiVo—it could lead to more sex! Record his or her favorite TV show. *Make love* during that time slot. (Hint: Choose his favorite *hour-long* show, not his favorite *half-hour* sit-com.)

170 Use *props* to enhance your lovemaking. Here's tonight's assignment: First, buy a derby. (Yes, a *derby.* One of those old-fashioned hats.) Then rent the movie, *The Unbearable Lightness of Being.* You'll learn how to make effective use of the derby.

Hang mistletoe over your bed. (Not just for Christmas only!)

The Playboy Catalog. Call 800-423-9494, or visit www.playboy.com

Love Notes (V)

171 Put a tiny little love note *inside* a balloon. Insert the message, blow up the balloon and tie it. Then attach a pin to the string.

"Love is that condition in which the happiness of another person is essential to your own."
—Robert A. Heinlein

172 Be prepared with greeting cards. Go out this weekend and buy $50 worth of greeting cards. Don't ask questions, *just do it!* Head for your nearest card shop and spend a solid hour reading *hundreds* of cards. Get some sentimental cards. Get some sexy cards. Get *several* birthday cards. Get some friendship cards. Get cards with no inscription, so you can exercise your creativity.
• Don't forget to file some of these cards at work.
• Pre-stamp the envelopes (with *Love Stamps*) to save time later.

173 Some creative twists to your basic love letters, love notes, poetry, verses, and romantic twists.
• Write them on nice parchment paper.
• Turn them into scrolls, tied with ribbon.
• Frame 'em.
• Have them rendered in calligraphy.
• Have your poem set to music.
• Have the new song recorded.
• Publish your love letters in a book.
• Place a love note in the newspaper classified section.
• Create a poster of a love poem.
• Write it up on your computer; add flourishes.
• Write a letter in *code.*

Cool idea! Have your poem set to music!

See the index listing for "Songsmith."

Love Notes (VI)

174 When traveling, give her a bouquet of roses; one rose for each day that you'll be away. Attach a note that says something like this:

> *"These three roses represent the three days*
> *I'll be away from you.*
> *They also symbolize the love, joy, and*
> *laughter we share together."*

Be creative and have fun with your love notes!

175 Another flower-and-note combination for when you're apart from one another: Give her forget-me-nots. The note:

> *"Forget-me-not while I'm away from you. You're never*
> *far from my thoughts as you're always in my heart."*

176 Send him *one rose.* The note: "This bud's for you!"

177 Remove all of the thorns from a dozen long-stem red roses before you give them to your lover. The note:

> *"These roses symbolize my love for you. Perfect, pure, and without*
> *the thorns of hurt. I'm not perfect but my love for you* is.*"*

178 Give her tulips. ("Tulips"—"Two lips.") *You* write the note!

Pun alert!

Lovesick

179 Send *five* large flower arrangements to her at work, timed to arrive one per hour, beginning at one o'clock. Write a five-part love note, with one part accompanying each flower arrangement.

180 During their first date she picked up a penny from the ground and said, "A penny for your thoughts." He shared his thoughts and she paid him. (He saved the penny.) As they continued to date they often gave each other pennies as special little love tokens. One day, two years later, he presented her with two ring boxes. As she opened them he said, "A penny for your thoughts...and a diamond for your heart. Will you marry me?"

They named their first daughter Penny. On their tenth anniversary he gave her a rare nineteenth-century penny made into a pendant. On their twentieth anniversary they visited the U.S. Mint on vacation. They now collect pennies in giant jars for their two grandchildren.

181 Attend a lousy movie (on *purpose*); sit in the balcony; make out in the dark.

Chapter
Theme Song:
"Love Sick,"
Bob Dylan

"The thing about falling in love is that if you do it right, you never have to hit the ground."

—Kendall Lepitzki

Prescriptions for Love

182 Prescription for Romance #1: Compliment her. Repeat every four to six hours.

183 Prescription for Romance #2: Say "I love you" at least three times today. Repeat dosage every day *for the rest of your life.*

184 Prescription for Romance #3: Hug. Often!

Chapter Theme Song: "Somebody Get Me a Doctor," Van Halen

185 Get an empty bottle of prescription pills. Fill it with green M&M's. Create a custom label, something like this:

PATIENT: (YOUR PET NAME FOR YOUR LOVER)
MEDICATION: LIBIDO LIBERATOR—EXTRA STRENGTH!
SIDE EFFECTS: LOVE SICKNESS & HOT FLASHES.
DOSAGE: A HANDFUL OR TWO.
REFILLS: SEE PRESCRIBING PHYSICIAN ONLY!
PHYSICIAN: DOCTOR OF LOVE, (YOUR NAME).

Additional ideas:
- Create a sexy prescription label for a bottle of massage oil.
- A custom prescription for a bottle of cough syrup filled with liqueur.
- Convince his or her doctor to "prescribe" one of these concoctions to your lover!
- Convince a local pharmacist to dispense one of these creations to your lover!

Write her a prescription for a dozen chocolate chip cookies. Then fill the order.

Help for the Hopeless

186 Romantic help is available online! Advice! Products! Books! All kinds of stuff available for free, and other stuff available for overnight delivery. A brief sampling:

- Get quotations to enhance your romantic notes: www.quoteland.com

- Get more quotations to enhance your romantic notes: www.quotationspage.com

- Lyrics to love songs are available at: www.romantic-lyrics.com

- Free cards, poems, ideas, etc. available at: www.lovingwhisper.com

- Romantic tips 'n stuff at: www.1001waystoberomantic.com

Know your anniversaries.
All of them…

The first time you made love
The day you first met
Your first big blow-out fight
Your first date
The day you moved in together
Your first kiss
The day you bought your home
The day you conceived your first child
The first time you said the words "I love you"

187 Are you ready? Take notes now. Here are fourteen creative ways to celebrate Valentine's Day:

1. Rent a local hotel's Honeymoon Suite.

2. Take the day off from work on Valentine's Day.

3. One day simply isn't enough! Celebrate for a solid week!

4. Buy ten boxes of kids' valentines, and *flood* your partner with them!

5. Give your partner one card every hour on the hour.

6. Make a batch of heart-shaped cookies.

7. Make a giant Valentine card on the back of a travel poster—

8. And have vacation tickets (to that location) taped to the poster.

9. Plan a solid day's worth of romantic music.

10. Stay at a local bed and breakfast.

11. Send ten Valentine's Day cards.

12. Send a *hundred* Valentine's Day cards!

13. Spend the entire day watching romantic movies.

14. Give your modern gal a piece of antique jewelry.

Hope for the Helpless

188 To help you with your romantic planning, here are
The 23 Kinds of Romantic Surprises:

1. Once-in-a-lifetime surprises
2. Unfolding surprises
3. Bait-and-switch surprises
4. Shocking surprises
5. Mystery-event surprises
6. Total surprises
7. Big surprises
8. Little surprises
9. Expected-but-not-right-now surprises
10. Expensive surprises
11. Surprise tickets
12. Group surprises
13. Surprise vacations
14. Public surprises
15. Private surprises
16. Surprises involving a collaborator
17. Midnight surprises
18. Surprises at work
19. Sexy surprises
20. Funny surprises
21. Meaningful surprises
22. Out-of-character surprises
23. Sweet surprises

> **A Romantic Surprise Coupon**
>
> Surprise!
>
> We're escaping together to a bed & breakfast this weekend!

Travel Tips

189 Sneak off to the airport the night before she's going to leave for a trip. Take one red rose. Rent one of those small storage lockers in the airline terminal. Put the flower in the locker. Sneak back home. Just before she leaves for the airport, hand her the key to the storage locker.

> I *love* this one!

190 When you're traveling without her: Mail a card or note to her the day *before* you leave town, so she'll get it while you're away.

191 When you'll be traveling without him, leave him one greeting card for each day you'll be gone.

192 When you'll be traveling for several days without her, leave behind a pile of "I'm Thinking of You" packets.
* Get a large manila envelope for each day you'll be away.
* Label each one with a day of the week, and fill each one with *stuff*. Stuff like: Her favorite candy, poems, little notes, magazines, a photo of you with a funny note, a "Love Coupon" for use when you're back, and an item of lingerie with a note saying, "Be wearing this when I return."

> If the two of you love the outdoors, keep your camping equipment in the trunk so you'll be ready for spontaneous overnight outings.

193 When you're going to be away, tape your photo to your pillow.

A Suitcase Full of Romance

194

- Pack a card inside his suitcase. Pack a dozen!
- Hide little "love notes" everywhere: in his socks and shoes and shirt pockets and pants pocket and suit pockets and briefcase and suitcase and wallet and notebooks and files.
- Pack his favorite candies (any kind that won't melt).

195
Give him a custom-made play list on his iPod just before he goes on a business trip. Tell him not to play it until the plane is airborne.

196
When she's going away by herself, give her a "Trip Survival Kit." (It would be nice to package it in a gift box or fancy bag—but you don't have to. You can make do with a grocery bag or shoebox labeled with a magic marker.) Fill the kit with fun stuff, candy, notes, etc.

Definition of *spontaneity:*

Deciding this afternoon to fly somewhere— *anywhere*—this evening. Traveling without any luggage at all. Buying what you need along the way.

Plan a surprise trip. Fill her suitcase with helium balloons. Attach to each balloon a note that gives clues about your destination.

197 Get help from hotel concierges! They're great resources, and they'll get nearly *anything* done for you: from normal things like delivering champagne and a note to his room, to the unusual—like filling his room with 100 balloons…or hiding a special gift in the bathtub…or whatever outrageous thing you can think up!

198 Send a greeting card *to her hotel*, so it's waiting for her when she arrives.

Fun & Games

199 Literally make a "game" out of being romantic. Take the spinner from an old board game; cover over the original instructions; divide the circle into twelve quadrants. Write different romantic activities in each quadrant. Take turns giving it a spin every week.

200 Go to a carnival, fair or amusement park together. Ride the rides. Play the games. Eat the hot dogs and cotton candy. Win her a stuffed animal. Kiss in the Tunnel of Love.

> Guys think they should get "points" for being romantic. Well, give it a try!—Make a "game" out of love, and award him "points." Might be the most fun you've had all year!

201 Visit a theater-supply shop together and rent some costumes. (Not just for Halloween, but for adventurous couples...)
• Guys: Be a cowboy, doctor, policeman, mechanic, astronaut.
• Gals: Be a ballerina, policewoman, doctor, cheerleader, elf.

202 Go on a mall-wide "Trinket Gift Hunt." Here's how it works: You each get ten dollars and thirty minutes to shop for each other. The goal is to buy as many different fun/crazy/significant/silly "Trinket Gifts" as possible for your partner. Meet back in the center of the mall, open your gifts, and be prepared for a hilarious time!

Weird & Wacky

203 Greet him at the door with confetti, noise-makers and party hats.

204 Practice "Telepathy Romance." When you're going to be apart, agree to stop whatever else you're doing and *think about each other and nothing else for one minute,* at a pre-determined time.

205 Practice "Leap Year Romance." When February 29th rolls around, take the day off work and declare it your own personal "Romance Day." Give the gift of time—twenty-four hours worth—to your lover!

206 Have you ever seen $10,000 in one dollar bills strewn about someone's living room? Well, neither have I—but one woman in the Romance Class reported that's what her husband did with a commission check he received one year after a big sale. He handed her a rake and said, "Honey, whatever you can fit into this paper bag is yours to spend!" (Being rather clever herself, she stacked the bills *neatly* and walked away with *all of it!*)

Cats & Dogs

207 Include his or her beloved pet in many of your times together. Pet-lovers can be fanatical, so don't force her to choose between you or Spot, because Spot will probably win!

Get special treats for her dog. Celebrate his cat's birthday. Find hotels that welcome pets.

208 There's a cat museum in Amsterdam, Holland. Called the Cat Cabinet, it features works of art highlighting the role of the cat in art and society. For more info call the Netherlands Board of Tourism at 312-856-0110, or write to them at 225 North Michigan Avenue, Suite 326, Chicago, Illinois 60601. Visit the museum website at www.kattenkabinet.nl

Eleven percent of cat owners have ended a romantic relationship because of their cat, according to one survey.

209 Not to be outdone, dog-lovers have a Dog Museum (the American Kennel Club Museum of the Dog) near St. Louis. The museum is devoted to the collection, preservation, and exhibition of works of art and literature related to Man's Best Friend. The museum is in the Trot Jarville House, a magnificent Greek Revival building in Queeny Park, 25 miles west of downtown St. Louis. Call 314-821-3647.

FYI:

Cat Fancy Magazine: 800-365-4421 or www.catchannel.com

Dog World Magazine: www.dogworldmag.com

Dog Fancy Magazine: 800-365-4421 or www.dogchannel.com

Also:

Aquarium Fish Magazine International and *Bird Talk Magazine* at www.animalnetwork.com/animalnetwork

210 Include his or her beloved pet in some of your romantic gestures:

- Attach a small gift to Fido's collar.
- Attach a little love note to Fluffy's collar.
- Float in the aquarium a bottle with a love note inside it.
- Place a diamond ring in a little treasure chest, sink it in the aquarium, then give clues about the location of the gift.

Satin & Lace

211 Ladies, regarding the sexual side of love, if you remember only *one thing* from this book, remember this: Men *love* lingerie.

Thousands of men in my Romance Classes have confided or complained that having their ladies wear lingerie more often is the one thing they want intensely that their women tend to hold back on.

> Remember, ladies: the more see-through, the better!

212 Go lingerie shopping together. Accompany her into the dressing room.

213 Timid about shopping in a lingerie shop? That's what *catalogs* are for!

- *Victoria's Secret* Catalog—800-888-8200, www.victoriassecret.com
- *Frederick's of Hollywood* Catalog—800-323-9525, www.fredericks.com
- *Playboy* Catalog—800-423-9494, www.playboy.com
- *Dream Dresser*—800-963-7326, www.wickedpassions.com/dreamdresser.html
- *Three Wishes Lingerie*—919-529-1800, ext. 1, www.3wisheslingerie.com
- *Moonliting Lingerie & Costume Company*—760-962-9904, www.lingerieandcostumeco.com
- *Coquette International*—800-668-5477, www.coquette.com

Lingerie Coupon

He gets to choose her lingerie outfit.

She gets to choose the sexual fantasy.

Participants must be at least 18 years of age.

Strategies & Examples

214 Use the particulars of your own personal love story to help you create gifts and gestures that are unique and meaningful. One couple had first met on the subway in Boston.

- He once gave her a Boston subway token in a jewelry box, along with this note: "Here's a 'token' of my affection for you."
- The following year he had that token made into a pendant by a local jeweler.

- She once held a "mobile birthday party" for him on a subway car. All of their friends got on board at different stops along Beacon Street in Boston.
- Because they'd met on the "Green Line," green was their "special color," and they used it in many of their gifts to one another.
- And, of course, their special song was "(Charlie on the) M.T.A." by The Kingston Trio.

215 Sometimes one simple concept can provide a *lifetime* of gift-giving opportunities. One guy in my Romance Class told us that he bought his wife a modest diamond necklace for their tenth anniversary: a nice gold chain with one "smallish" diamond on it. For their eleventh anniversary he added another diamond; for Christmas he added *another* diamond; for her birthday he added yet *another* diamond. He's been doing this for twenty-three years now!

During years when money is tight, he simply buys less expensive diamonds. Then, when times are good, he replaces a cheaper diamond with a more expensive one!

He's happy because he saves *tons* of time by not having to really go shopping(!)—and his wife is happy because she really believes that "Diamonds are a girl's best friend!"

"The relationship between commitment and doubt is by no means an antagonistic one. Commitment is healthiest when it's not without doubt but in spite of doubt."

—Rollo May

Bed & Breakfasts

216

- Andrie Rose Inn, Ludlow, Vermont. "The most romantic of a dozen inns we've visited over the years." A variety of rooms and suites in nineteenth-century surroundings welcome guests at the base of Okemo Mountain. Call 800-223-4846 or visit their website at www.andrieroseinn.com.
- Blue Lake Ranch, outside Durango, Colorado. "So private that there's no sign out front." Choose from the main inn or private cottages near picturesque Blue Lake. Call 888-258-3525 or visit their website at www.bluelakeranch.com.
- The Inn on Mount Ada, Avalon, California. "The definition of romance: A Pacific California island that doesn't allow cars!" Six rooms in a stately mansion are elegantly appointed with antiques and working fireplaces. Call 800-608-7669 or visit their website at www.innonmtada.com.
- The Don Gaspar Compound, Santa Fe, New Mexico. This classic Mission- and Adobe-style home has six private suites that enjoy a secluded garden courtyard. Call 888-986-8664 or visit their website at www.dongaspar.com.
- The Inn at Long Lake, Naples, Maine. The guest rooms have been restored to their original country warmth with elegant antique furnishings, fluffy comforters, and pillows. Call 800-437-0328 or 207-693-6226, or visit their website at www.innatlonglake.com.
- The Terrell House, New Orleans, Louisiana. Circa 1858, this inn is located in the Lower Garden District of New Orleans. The house surrounds you with Southern charm, antique chandeliers, marble fireplaces and elegant parlors. It's located on a street of antique shops and jazz clubs. Call 866-261-9687, or visit their website at www.terrellhouse.com.

• The San Ysidro Ranch, Santa Barbara, California. A favorite of the Hollywood elite: Vivien Leigh and Laurence Olivier got married here; frequented by Jean Harlow, Audrey Hepburn, Fred Astaire. Call 800-368-6788, or visit their website at www.sanysidroranch.com.

Internet resources for B&Bs:

www.innplace.com
www.innfinder.com
www.bedandbreakfast.com
www.bbonline.com
www.bedandbreakfastnetwork.com

Gifts & Presents

217 Understand the difference between a *gift* and a *present*.
- A present is something you're giving the receiver because it's something you want him or her to have.
- A gift is something that you're sure the receiver *wants*.

(Don't bother looking up the words "gift" and "present" in the dictionary. Technically, they're synonyms. But then, what does *Webster's* know about romance?)

When a man gives a woman lingerie—guess what?!—nine times out of ten it's a *present*. When he gives her favorite perfume, it's a *gift*. This is not to say that one is better than the other. Gifts and presents are just *different*. Knowing the difference between a gift and a present will help both of you stay "in tune" with each other and avoid unrealistic expectations and possible hard feelings.

Note: Items can sometimes be both gifts and presents at the same time. It depends on the item in combination with the recipient's individual personality.

Gift—Tickets to see his favorite team.
Present—Tickets to the opera.
Gift—Elegant, satin lingerie.
Present—Peek-a-boo panties.
Gift—A new Ping putter.
Present—Clothes you'd like him to wear.
Gift—A book by her favorite author.
Present—A book you'd like her to read.

218 Consciously choose gifts and presents that *symbolize* your love.

Gifts and presents are *things* we give to symbolize our love. It's not about the *stuff*, it's about what the stuff *means*. Frankly, what lovers *really* want is *more of each other!* More time together, more shared experiences, more opportunities to be loving.

The role of gifts and presents is to stand in for you, to represent you, when you're not physically there. So choose them wisely.

What has he *really wanted* for a long time, but held back from buying? Get it for him!

Presents & Gifts

219 Create "theme" gifts and gestures. Combine similar items and ideas to create fun, meaningful gifts.

Give her these three gifts, wrapped separately but tied together with a ribbon:

- The book *Best of Friends: A Coupon Gift of Love and Thanks,* by Source-books, Inc.
- The CD *Forever Friends,* by Justo Almario
- The song "My Best Friend," by Tim McGraw

220 Another "theme" gift: Give him *all* of Leo Buscaglia's "love" books:

- *Love*
- *Personhood*
- *Living, Loving & Learning*
- *Born for Love*
- And get some of Leo's wonderful lectures on DVD.

Give a *funny* gift.
Give an *artistic* gift.
Give a *sexy* gift.
Give a *timely* gift.
Give a *meaningful* gift.
Give a *musical* gift.
Give a *tiny* gift.
Give a *seasonal* gift.
Give a *tasty* gift.

221
- "Diamonds are a girl's best friend." Get her one.
- "Dogs are a man's best friend." Get him one.

222 And another "theme" gift:
- Give her a new pair of walking shoes or hiking boots.
- And a copy of the book *Off the Beaten Path—A travel guide to more than 1,000 scenic and interesting places still uncrowded and inviting.*
- And a written invitation to a three-day hiking vacation.

Daily & Weekly

223a A *Daily* Romantic Checklist:
- Spend twenty minutes of uninterrupted time together.
- Check in with each other during the day.
- Perform one small—and *unexpected*—gesture.
- Say "I love you" at least three times.
- Thank your partner for *something*.
- Look for romantic concepts in the newspaper.
- Take an extra minute when kissing good-bye.

On Sunday: Be *debonair*.
On Monday: Be *zany*.
On Tuesday: Be *enchanting*.
On Wednesday: Be *sexy*.
On Thursday: Be *funny*.
On Friday: Be *playful*.
On Saturday: Be *romantic*.

223b A *Weekly* Romantic Checklist
- Bring home one *small*, unexpected gift or present.
- Share some form of physical intimacy.
- Share an *entire* afternoon or evening together.
- Share two insights you gained this week.
- Write at least one little love note.
- Mail *something* to your partner.
- Make love!
- Plan something *special* for the upcoming weekend.

Focus on a different sense each day:
Sunday: Sense of *sight*.
Monday: Sense of *hearing*.
Tuesday: Sense of *smell*.
Wednesday: Sense of *touch*.
Thursday: Sense of *taste*.
Friday: Common *sense*.
Saturday: Sense of *humor*.

Monthly & Yearly

223c A *Monthly* Romantic Checklist
- Plan one romantic *surprise* for this month.
- Re-stock your stash of greeting cards.
- Go out to dinner once or twice.
- Rent at least two romantic movies.
- Make love several times!
- Make plans for a three-day romantic weekend sometime in the next three months.
- Plan one romantic event with a *seasonal theme*.

223d A *Yearly* Romantic Checklist
- Make a New Year's Resolution to be a more *creative* romantic.
- Make plans for your next anniversary.
- Think of an *unusual* way to celebrate your partner's birthday.
- Review your plans for your next vacation.
- Create a special "Romance" category in your household budget.
- Make plans for Valentine's Day—well in advance!

Rent one romantic comedy every month:
January: *Serendipity*
February: *America's Sweethearts*
March: *Garden State*
April: *Love Actually*
May: *Sweet Home Alabama*
June: *As Good as it Gets*
July: *Return to Me*
August: *Never Been Kissed*
September: *The Princess Bride*
October: *How to Lose a Guy in 10 Days*
November: *The Wedding Singer*
December: *You've Got Mail*

Yin & Yang

224a A lot of problems and misunderstandings—from marital spats to world wars—are caused by people ignoring the fact that everything operates under the principles of Yin and Yang. Everything includes, or works together with, its opposite: masculine and feminine; love and hate; give and take; funny and serious; life and death.

There is great wisdom and truth in every pair of ideas below—even though each pair represents two *opposite* suggestions! These paradoxes are part of the mystery and magic of life and love.

Chapter Theme Song: "Yin & Yang," Adam Ant

- Celebrate your differences.
- Take comfort in your similarities.

- Live in the present! *Now* is all there is! Free yourself from the past.
- Keep your memories alive. Nostalgia fuels romance.

Romantics are particularly good at balancing opposites.

- Read books! They contain wisdom, great ideas, and inspiration!
- Throw the books away! Listen to your inner voice.

- Say what you feel when you feel it. Be *totally honest* with each other.
- Choose your words carefully. What you say creates your reality.

Yang & Yin

224b

- Treat her as your *best friend*—You'll build intimacy.
- Treat her as a *stranger*—It will add spice to your life!

- Lighten up! Have more *fun* together. Experience the joy of life!
- Get serious! Successful relationships require work!

- Romance is easy! Just express yourself. Romance is "adult play"!
- Romance is hard! Plan, shop, hide, wrap, write, surprise, deliver, drive, call, remember, woo!

- Actions speak louder than words. *Do* something, don't just *talk*—Talk is cheap!
- Communication is the cornerstone of a good relationship.

"Love is a force more formidable than any other. It is invisible—it cannot be seen or measured, yet it is powerful enough to transform you in a moment, and offer you more joy than any material possession could."

—Barbara De Angelis

Romantics *thrive* on dynamic tension!

- Travel inspires romance: exotic locales, foreign food, new experiences, high adventure!
- Home is where the heart is: A cozy fire, a romantic bedroom, and a hot tub!

- "Shake up" your life! Go to a motivational seminar! Do something outrageous! Go skydiving!
- "Slow down" your life. Meditate. Find your center. Listen. Shhh.

Mozart

225 The dozen most romantic classical compositions of all time?

1. Liszt-Siloti: "Un Sospiro (A Sigh)," Concert Etude in D Flat Major
2. Debussy: "Girl with the Flaxen Hair"
3. Beethoven: "Moonlight Sonata," 1st Movement Op. 27, No. 2
4. Debussy: Arabesque No. 1
5. Mendelssohn: "Venetian Boat Song," Op. 30, No. 6
6. Chopin: Waltz in C Sharp Minor, Op. 64, No. 2
7. Beethoven: "Fur Elise"
8. Mendelssohn: "Song Without Words," Op. 62, No. 1
9. Chopin: Nocturne in F Sharp Minor, Op. 48, No. 2
10. Brahms: Waltz in A Major, Op. 39, No. 15
11. Brahms: Waltz in E Major, Op. 39, No. 2
12. Saint-Seans: "The Swan" from *Carnival of the Animals*

226 The next twelve most romantic classical compositions of all time?

13. Rachmaninoff: "A Night for Love"

14. Debussy: "Clair de Lune"

15. Granados: Spanish Dance No. 2 ("Oriental")

16. Chopin: Rondo in C Major, Op. 73

17. Scriabin: Fantasy in A Minor, Op. Posthumous

18. Debussy: "Prelude to the Afternoon of a Fawn"

19. Bach: "Jesu, Joy of Man's Desiring"

20. Schubert: Impromptu in G Flat

21. Ravel: "Jeux d'eau"

22. Rameau: Gavotte and Six Doubles

23. Schubert-Liszt: "Serenade"

24. Ravel: "Bolero"

Elvis

227 For your Elvis fan:

• Visit Graceland on your next vacation.

• Hold a yearly birthday party on January 8th.

• Use Elvis stamps *every time* you mail something to him or her.

• Get all 147 Elvis records that were certified gold, platinum, or multiplatinum.

• Plan your vacations with the help of the book, *The Field Guide to Elvis Shrines*, by Bill Yenne. It's a truly *astounding* resource.

Everybody has a favorite singer, song, group, or type of music. Use this knowledge in your romantic gestures!

228 Take a favorite CD and paste a new label over the original one: Retitle the album using her name or some personal reference. Or simply rename it "Our Songs."

229 Get *every recording ever made* by his or her favorite musical group.

230

• Musical love note: "Play the CD *The Emancipation of Mimi,* by Mariah Carey. My message to you is song number two."

Song #2: "We Belong Together"

• Musical love note: "Play the CD *Come Away With Me,* by Norah Jones. My message to you is song number one."

Song #1: "Turn Me On"

• Musical love note: "Play the CD *Surfacing,* by Sarah McLachlan. Listen to song number two."

Song #2: "I Love You"

• Musical love note: "Play the CD *No Name Face,* by Lifehouse; my message to you is song number twelve."

Song #12: "Everything"

• Musical love note: "Play the CD *A Day at the Races,* by Queen. My message to you is song number two."

Song #2: "You Take My Breath Away"

Lame Excuses (#'s 1-4)

231a Lame Excuse #1: "Real Men aren't romantic."

> Not true!

Says who?? Somebody on a TV talk show? Some character in a movie? Your buddies? (Experts all, on matters of the heart, no doubt.) Let me tell you something: If Real Men aren't romantic, then Real Men are *lonely*.

231b Lame Excuse #2: "Being romantic is going to cost me a fortune!"

> Not necessarily!

As the Beatles said, "Money can't buy me love." It's true. Money can buy you companionship, attention, sex, and status—but it *can't* buy you *love* or *happiness*. Being romantic *can* cost you a fortune, but it doesn't *have* to. There is no correlation whatsoever between the size of the sentiment and the size of the price tag.

231c Lame Excuse #3: "I don't have time."

> Give me a break!

Bull! You have 1,440 minutes every day—the same as everybody else. How you use those minutes is up to you. Yes, work is important. Yes, your golf game is important. But do you really need to watch that rerun of *Gilligan's Island* again? The truth is, we all have time for what's *truly important* to us.

231d Lame Excuse #4: "I forgot."

> Uh-Uh!

That's okay. *Just don't do it again.* You're allowed to forget *occasionally*, but not consistently. If forgetting is a *habit*, you're sending a clear signal that he or she just is not that important to you.

Lame Excuses (#'s 5-8)

231e Lame Excuse #5: "I'll be romantic later—after I get my career in order."

> The busy executive excuse.

"Later" usually comes in about *forty years*—much too late for most partners to wait. And I know this next comment is a cliché, but it's so, so true: No one, on his death bed, ever wished that he'd spent more time at work.

231f Lame Excuse #6: "I shouldn't have to *prove* my love by being romantic."

> The belligerent excuse.

Romance isn't about *proving* anything. It's about *expressing* something.

231g Lame Excuse #7: "Maybe *next* week."
- Question 1: How many weeks have you been saying this??
- Question 2: (Sorry to be morbid—*but...*) How would you feel if your lover passed away without you having expressed your true love for him or her?

> The procrastinator's excuse.

231h Lame Excuse #8: "What will the *guys* think?"

First, why should you *care* what the guys think? Second, who says that you need to *tell* the guys how romantic you are? Third, even though many guys won't admit it, most of them would *love* to know the relationship secrets of romantic guys!

> The pseudo-macho excuse.

Lame Excuses (#'s 9-12)

231i Lame Excuse #9: "Oh, heck, she *knows* I love her."

> One of the most common excuses.

She knows that you loved her *at one time*—but she may not be so sure about *right now*. Love must be *expressed* in order stay alive. Otherwise it simply withers away.

231j Lame Excuse #10: "It's simply not *me* to be romantic."

What you *probably* mean is that you're not "typically" romantic, or that you're not very *openly* demonstrative. This is fine, as long as you do express your love in *some* way, in a way that works for you *and* that your partner recognizes.

> A really *feeble* excuse.

231k Lame Excuse #11: "I'm just not creative."

> A lazy excuse.

Untrue. *Everyone* is creative. It's simply a matter of *where* you apply your creativity. Most people use their creativity all day at work, then come home and shut it off.

231l Lame Excuse #12: "I'm simply not eloquent."

Great news, Shakespeare! You don't *have* to be eloquent in order to be romantic! A simple "I love you" usually does the trick. And besides, I'll *bet* that she knows you well enough to suspect that your talents lie in areas other than poetry.

> Grasping at straws!

Lame Excuses (#'s 13-14)

231m Lame Excuse #13: "I'm just too *tired* to be romantic."

Oh, my! Poor baby! Let's help. No, not by propping up your feet so you can watch TV more comfortably—but by *really* helping you. First, we'll take you to the doctor, to make sure you're not anemic. Then we'll start you on an exercise program. Then we'll improve your diet. Then we'll get you started on a yoga program. Then we'll make sure you stop working overtime, and get home to your loving partner at a reasonable hour.

> Zzzzzzzzzzzzzz...

231n Lame Excuse #14: "It's been so long since I've been romantic that if I brought home a dozen roses her first reaction would be to ask me what I've been up to."

I'd say she has a *right* to be skeptical, don't you? She really wants to be reassured that this romantic gesture isn't just something you've done because you read it in a book(!). She needs to know that the gesture is genuine—and that it's not a one-time occurrence. You're just going to have to prove yourself over time. (Believe me, it's worth it!)

> Get over it!

> *Bonus* Lame Excuse!
>
> "I'm afraid she'd be so shocked if I were to be romantic that she'd have a heart attack and die."

For Men Only

232 Wear a tuxedo home from work.

233 A shopping trip for men (store-specific). Buy one item from each store. Gift wrap in separate boxes.

- A bath shop
- A lingerie boutique
- A card shop
- A liquor store
- A flower shop
- A quality jewelry store

> Women *love* how a man looks in a tuxedo. I think it's genetic.

234 Another shopping trip for men (product-specific): Pick up all these items in coordinated fragrances:

- Body lotion
- Hand lotion
- Foaming bath gel
- Dusting powder
- Potpourri
- Shampoo
- Conditioner
- Perfumed soap
- Fragrance candles
- Oils

235 Secret Romantic Idea for Guys Only. Record or TiVo the Super Bowl—and take your wife out to dinner during the game! Think about it: You only have to do this *once*. She'll be *thrilled*. She'll be telling all her friends how wonderful you are. (More bonus points for you!) And you *will* get to see the game—just three hours later than everyone else. And heck, the game is usually a letdown anyway.

> This one is worth *10 zillion* points in the Relationship Accounting Department!

For Women Only

236 Send him a letter sealed with a kiss. (Use your reddest lipstick.)

237 Send him a *perfumed* love letter.

238 Send flowers to him at work.

239 Don't position yourself against his passions. Please don't force him to choose between you and his golf/football/basketball/cars/fishing! There's room for football *and* females in most guys' lives. If you're in love with a fanatic, you have to remind him why he *used to be* fanatical about you, too—and why it's worth his while to be a fan once more!

240 Read the book *Iron John*, by Robert Bly. It offers a fresh and insightful look at masculinity. Learn that the "Wild Man" inside him need not turn him into an insensitive macho guy; see the partnership that the book offers between the masculine and the feminine. (If your guy hasn't already read this book, give it to him when you're finished with it.)

Chapter Theme Song: "Ain't No Other Man," Christina Aguilera

The rules have changed: It's now appropriate and acceptable for women to give flowers to men.

A heartfelt appreciation for the positive, powerful, endearing, and enduring qualities of men: *What Men Won't Tell You but Women Need to Know*, by Bob Berkowitz and Roger Gittines.

For Singles Only

241a Think Like a Married Person: Strategy #1

Build Intimacy

Dating as a "lifestyle" is okay for a few years, but most singles long for a serious, monogamous, intimate relationship. Ask yourself what your *real* goals in dating are. (Making the scene? Looking good? Scoring?) If, instead, intimacy is your goal, you'll share more of yourself sooner, you'll communicate honestly, and you'll listen to one another more attentively.

Chapter
Theme Song:
"Soulmate," Audio
Adrenaline

241b Think Like a Married Person: Strategy #2

Think Long-term

The single brain is consumed with short-term goals. (This Saturday night. What will I wear? Will he kiss me tonight? Will she sleep with me on the second date?) *Chill out,* singles! A *long-term* mindset will relieve a lot of your stress, help you be more "yourself," and give you a better perspective on things.

Think like a
married person!

241c Think Like a Married Person: Strategy #3

Communicate!

Have you ever noticed that single people often do a lot of *talking* without really *communicating*? The singles scene is characterized by a lot of posturing, boasting and clever bantering. Those who get beyond these superficial things most quickly tend to end up in the best relationships.

For Marrieds Only

242a Think Like a Single Person: Strategy #1

Flirt!

When's the last time you actually flirted with your own spouse? Try it the next time you're out in public together. You'll give your partner a pleasant jolt—and you'll have fun, too. Think back to all those little things you used to do while you were courting one another—and try them out again.

Chapter
Theme Song:
"Love and Marriage,"
Frank Sinatra

242b Think Like a Single Person: Strategy #2

Pursue Instant Gratification

The typical mindset of a married person is long-term. The positive side of this is that long-term can mean security, commitment and comfort. The negative side is that it can also mean boredom, laziness, and complacency. One way to combat this negative side is to adopt the mindset of a single person: It's a mindset of instant gratification. Horny?—Make love now. Thinking of her?—Call her now. Appreciate him?—Hug him now. Walking through a mall?—Pick up a little love-gift now.

"A happy marriage has in it all the pleasures of friendships, all the enjoyment of sense and reason—and indeed all the sweets of life."
—Joseph Addison

242c Think Like a Single Person: Strategy #3

Seduction

When's the last time you seduced your spouse? How often do you bother to set the mood, play the music, dress the part, say the right words, do the little things? Think back to your seduction techniques from when you were single. (C'mon—don't play innocent with us here!)

Think like a *single* person.

A Month of Romance: Week 1

243 **Sunday**: Buy a guidebook for the city or region in which you live. Visit someplace you've never been before.

244 **Monday**: Clip your partner's horoscope from the newspaper. Attach a note describing how you're going to make certain that the astrological prediction comes true. Give it to your partner as you part ways for work.

245 **Tuesday**: After you say good-bye, turn back one more time and blow her a kiss.

246 **Wednesday**: Buy a lottery ticket. Give it to her with a little note attached:

"I hit the jackpot when I married you!"

247 **Thursday**: Thursday is "Gift Day"! (*Why? Because I said so, that's why!*) Bring home a bottle of scented massage oil. Use it!

Chapter Theme Songs:

"Sunday," No Doubt

"A Sunday," Jimmy Eat World

"Loving You Sunday Morning," Scorpions

"Sunday Morning," Maroon 5

"On Sunday," 'Til Tuesday

"Sunday Kind of Love," Ella Fitzgerald

"Tell Me on a Sunday," Sarah Brightman

Alternative notes:
"Take a chance on me!"
"You're one-in-a-million!"

248 **Friday:** Page through your photo albums together. Relive the memories.

249 **Saturday:** Touch more. Hold hands. Rub her neck. Massage his feet. Hug! Cuddle!

A Month of Romance: Week 2

250 **Sunday:** Go for a walk. (No headphones allowed.) Hold hands.

251 **Monday:** Get up with the sun. Enjoy the morning for a change, instead of rushing through your shower, grabbing your coffee, and dashing out the door.

252 **Tuesday:** Get up with the sun. Make love. Go to work.

253 **Wednesday:** Take a class together. Sign up for a dance class. Or a cooking class. Or a wine-tasting class. Or a massage class.

254 **Thursday:** Thursday is Gift Day! Bring home a bouquet of flowers. Write a poetic note about their symbolic significance.

255 **Friday:** Have "your song" playing on the stereo when your partner returns home from work.

256 **Saturday:** Visit a museum gift shop and get a poster print by her favorite artist. Have it framed for her. They may also have greeting cards, note cards, journals, or blank books featuring the artwork of her favorite artist.

Chapter Theme Songs:

"Come Monday," Jimmy Buffett

"Another Monday," John Renbourn

"Born on a Monday," Michael Quatro

"Blue Monday," New Order

"Monday Monday," The Mamas & The Papas

"Manic Monday," Bangles

"Monday Love," Tara Kemp

"Monday Morning in Paradise," Tom Paxton

• • •

"Tuesday's Gone," Lynyrd Skynyrd

"Ruby Tuesday," Cat Stevens

"Barely out of Tuesday," Counting Crows

"Love You 'Til Tuesday," David Bowie

"Sweet Tuesday Morning," Badfinger

A Month of Romance: Week 3

257 **Sunday:** Remove the light bulbs from the lamps in your bedroom. Replace them with candles. You take it from there.

258 **Monday:** Head to your local music store. Get the *Come Away with Me* CD by Norah Jones.

259 **Tuesday:** Start the day in a special way. Read out loud an inspirational passage from a favorite book.

260 **Wednesday:** End the day in a special way. Give him or her a massage.

261 **Thursday:** Yes—today is Gift Day! Buy him a wild tie. Buy her a stuffed animal.

262 **Friday:** Share a bubble bath.

263 **Saturday:** Make love tonight—*without using your hands.*

Chapter Theme Songs:

"Waiting for Wednesdays," Lisa Loeb

"Wednesday," Tori Amos

"It's Already Wednesday," Freya

• • •

"Misty Thursday," Duke Jordan

"Thursday's Child," David Bowie

"Thursday Afternoon," Brian Eno

A Month of Romance: Week 4

264 **Sunday:** Spend *all day* in bed. Read the Sunday funnies aloud to her. Make love. Enjoy breakfast in bed. Take a nap. Watch old movies on TV. Make love again. Have Domino's Pizza deliver dinner. Make love again.

265 **Monday:** Call in sick to work. Repeat yesterday.

266 **Tuesday:** Send loving thoughts to your lover via mental telepathy.

267 **Wednesday:** Pack a picnic lunch. Meet him at work. Close his office door. *Bon appétit!*

268 **Thursday:** Another Gift Day. Today's gift won't cost you a *dime.* Write a list titled "Ten Reasons I Love You." Present it to him or her over dinner.

Chapter Theme Songs:

"Friday," Daniel Bedingfield

"Friday I'm in Love," The Cure

"Friday's Angels," Generation X

"Thank God it's Friday," R. Kelly

"A Few Minutes on Friday," Bright Eyes

• • •

"Saturday," Fall Out Boy

"Drive-In Saturday," David Bowie

"Saturday Afternoon," Jefferson Airplane

"Sentimental Saturday," Sarah Hudson

"Saturday in the Park," Chicago

269 **Friday:** Today's assignment is to find one romantic idea/concept/gift in the newspaper. Act on it within the next two weeks.

270 **Saturday:** Make a couple of *incredible* banana splits. Make sure to use your partner's favorite ice cream flavors.

The Golden Rules of Romance

271a Time and effort expended are more appreciated than money spent.

Gifts are great, but they can't make up for lost time. Maintaining a loving, romantic connection with your lover means lingering over dinner, spending lazy Sunday afternoons together, walking and talking, etc.

271b Planning doesn't destroy spontaneity—it creates opportunity.

Plan a special gesture for your next anniversary. Plan a surprise birthday party. Plan your work life with time built in for romance.

> Romance is often—but not *always*—a spontaneous thing. Sometimes it's the *planning* that makes the romance come alive.

271c The *receiver* defines what's romantic.
- If you give her flowers, and she hates flowers, it ain't romantic.
- If you've spent all day cooking a gourmet meal, and he'd rather call Domino's for a pizza...guess what?

- If you've spent a fortune on an outfit for her, and she says it isn't her style, you have no right to be resentful. (This is why you must listen to her and learn her likes and dislikes.)

271d Romantics give their relationship the top priority in their lives.

> "The way to love anything is to realize that it might be lost."
> —G. K. Chesterton

Everything else flows *from* the relationship, *through* the relationship, and *because* of the primary love relationship, if your life is operating in a successfully dynamic manner. This does not mean that one becomes a martyr on behalf of the other. Martyrs hurt themselves, and thus harm the relationship. Healthy relationships always support and nurture each member of the couple.

Rules Were Made to Be Broken

272

- ■ Rule: *Don't* give cash as a gift.
- ❑ Breaking the Rule: Unless it's done *creatively.*
  - Tape one hundred one-dollar bills together, creating a long banner out of them, and string them throughout the house. If his favorite color is green, tie a stack of one-dollar bills with a green ribbon.

> Chapter Theme Song:
> "Breaking the Rules," AC/DC

- Attach a one-hundred-dollar bill to a Victoria's Secret catalog, along with a note saying, "You choose."
- Wrap a one-hundred-dollar bill around the stem of a flower.

273

■ Rule: *Don't* give gift certificates.

❏ Breaking the Rule: Gift certificates generally don't work because they're too generic. So if you can make them specific, personalized, and "just right" for your partner, go for it!

- For gals: A generous gift certificate for her all-time favorite boutique, catalog, or service.
- For guys: A gift certificate from Brookstone, The Sharper Image, or Radio Shack.
- Exception #3, for both: Custom-made gift certificates that express your affection in a special, creative, unique, and/or touching way.

> Romantics like to break the rules, be unconventional, express themselves, and be spontaneous.

Be My Valentine!

274 For future reference: Buy an *extra* bag of Valentine Conversation Heart candies and save them for use *six months later.*

Peanuts © 1992. Reprinted by permission of United Features Syndicate, Inc.

275 While sharing stories from their childhoods, Pete told Deb that, because he grew up poor, he was unpopular in grammar school. Every Valentine's Day when the children would decorate their shoeboxes so they could deliver Valentines to each other, Pete's box always remained empty. Deb thought this was the saddest thing she'd ever heard.

For the next Valentine's Day she decorated a shoebox and *filled* it with Valentines. And Deb promised him that he would *never* go without a Valentine again.

276 Gals: Stumped about what to get him for Valentine's Day? Try this idea this year: Forget the *gift!* Just greet him at the front door wearing a big red ribbon—*and nothing else.*

Kiss Me, You Fool!

277 Of course you know how to kiss, but perhaps a refresher course might add a little spark to your lives. Pick up a copy of a fun little book called *The Art of Kissing,* by William Cane. In it are instructions for (among other things)…

- The Candy Kiss
- The Sliding Kiss
- The Counter Kiss
- The Music Kiss
- The Surprise Kiss
- The Vacuum Kiss
- The Perfume Kiss
- The French Kiss
- The Japanese Kiss

Trivia: The rock group Kiss has not recorded *any* romantic songs.

278 "Butterfly Kisses": You're butterfly kissing when your face is very close to your lover's cheek, and you blink your eye rapidly, softly grazing your eyelashes against her skin.

"Any man who can drive safely while kissing a pretty girl is simply not giving the kiss the attention it deserves."

—Albert Einstein

279 Rent the classic movie *Singin' in the Rain.* Then…

- Take a walk the next time it rains—
- And sing and dance in the rain together!
- Buy her an umbrella in her favorite color.

GREGORY J.P. GODEK • 123

- Buy a golf umbrella—so you can walk comfortably together.
- Buy a tiny travel umbrella—so you have to huddle together!
- Get him a new overcoat; stuff the pockets with your lingerie.
- Vacation in Seattle.

1) Steal a kiss.
2) Give it back.

The Mathematics of Romance

280 Great relationships aren't 50/50. They're 100/100. Having a "fifty-fifty" relationship *sounds* like a good goal—but it's *not*. An *equitable* relationship is not the same thing as a *loving* relationship. Fifty-fifty *really* means "I'll meet you halfway." In other words, "I'll work only this hard, I'll give only this much, then it's your turn to meet me halfway." Love is about giving 100%, not merely 50%.

Give 100% to your relationship. But don't fall into the trap of trying to give "150%." It sounds impressive, but it's impossible to give more than you have. It will just frustrate you and make you feel guilty.

Nobody can give 100% of himself 100% of the time—it's impossible. But you *can* aim for it, and when you (inevitably) fall short, it'll still be okay. Even if you each fall short by as much as 50%, you'll still be in fine shape; it'll still add up to something close to 100%. The problem is when you're both trying to limit your giving to your "fair share"— usually defined as 50%. If you do that, you'll *definitely* fall short of 100%.

281 5 minutes devoted to romance = 1 day of harmony.

Think of all the times that your failure to do some *little thing*—like calling to tell her you'll be home late from work, or mailing her birthday card on time—has caused a full day of unhappiness. Consistent attention to your lover will keep your relationship balanced and happy. It doesn't take much! Little gestures go a long way.

Here's the mathematical formula for romance:
$$r = a(1-\cos A)$$
Actually, this is the formula for a "cardioid"—a somewhat *heart-shaped curve*. More precisely, for you romantic mathematicians, a cardioid is "the path of a point on a circle that rolls externally, without slipping, on another equal circle." (Who *says* nerds can't be romantic?!)

Best Mathematical Love Poem of All Time: See the story titled, "Trurl's Electronic Bard," in *The Cyberiad* by Stanislaw Lem.

282

- Celebrate your 1,000th day together. (That's about 2 years, 8 months, and 26 days—depending on when the leap years fall.)
- Celebrate your 10,000th day together! (That's about 27 years, 4 months, and 23 days.)

The Calculus of Love

283

Be prepared for romantic weekend getaways. Get a road map of your state. Now draw a circle on the map. Make your house the center of the circle, and measure a radius of 120 miles. You've just identified a 45,238-square-mile region that lies within a mere two-hour drive of where you live. Unless you live in *Antarctica,** there must be *many* romantic, exciting, new and different things to do within a 45,238-square-mile area!

*Romantic things to do in Antarctica:

- Go tobogganing.
- Host a formal party. Invite penguins.
- Stay in bed all night. (Nights last *six months!*)

Once you've got your circle inscribed on your map, it's time to do a little research:

- Locate every bed & breakfast in your circle.
- Find every park and walking path.
- Locate every art gallery, museum, and theater.
- Find every mall and store of interest to you and your partner.
- Make a list of twenty restaurants that look interesting.

284 Figure out how many *days* you've been together (don't forget to add in leap years). In ten years you'll have spent 3,652 days together! Reflect on the highlights of your time together. How have you changed? What have you accomplished together?

- Write a short letter sharing your feelings about your time together.
- Create a timeline, noting highlights of your relationship.

> Once you've figured out how many *days* you've been together, figure out how many *hours, minutes,* or *seconds* you've been together!

285 Use *numbers* to create *theme* gifts and gestures. Use your partner's *age,* or the number of *years* you've been together, or his or her lucky number. Send that number of greeting cards. Spend that amount of money on a gift. Get that *number* of gifts. Spend that many days on vacation. Spend that many minutes giving him or her a massage. Buy a piece of jewelry with that number of gemstones in it.

Couplehood

286 15 Ways to Really Be a Couple in Public

1. Always make your "entrance" arm-in-arm.
2. Wear outfits that match in a subtle way.
3. Compliment her in front of her friends.
4. Hold her chair for her at the table.
5. Whisper your pet name to her.
6. PDA.*
7. Brush against him in a sexually suggestive way.
8. Wear matching baseball caps.
9. Open doors for her with an extra little flourish.
10. Hold hands.
11. Give him a seductive smile.
12. Order for her when dining out.
13. Wink at him from across the room.
14. Blow her a kiss.
15. Buy her one rose from a street vendor.

*PDA—Public Displays of Affection

Very funny (and insightful) books, both by Paul Reiser:

Couplehood
Babyhood

Q: How do you know when you're a "couple"?
A: When you say, "Hi, it's *me*," on the phone—and he or she *knows* it's you.

• • •

Q: How do you know when it's *really* love?
A: When it doesn't feel like you're *pretending* or *hoping* it's love.

287 Switch roles with your lover for a day, a weekend or a week. Trade responsibilities, chores, and daily routines; trade sides of the bed, trade as many aspects of your lives as you possibly can. You'll gain new insights into your partner. You'll get to know him or her better. Guaranteed. And this knowledge will make you both more patient and understanding with each other. It will also help you make romantic gestures that are more personal, intimate, appropriate, and appreciated.

Parenthood

288 Guys: Hang this sign on your wall at work:

"The best thing a father can do for his children is to love their mother."

289 Create a neighborhood "Child-Sharing Program." Arrange entire weekends when one family on the block plays host to "The World's Biggest Slumber Party," while the rest of you get romantic.

"Why do ya want to be romantic? You're already married!"

Erotica

290 "Christen" every room in your house or apartment by making love in it. (Don't forget to include the stairways, hallways, and closets.)

Chapter
Theme Song:
"The Need to Be
Naked," Amber

The goal of this fantasy is to get your guy to react the way Roger Rabbit does when he sees Jessica!

291 For women: Fulfill a fantasy—Greet him at the door wearing the lingerie outfit that you *know* makes his eyes bulge out of his head!

292 For men: Fulfill a fantasy—Become her vision of Prince Charming, whether it involves dressing in a tuxedo or in a sexy muscle shirt and hard hat! Indulge her.

293 When he's traveling on business, give him a sexy wake-up call at 6 a.m.

"Love never dies a natural death. It dies because we don't know how to replenish its source..."

—Anaïs Nin

294 Kiss every square inch of her body...S-L-O-W-L-Y.

295 Why not mail a lingerie gift to her—*at work.*

Picture this: She opens her mail about 11 a.m.; she gets your package. After she recovers and regains her composure, she's totally distracted for the rest of the day. Sounds good to me!

Exotica

296 One of the most exotic places in the world you could *possibly* visit is Nepal—the tiny Asian country where Mount Everest resides. If your partner loves adventure, just imagine trekking through the Himalayas, discovering the Nepalese culture, shopping in the open-air markets, exploring Katmandu. The expert on trekking in Nepal (and in trekking vacations to other countries, as well) is Steve Conlon, founder of Above the Clouds Trekking. (Isn't that a *fabulous* name for a company?!) Call 800-233-4499 or write to P.O. Box 398, Worcester, Massachusetts 01602. Visit www.aboveclouds.com or www.gorp.com.

Everyone has a different idea of what constitutes an "exotic" experience or location. For some folks, exotic means roughing it in Africa. For others it means lounging in Tahiti. For some, New York City is exotic. Others prefer Paris.

297 If you'd rather ride than walk, consider a trip on the Trans-Siberian Railroad in a vintage private train! You'll travel in original antique carriages that were once part of the fabled Orient Express. Call TCS Expeditions at 800-727-7477, or write to 710 Second Avenue, Suite 840, Seattle, Washington 98104; or visit www.tcs-expeditions.com.

298 Equitour organizes horseback vacations as far afield as India and Australia. Trips through the American Wild West are also available. The trips are wonderfully diverse: On the Wyoming trip you camp out in tents, while on the Vermont trip you stay in quaint country inns. Call Equitour at 800-545-0019; or visit www.ridingtours.com.

Creating an A+ Relationship

299 The A+ Relationship is a powerful concept that reveals unique insights into loving relationships. It is a technique, a tool that can help you accomplish two things. First, it helps you *understand* your loving relationship on a deep level that is impossible to achieve in any other way. And second, it helps you *take action* on your love in ways that fulfill you and your partner as individuals and nurture the two of you as a couple.

Chapter Theme Song:
"Straight A's,"
Dead Kennedys

My twenty years of teaching Relationship Seminars, my research, and my discussions with *thousands* of couples have convinced me that the A+ Relationship concept can help any couple improve their relationship.

How do you *achieve* an A+ Relationship? You commit yourself to excellence, you work hard (and *play* hard!), and you work on your relationship skills together. In other words, to the best of your ability, you *live your love.* Great relationships are acts of conscious creation, and the two of you are artists working to create one life out of two. While falling in love *does* "just happen," *staying* in love *never* happens by itself.

A+ Relationship
(a • plus • ri la' shen ship), n.

1. The best intimate relationship you can possibly create. 2. A loving monogamous relationship that is excellent, superior, awesome, exciting, passionate, growing, fulfilling, fascinating, and romantic. 3. An act of creation involving two individuals—two artists whose lifework is creating love through the medium of their relationship. 4. A relationship that, while not perfect, ranks in the ninety-fifth percentile.

You—and every couple—have the power to establish your own "rules" and expectations for your relationship. This is one of the great benefits of the social changes we've been experiencing since the 1960s. This kind of empowerment is a major factor in why the twenty-first century marks a new epoch in the evolution of human relationships: We're free to break away from the rigid, stereotyped thinking that characterized relationships in the 1950s. You have the opportunity to create a "custom-fit" relationship that incorporates the best of the timeless values (commitment, faith, honesty, etc.) with the best of the modern values (equality, flexibility, creativity, etc.). You can create your *own* set of standards and establish your own goals for your relationship.

The A+ Relationship concept focuses on *behavior,* not on *personality.* It's not about making value judgments of people, it's about making honest evaluations of people's behavior. It helps you look directly at how you're doing right now, and then helps you achieve your future relationship goals. What more could you ask for?!

The Relationship Report Card

3OO Fill out the "Relationship Report Card" on the next page.

Instructions:
- You grade yourself and your partner.
- Get your partner to grade him or herself and you.
- Compare and discuss your grades; you'll gain great insight into your relationship.
- Celebrate everything from a B– to an A+.
- Work to improve your Cs and Ds.

Don't be deceived by the seeming simplicity of this exercise!

It opens communication, uncovers profound insights, and provides a practical tool for change and improvement.

---

*How would you grade your relationship?

A = Passionate, exciting, loving, fulfilling; not *perfect*— but clearly excellent.

B = Very good, solid, better-than-most, consistent, *improving.*

C = Average, acceptable, status quo, okay—but static, ho-hum, sometimes *boring.*

D = Below average, unhappy, dismal; bad—but not hopeless.

F = Hopeless, depressing, dangerous; tried everything, it didn't work.

Master These Skills for an A+ Relationship

Fill out the "Relationship Report Card": Grade yourself and your partner (A+ through F, like in school).

	Grade Yourself	Grade Partner
Affection	_____	_____
Arguing Skills	_____	_____
Attitude	_____	_____
Commitment	_____	_____
Communication	_____	_____
Considerate	_____	_____
Couple Thinking	_____	_____
Creativity	_____	_____
Empathy	_____	_____
Flexibility	_____	_____
Friendship	_____	_____
Generosity	_____	_____
Gift-giving Skills	_____	_____
Honesty	_____	_____
Household Mgmt.	_____	_____
Listening Skills	_____	_____
Lovemaking	_____	_____
Patience	_____	_____
Playfulness	_____	_____
Romance	_____	_____
Self-Awareness	_____	_____
Self-Esteem	_____	_____
Sense of Humor	_____	_____
Sensitivity	_____	_____
Spontaneity	_____	_____
Tolerance	_____	_____

Common Sense

301 Common sense says, "Do what you do best," and "Use your talents." Sounds good, but the problem is that *simple* advice is rarely *easy* to apply.

In a great book, *The Acorn Principle,* Jim Cathcart explains in detail how you can "nurture your nature." He provides exercises and examples that will help you discover, explore, and grow the seeds of your greatest potential. *The Acorn Principle* is one of those rare books that will help you improve your work life *and* your love life.

302 Dot your i's and cross your t's. In other words, pay attention to details.

- Don't buy just *any* flowers—get her *favorites.*
- Make a point of *always* wrapping his gifts in his favorite color.
- Don't buy her *gold* jewelry when she prefers *silver.*

303 Remember that relationships are not self-regulating! They're delicate creations that require attention, adjustment, and regular oiling.

You fell in love. You decided to spend your lives together. Isn't it simply common sense to make the most of it??

"Love is what we were born with. Fear is what we learned here."

—Marianne Williamson

304 "Walk a mile in his shoes," then rethink your romantic gestures.
- After an especially tough week, he'd probably prefer a massage to going out dancing.
- Don't bring her flowers when what she *really* needs is two hours of peace and quiet.
- Does she need a quiet respite—or an exciting change of pace? Plan accordingly.

Uncommon Sense

305 The "Golden Rule" doesn't always work: *"Do unto others as you would have them do unto you,"* would lead sports fans to get Super Bowl tickets for their wives; clothes-lovers to buy their partners outfits; workaholics to buy their partners briefcases; and handymen to buy their gals tools!

Try the "Platinum Rule" instead: *"Do unto others as they want to be done unto,"* is a philosophy that gives you deeper insights into your partner. The Platinum Rule helps you see the world through your lover's eyes; it enhances your intuition; it improves your gift-giving skills.

For further insights into this way of thinking, I highly recommend the book *The Platinum Rule,* by Tony Alessandra and Michael J. O'Connor.

Romantics are good at thinking in uncommon ways.

Rose Is Rose reprinted by permission of United Feature Syndicate, Inc. © 1990.

306 Contrary to popular belief, you should *not* use romance to apologize after a fight! If you do, you'll taint *all* your romantic gestures for a long time to come. (After a fight, a simple, sincere apology is best. Resume romantic gestures *after* you've both cooled down, or after a week—whichever is later.)

It's the Thought That Counts

307 Couples with A+ Relationships understand that they need to balance these two concepts in their lives: 1) Actions speak louder than words, and 2) It's the thought that counts.

These concepts are two sides of the same coin. Sometimes the action, the gesture, the gift says it all. And other times it's the thought, the meaning, the intention, the words that say it all.

Chapter
Theme Song:
"Thinking About You," Norah Jones

308

- Guys, let's stop: stereotyping women, assuming we know what they think, feeling threatened by feminism, ignoring our feelings, acting macho and superior...
- And start: being real, getting in touch, reviving gallantry, giving of ourselves, making our relationships a top priority, listening more.

309

- Gals, let's stop: male-bashing, assuming that *all* men are romantic boneheads, feeling superior about your relationship skills (which, admittedly, very often *are* superior), putting down the fledgling men's movement, being a martyr...
- And start: giving him the benefit of the doubt, appreciating his quirks, putting yourselves in his shoes, sending him flowers.

310
If you're like me, you probably can't afford to buy an original Renoir for your partner. You might be happy with a poster print, but that may not seem classy enough. Well, now you can get replicas of famous paintings on canvas. Many classic masterpieces are available from The Masters' Collection. Call 800-2-CANVAS, or visit www.masterscollection.com.

Actions Speak Louder Than Words

311 Cuddle up in front of a roaring fire. (No TV. No kids. No phone.)

312 Carve her initials and yours into a tree.

313 Leave a trail of your clothes, leading from the front door to your bedroom.

G.G.
+
K.R.

314 Fill a basin with hot water. Take off his shoes and socks for him. Sit him down in his favorite chair. Wash his feet. Let them soak for ten minutes. Dry off his feet. Resume life as before.

315 Sara loved Christmas, especially those classic, snowy New England Christmases in Boston. One December was unseasonably warm. And as Christmas approached, Sara was downhearted—and doubly so when her husband Jim announced that he had to work on Christmas Eve.

Jim, a contractor, secretly drove his dump truck three hours north into Maine, loaded it with man-made snow from a ski resort, then drove home, spread the snow on the front lawn, and presented a delighted Sara with a White Christmas.

S.W.A.K.

316 FYI, you can get postage stamps for almost *any* interest or passion your partner may have. The U.S. Postal Service has issued stamps over the years that illustrate *thousands and thousands* of topics. This book is a great resource: *The Postal Service Guide to U.S. Stamps.* Call 800-STAMP-24 and ask for the Philatelic catalog.

Patsy Cline & Hank Williams & Bob Wills
Dogs & cats & fish & birds
Spacecraft & astronauts & planets & stars
All fifty states
Lions & tigers & bears (Oh, my!)
Flowers & flowers & flowers & more flowers
State birds & state flowers & state flags
Historical themes & places & people
The Olympics
Inventions & contraptions
Gone with the Wind, The Wizard of Oz
Trains, planes, & automobiles
Peace themes & ecology themes
Presidents, presidents, presidents!
Elvis & Marilyn Monroe & James Dean
Glenn Miller & Count Basie
Cancer awareness
Fruits & rocks & shells
American history, decade by decade
Christmas & holiday themes
Bugs Bunny!
Dinosaurs & comic strips
Frank Lloyd Wright & the Wright Brothers
And, of course, *Love*

317 Did you know that the United States federal government actively promotes love and romance? Well, sort of. They *do* issue Love Stamps through the U.S. Post Office. Use the latest Love Stamps for all of your love letters, cards, and gifts sent via mail.

318 Mail a greeting card to him or her *at work*. A sure way to brighten your lover's work day.

319
- Get a framed print of "The Kiss," by Gustav Klimt.
- Get a reproduction of the sculpture "The Kiss" by Auguste Rodin.
- A romantic ritual: Pause and kiss at your front door.
- Ask him to pick a number between one and fifty. Reward him with that number of kisses.

G.M.F.L.

320 G.M.F.L. ("Geese Mate For Life.") This phrase reflects that eternal love is symbolized by two geese.
- Some people sign their love letters with G.M.F.L.
- Some couples have G.M.F.L. engraved on the inside of their wedding bands.
- Some folks have gotten the 14K gold G.M.F.L. pin from Cross Jewelers. Call 800-433-2988.

> "The first duty of love is to listen."
> —Paul Tillich

321 Jill gave Howard a birthday card with this inscription:

For your birthday I'm giving you a week of E.S.P.N.*

Love, Jill

*E.S.P.N. stands for "Exciting Sex Practiced Nightly."

322 For true romantics...
- CEO means "Chief Erotic Officer."
- RN means "Really Naughty" or "Romantic Nut."
- CPA means "Cupid's Personal Agent."
- MD means "My Darling."
- CFO means something really, really dirty.
- ASAP means "As Sexy As Possible."

Can't Buy Me Love

323a The best way to spend the *most* money on a car is to buy a *Lamborghini Diablo*. (The *second* best way is to buy a *Ferrari F50*.)

323b The best way to spend the *most* money for a *show* is to get *front row center seats* for whatever is the current hottest show on Broadway.

323c The best way to spend the *most* money for *stereo equipment* is to get one of Bang & Olufsen's amazing, high tech, beautifully designed systems. Visit www.bang-olufsen.com.

Chapter Theme Song:
"If I had $1,000,000," Barenaked Ladies

324 You *could* update his *entire* music collection! Convert his aging LP collection of beloved Beatles albums, Moody Blues tunes, and Rolling Stones records to compact discs or MP3s. With new conversion technology available, converting a lifetime collection of five-hundred-some albums could cost less than $1,000 (up to $400 for the LP-to-CD converter and then the cost of CDs and jewel cases). Visit www.hammacher.com.

Give your partner a proof set of coins from the year you were married.

325 Consider buying a fine vintage wine from the year of your lover's birth—or the year of your anniversary. The Antique Wine Company of Great Britain Ltd., has a huge wine cellar of aged fine wines, dating back to 1893. The value of each gift depends on the year. Call 800-827-7153, or visit www.antique-wine.com.

I Want to Hold Your Hand

326

- Simple question: When is the last time the two of you simply went for a *walk* together?
- Complex answer: Now let's be specific here: Part of the definition of "a walk" is that you must hold hands. Also, neither of you can be wearing a Walkman during the so-called "walk." Your speed is important, too. Running and jogging are obviously not romantic. The proper speed is a saunter.

> The speed of love is 1.7 mph—the speed of a casual saunter.

327

Does your partner like *speed* and *thrills*? Plan your vacations around some of the best roller coasters in the U.S., according to *Park World* magazine:

- Superman the Escape, at Six Flags Magic Mountain, in Valencia, California: accelerates from zero to 100 mph in seven seconds.
- Georgia Cyclone, at Six Flags Over Georgia, in Atlanta, Georgia: based on the famous Coney Island Cyclone.
- Magnum XL-200, at Cedar Point, in Sandusky, Ohio: during portions of the ride you actually float off your seat!
- Thunderbolt, at Kennywood, in West Mifflin, Pennsylvania: begins with a terrifying drop into a ravine.
- Beast, at Kings Island, Ohio: the world's longest wooden roller coaster.

> Definition:
>
> Interdigitation: Holding hands.

328 As a couple, dedicate yourselves to *learning something new every day.*

It might be a new word, it might be a fact from the newspaper, it might be something new about each other. And on a regular basis, take a class together. Learn to paint, learn to play piano, learn to speak French, learn new massage techniques.

Help!

329 Give your partner choices: Classic or avant-garde? Conservative or outrageous? Public or private? Here or there? Loud or quiet? McDonald's or Burger King? Big or small? Light or dark? Fast or slow? Today or tomorrow? Active or lazy? One or many? Gold or silver? Red or blue? Day or night? Expensive or inexpensive? Now or later? Right or left? Modern or antique? Serious or funny?

Sally Forth © 1998. Reprinted by permission of North America Syndicate, Inc.

330 A basic romantic concept: "The Gift-of-the-Month Clubs." Here are some creative twists: Create your own...
- Beer-of-the-Month Club
- Romantic-Restaurant-of-the-Month Club
- New-Ice-Cream-Flavor-of-the-Month Club
- Lingerie-Outfit-of-the-Month Club
- New-Sexual-Position-of-the-Month Club
- Stuffed-Animal-of-the-Month Club

Knowing your lover's interests and preferences will help you create your own, unique Gift-of-the-Month Clubs.

All You Need Is Love

331 You've heard it said that "There are no guarantees in life." Well, that's true. You can't get a *guarantee*—but you just may be able to get a *warranty*. One fellow in my Romance Class told us that he surprised his new bride at the conclusion of their wedding ceremony by presenting her with a written "Lifetime Relationship Warranty."

Chapter Theme Song:
"Eternity,"
Robbie Williams

332 It's winter, it's ten degrees below zero, and the wind chill factor makes it feel like forty below. At a time like this, love isn't about preparing a cup of tea—it's about going outside to warm up her car for her!

333

- Once a week for a year: Jot down two reasons why you love him or her.
- Once a week for a year: Jot down one great thing he or she did.
- Once a week for a year: Jot down one inspirational thought.

At the end of the year: Print all this out on a big scroll and present it to your lover.

"Let him kiss me with the kisses of his mouth: for thy love is better than wine."
—Song of Solomon 1:2

334

Number One Tip for Being Romantic in the Twenty-first Century: *Remove yourself from the electronic and media grid* on a regular basis—over a weekend, during vacations, and on random days.

In order to slow down and connect one-on-one with your lover, it helps immensely if you occasionally disconnect from the internet and e-mail, from TV and radio, from newspapers and magazines, from cable and videos, from mobile phones and pagers, from computers and gizmos, from ATMs and credit cards, and from the media in all its forms.

At Home

335 Carry her over the threshold of your house or apartment.

Not for newlyweds only!

336 Your home should be a *romantic hideaway.* You should be ready at a moment's notice to transform your house or apartment into a love nest through the creative use of candles, music, flowers, wine, and food.

337 Make a path of lighted candles leading from the front door to your bedroom. Be waiting for your lover, and let your own flame burn bright!

When dining at home, enhance the mood with soft candlelight.

338 Don't wait until Saturday night to go out dancing. Dance by yourselves at home in your living room. Move the furniture and roll up the rug!

339 When most people decorate or redesign their homes, they plan and sketch, read home-improvement magazines, hire interior designers, spend big bucks, consider color, space, texture, and style. But how many of them consider "romance" as a design element or a goal of the entire project? Consider designing a home with "romance" as its primary guiding principle.

Jot a little love note on a sheet of paper, fold it into a paper airplane, and sail it across the living room to your partner.

At Work

340 Find out where he's having lunch today. Then have flowers delivered there. (Or deliver them yourself!)

341 Instruct your secretary that *all* calls from your wife are to be put through—regardless of what you're doing, or with whom you're meeting. (*Prove* to your wife that she's the top priority in your life.)

342 Copy your face (or other body parts) on the Xerox machine. Mail it to him with a funny or suggestive note.

Call from work simply to say "I love you!" (There's rarely an acceptable reason to go eight straight hours without touching base.)

343 Pack a pillow and a blanket in a picnic basket and surprise your partner by appearing in the office at noon. Tell the secretary to hold all calls. Lock the office door. Turn off the intercom. Close the blinds. Make love on the desk.

344 Same as above, but pack a *real* lunch. (Not as much fun, but more nutritious.)

345 Mail him a Rolodex card with your name and number on it. Write on it: "Your instant resource for love. Call when lonely."

Sweet Stuff

346 Fill a Victoria's Secret box full of green M&M's. Fill an M&M's bag with new lingerie. Present both of them to her in bed.

347
- Smooth the top of an Oreo cookie, then scratch a heart and your initials into the surface.
- Remove the white frosting from the top of a Hostess Cupcake, then write your *own* message using red frosting.

348 Give your partner his or her favorite kind of Girl Scout cookie.

349 Think up fun/clever/suggestive notes to attach to these candies: Good 'n Plenty, Mounds, Snickers, Almond Joy, Fire Balls, Double Bubble, Life Savers, or Hershey's Kisses.
- "Where would I be without you, gal? You really are a *Life Saver.*"
- "Wow! You certainly were a *Fire Ball* last night!"

> **Chapter Theme Song:**
> "Sweet Surrender,"
> Sarah McLachlan

French Chocolate Twigs, Chocolate- and Almond-Dipped Apricots, Cheesecake Lollipops! From the Norm Thompson catalog: 800-547-1160; or visit www.normthompson.com.

- "Here are a few *Kisses* to hold you over until we're together again."

350 Fill the cookie jar with love notes. Fill the mailbox with cookies.

> And if you want to be scandalously romantic, you can get "adult" pastries and chocolate body parts!

Kid Stuff

351 Rediscover and nurture the "child" inside of you. It's the key to your creativity, spontaneity, sense of wonder and joy.

352 When's the last time you watched cloud formations? Take your lover for a walk in a field. Find an unobstructed view. Flop down on a hilltop. What do you see in the clouds? What do you imagine?

> What *else* might you be able to do together in a field??

353
- Surprise her with a little "Trinket Gift" hidden inside a McDonald's Big Mac container.
- Surprise him by hiding a favorite stuffed animal inside his gym bag.

354 Seventy-eight percent of all women love stuffed animals.

355 Most men love gadgets, electronic stuff or tools…"boys' toys." Men never really grow up—our toys simply get more expensive.

366 Get a favorite toy or item from his childhood: a toy, book, report card, or picture from the wall. (Call his parents; they'll *love* to be a part of this idea.) Wrap it up and include a touching note.

Funny Stuff

357 Make copies of some favorite comic strips, then rewrite the captions to make them refer to you and your partner! With the application of a little White-Out and a little creativity, you can have lots of fun turning Blondie and Dagwood into the two of you. Or, picture her as Cathy or Sylvia, or him as Snoopy or Doonesbury.

358 Basic: Tape relevant comics to the refrigerator or the bathroom mirror.

359 Give him a book of collected comics. What's his favorite? "The Far Side," "Calvin and Hobbes," "Peanuts," "Cathy," "Funky Winkerbean," "For Better or For Worse," "Blondie," "Andy Capp," "Pogo"?

360 Beyond "basic":
- Tape a comic to the rearview mirror in his car.
- Insert comics in dinner napkins.
- Stick them in cereal boxes.
- Attach them to the underside of the toilet seat.

361 Funny stuff? You want *funny stuff*?! Why didn't you *say* so? If you want *funny stuff*, you've got to check out The Lighter Side catalog. They've got piles of silly, funny, curious, and odd things. Call 'em at 800-232-0963, visit their website at www.lighterside.com, or write to Post Office Box 25600, Bradenton, Florida 34206.

Cool Stuff

362
- Wouldn't it be cool to take a Japanese flower-arranging course?
- Wouldn't it be wild to rent a classic roadster for an afternoon?
- Wouldn't it be fun to stay in bed together all day on Sunday?

363 Place a full-page ad in your local hometown newspaper to announce your anniversary, or celebrate his birthday, or simply to celebrate your love!

How would your partner define "cool"?

364 Present him with a "favor" (a gift bestowed as a token of goodwill; as a maiden's kerchief given to a knight)— something he'll carry around with him as a reminder of you.

- Classic: a kerchief or scarf
- Meaningful: a short verse printed on a tiny slip of paper
- Intimate: panties
- Silly: a little toy
- Personal: a lock of your hair

Get a kit of Magnetic Poetry, and write little poems to each other on the refrigerator door.

365 If your partner is into puzzles— jigsaw puzzles—then you've got to get in touch with Stave Puzzles and Bits & Pieces. They create the most wonderful, fun, beautiful, and challenging jigsaw puzzles in the world.

These companies will also create custom puzzles that you can use for all kinds of personal occasions. People have used them to spell out marriage proposals, to send personalized birthday greetings, and to help celebrate anniversaries.

- Stave Puzzles: 802-295-5200, www.stave.com
- Bits & Pieces: 1-800-JIGSAWS, www.bitsandpieces.com

Dirty Stuff

366 Plant and care for a garden together. Crawling around in the dirt together has a funny way of bringing a couple closer.

367 They shared a love of gardening. But while his flower garden was a wild riot, her vegetable garden was organized and labeled. One day she did a double-take as she noticed the seed-packet sign on her row of carrots had been changed to read "karats." While her husband barely suppressed a smile, she dug carefully until she found a sealed box containing a three-karat diamond ring!

368 If the two of you enjoy hiking together, try *barefoot* hiking! The Dirty Sole Society can help you find the best trails. Check them out at www.barefooters.org/hikers/.

369 He was an avid gardener. One year, as a surprise for his wife, he planted his flowers in a pattern that spelled out "I LOVE YOU." The message appears only when the flowers are in bloom, and can only be read from their second-story bedroom window.

He changes the message every year. He has great fun, and his wife is thrilled every spring.

Sex!

370 Here's how one couple turned fore-play into a "game," using five dice. First they erased the dots using White-Out. Then they re-labeled all the dice in this manner:

- On a pink ("Hers") die: They wrote a different body part on each of the six sides.
- On a blue ("His") die: They wrote a different body part on each of the six sides.
- On the third die: They wrote a *verb* on each side: "Rub," "Lick," "Kiss," "Massage," etc.
- On the fourth die: They wrote an *adverb* on each side: "Softly," "Quickly," "Slowly," etc.
- On the fifth die: They wrote *time-related* words: "Five minutes," "Half an hour," "As fast as you can," etc.

371 Do you always make love *at night*? How about a little *afternoon delight*?

372 Go in search of her G Spot. You may not find it, but you'll have a great time looking! (Pick up a copy of *Unleashing Her G-Spot Orgasm,* by Donald L. Hicks.)

Chapter
Theme Song:
"Let's Talk About
Sex," Salt-N-Pepa

Funniest
relationship book
ever written: *Is Sex
Necessary?* by
James Thurber &
E.B. White.

Surprise!

373 Surprise her by giving *her* a gift on *your* birthday.

> This is one *heck* of a great surprise!

374 *The Time-Delay Tactic.* Learn what she likes/wants. Get it for her, but hold on to it for a few weeks—or months. (This gives her time to forget about it, or think that you've forgotten.) Surprise her with it when she least expects it.

375 *The Little White Lie.* Setting up surprises sometimes involves a subtle touch, a smooth manner, or outright lying.

> Don't worry, lying in the service of romance is *not* a sin. Lovers receive special dispensation.

376 Surprise him by performing one of his chores for him. (And I don't mean a little thirty-second chore like taking out the garbage! I mean something *time-consuming,* like cutting the lawn or washing his car.)

377 Surprise her by performing one of her chores for her. (And I don't mean something *easy* like carrying the groceries in from the car! I mean something that requires some time and effort. Something like cooking all the meals over a weekend, or cleaning the entire house.)

Note: Because I'm addressing *millions* of people here, I've chosen chores that a majority of people assign along classic gender lines. You certainly have the freedom to choose who does what in *your* household!

Celebrate!

378 *Balloons!* Balloon bouquets. Helium-filled balloons. Heart-shaped red balloons. Mickey Mouse/Snoopy/Garfield balloons. Silvery, shiny Mylar balloons. Giant-sized balloons. Balloons with your names on them. Balloons with personalized messages on them.

Chapter
Theme Song:
"A Celebration," U2

379 New Year's Eve in Times Square! It's a little crowded, but it's tons o' fun!

380 Celebrate the birthday of your partner's favorite cartoon or comic strip character. Buy a birthday cake. Get a book of collected comic strips. Get a T-shirt picturing this character.
* Bugs Bunny's birthday: July 27th
* Garfield's birthday: June 19th
* Mickey Mouse's birthday: November 18th
* Snoopy's birthday: October 2nd

381 Create a "Count-Down Calendar" to mark the time remaining until a birthday, wedding, anniversary, vacation, or "Mystery Day."

382 Celebrate your partner's favorite movie star's birthday. Go out to dinner. Toast the chosen star. Recite the star's famous lines; maybe have these lines rendered in calligraphy or printed on a scroll. Make a gift of a book about this star.

Celebrate the 4th of July: with fireworks—in bed.

Celebrate Thanksgiving: by vowing to stop being a turkey.

Celebrate Halloween: by dressing as sexy fantasy characters.

Celebrate Valentine's Day: at the most elegant B&B within one hundred miles.

Celebrate your anniversary: with a bottle of Dom Perignon.

Celebrate her birthday: aboard a cruise ship in the Mediterranean.

Celebrate his birthday: at the Indianapolis 500.

Celebrate next Tuesday: by playing hooky from work together.

Outrageous!

383 "The Grand Gesture." The once-in-a-lifetime event.

Wouldn't it be a shame to look back on your life and not be able to say that you did one *incredible, unbelievable, outrageous, and wonderful thing* for and with your lover?

- One bold husband in the Romance Class went out and *replaced his wife's entire wardrobe* instead of going on vacation one year! "It cost me $7,500, but it was worth it!" he exclaimed.
- One woman, whose husband is a partner in a prestigious law firm, arranged a *surprise three-week vacation tour of Europe's vineyards* for her husband. He nearly had a heart attack when he realized that his flight to Chicago was really a flight to *Paris*, that his wife was on board the flight, and that all his work was being taken care of by another partner. His wife reports that he *did* finally calm down and had the time of his life.

384 Gals: Greet him at the front door wearing your wedding gown.

385 *Do the impossible* for your lover:
- Get Super Bowl tickets.
- Find that out-of-print book for her.
- Meet her at the airport—when she knows you're busy elsewhere.
- Get tickets to the World Series.
- Get tickets to the NBA or Stanley Cup finals.
- Cook a meal.
- Get tickets to a *sold-out* Broadway show.

Outrageous!

The surprise three-week vacation.
The new red Porsche.
The dancing lessons.
The *ten* dozen red roses.

Passionate!

386 Romantics are Passionate (#1)

I'm not talking about *sexual* passion here, but about a passion for *life*. (Don't worry, we'll get to sexual passion in just a moment!) Romantics don't allow any aspect of their lives to slide into boredom.

- What is your *partner* passionate about? What are you passionate about? What passions do you share?
- List three specific ways that you could enhance your partner's enjoyment of his or her passion.
- Within the next week, figure out a way to give your partner five hours of uninterrupted time to pursue and enjoy his or her passion.

387 Romantics are Passionate (#2)

Yes, as a matter of fact, romantics *do* tend to be more sexually passionate than the average mortal. (Just another of the many side-benefits of the romantic lifestyle!)

Being romantic means *expressing* love. And that expression is often a *physical* expression. The real magic of romance lies in the fact that it includes/weaves together/reflects all facets of love: physical, spiritual, and emotional.

> "Kissing is like drinking salted water. You drink, and your thirst increases."
> —Chinese Proverb

388 Gals, if you want to stimulate a little bedroom passion, try wearing one of his dress shirts to bed. A surprising number of men and women find this to be a great turn-on!

Games People Play

389 *"The First Date Game."* A role-playing game. Pretend that you're going out on your first date together. Re-enact your fondest memories of that first date. (Where did you go? What did you do? What did you eat? What did you talk about?)

People with A+ Relationships don't take themselves too seriously. But they *do* take their partners seriously.

390 Many couples play a curious little game that goes by various names: "Where's the Bunny?" or "Hide and Go Seek" are two favorites.

The rules are simple: You pick a small inanimate object (like a little stuffed animal, a wind-up toy, seashell, piece of plastic fruit, etc.). You take turns giving it to each other in creative, funny ways. Some couples keep the object in constant rotation. Others will wait *months* before giving it back, and go to *incredible* lengths to surprise their partners. World-class players have reportedly:

- Had the object sealed inside a Coke can.
- Sent the object via Federal Express.
- Had an airline attendant deliver it while in flight.
- Had the object appear in a corporate board room.
- Had it delivered by a parachutist.
- Had the object frozen in an ice cube.
- Placed the object in a store display window.

Declare today "Couple's Day." Do *everything* as a couple. Don't leave one another's sight—even for a moment!—from the time you wake up until the time you go to sleep tonight.

Games Lovers Play

391 *"All-Day Foreplay."* Plan in the morning to make love tonight. Call each other all day long with "reminders," ideas, and suggestive suggestions. By the time evening rolls around you'll both feel like you've engaged in foreplay all day long!

392 A surprising number of couples in my Romance Classes play various "Car Games." Here are some of them:
- Kissing at every stop light.
- Kissing whenever you spot a red Corvette.
- Making love at highway rest areas.
- And variations of *"How Far Will You Go?"*

Book recommendation: *The Couple's Guide to Erotic Games,* by Gerald Schoenewolf.

393 *"The Affair Game."* (Recommended especially for those married ten-plus years.) Another role-playing game. Pretend that you're not married to him or her, but you're having an affair with your spouse. How would you act? Where would you go? What would you do? What would you talk about? How and where and when would you make love?

Here's a sexy game: "Connect the Freckles"!

394 *"An Enchanting Evening."* A fun and revealing board game. Check your local toy store or call 800-776-7662, extension 105; or write to Time for Two, 7349 Via Paseo Del Sur, Suite 515, Scottsdale, Arizona, 85258; or visit www.timefortwo.com.

Off the Wall

395

- Tie a piece of string to the inside doorknob of your front door. String it throughout the house, tracing a path that leads to the bathtub, which you've prepared especially for him.
- Variation on a theme: Tie one end of the string to the doorknob, string it through the house—then tie the other end of the string to *yourself.* Wait patiently in the bedroom.

> ### Chapter Theme Song:
> "Crazy," Gnarls Barkley

396 Write her a check for a million kisses.

397 Test drive a Porsche together.

398 Hide a (very) small gift somewhere on your body.

Then say to your lover, "I've got a gift for you, and it's hidden on me somewhere! Find it and it's yours!" Use your imagination—and be sure to leave enough time to participate in any "extracurricular activities" that may result from the search!

399 Some custom T-shirts that Romance Class participants have created:

- *It's the real thing. Love.*
- *Just do it. Love.*
- *W.W.R.D. (What Would Romeo Do?)*
- *Got romance?*

On the Wall

400 Several "off the wall"—or rather, "*on* the wall"—ideas from Romance Class participants:

- The Mosaic Room: A bulletin board for tacking up mementos overflowed onto the wall and eventually took over the entire den!
- The Photo Gallery: Many couples have special walls full of funny, sentimental, meaningful, and romantic photos.
- The Memory Wall: Some couples frame everything from ticket stubs and menus to dried flowers and greeting cards.
- The Wine Wall: Two wine enthusiasts have wallpapered their dining room with wine labels from their favorite bottles.
- The Travelogue Room: Two travel bugs have wallpapered two rooms (soon to be three) with maps of all the places they've visited.

One creative guy wrote a "proposal poem" with which to ask his girlfriend to marry him. He had the poem written in calligraphy and beautifully framed. He then went to the owner of a romantic little restaurant and arranged to have his poem hung on the wall next to a cozy booth. He then took his gal out to dinner and waited for her to notice the "unique" artwork on the wall!

401 Make a collage for her. The theme: her favorite fairy tale. Clip illustrations from several different books. Intersperse photos of the two of you! Combine classic verses from the story with phrases from your own lives.

"Where there is love there is life."
—Gandhi

402 Hire an artist to create a poster illustrating her favorite fairy tale or children's story—and have *her* pictured as the heroine!

The Myths of Romance (I)

403 Myth: "The Battle of the Sexes."

What a *foolish* concept! Yes, it makes cute headlines in women's magazines, and exciting segments on TV talk shows, and funny scenes on sitcoms. However, *there ain't no such thing as a battle of the sexes.* There certainly are some psychological and physical differences ("*Vive la différence!*"), but there's nothing worth terming a "battle."

Beware the power of metaphors!

Here's the problem with this kind of thinking: It leads to stereotyping. You end up treating your partner like "all men" or "all women," and ignore the fact that he or she is really a unique individual. This stereotyping blocks *real* communication, it short circuits *true* intimacy, and it becomes a barrier to true love.

404 Myth: "Nice guys finish last."

Think about it: If you believe that "Nice guys finish last," I suppose that means that "Jerks and bullies finish first." Perhaps this *is* true in the business world and maybe in the world of sports, but it is *definitely* not true in the realm of intimate human relationships.

> True or False?—
> "Nice guys finish last."

Note: "Nice" doesn't mean "wimpy" or "feminine." Nice means *courteous, mature, gentlemanly, thoughtful, loving.*

405 Myth: "Romance will save my relationship."

It's not quite that simple. If the romance is an expression of the love you feel, then it *will* save your relationship. But if the romance is just a *show,* just something you do to pacify your partner, then it *won't.*

The Myths of Romance (II)

406 Myth: "Romance will cover up my faults."

Sorry. A jerk who gives flowers is *still* a jerk. Romantic gestures may disguise your faults in the short-run—but your true personality will always reveal itself. Having realistic expectations about romance will enhance your relationship and help your love grow.

> True or False?—
> "Give her an inch and she'll take a mile."

407 Myth: "Give her an inch and she'll take a mile."

This is a myth promulgated in men's locker rooms and in high school bull sessions. The key word here is "bull."

If you "give an inch" on a consistent basis, you'll satisfy nearly *any* woman. It's when you're stingy with those romantic gestures that a woman builds up so much resentment that she demands "a mile" from you. And rightfully so.

408 Myth: "I can change him."

No you can't. People can be *influenced*, they can be *adjusted*, they can be *manipulated*—but they can't be *changed* or "fixed."

What you *can* do is help your partner learn better skills for expressing his or her feelings. If the feelings of love are in there somewhere, then you can help him to be more romantic.

Men Are from Mars

409 Be aware that *men and women tend to have different styles of communicating.* Deborah Tannen, author of *You Just Don't Understand,* says that a man engages the world as "an individual in a hierarchical world social order in which he [is] either one-up or one-down." A woman, on the other hand, approaches the world as "an individual in the world of connections. In this world, conversations are negotiations for closeness in which people try to seek and give confirmation and support, and to reach consensus."

Without falling into the trap of simplistic stereotypes, Tannen explores the communication styles of men and women, and helps build bridges.

410 Ladies: Do you really think that *he* thinks the way *you* think?

Gentlemen: Do you really think that *she* thinks the way *you* think? Everyone: *Think again!*

- He gives her lingerie:
  - *What he means:* "You'd look great in this."
  - *How she takes it:* "He wants me to look like a slut!"
- She wants to go out for dinner and a movie:
  - *What she means:* "I want to go out for dinner and a movie."
  - *How he takes it:* "I'm going to go broke!"
- He gives her one red rose:
  - *What he means:* "This symbolizes my love for you."
  - *How she takes it:* "He's too cheap to buy a dozen."
- She gives him this book:
  - *What she means:* "This will improve our relationship."
  - *How he takes it:* "She's trying to turn me into someone else."

What to do? Talk more. Assume less. Listen more. Open your heart. Check your assumptions. And keep trying.

Chapter Theme Song:
"Why Can't a Woman Be More Like a Man?" from *My Fair Lady*

Women Are from Venus

411 When women use the word "romance," they're usually referring to *love*. When men use the word "romance," they're often referring to *sex*. (So be careful! The word "romance" can be slippery.)

412 Sales figures show that women tend to prefer pink and white and pastel colors for lingerie, while men prefer to see women in black and red.

- Women: Ask yourself if you're dressing to please him or yourself.
- Men: Ask yourself if the goal of your lingerie gift is to please her or please yourself.

413
- Women: Stop nagging. Even if you're right. (*Especially* if you're right!) Hundreds of women in the Romance Class have told me that nagging and complaining are the quickest ways to drive a man into a resentful—and far from romantic— silence.
- Men: Stop judging. Stop correcting. Stop lecturing. She doesn't need it and doesn't want it. You're not her father or teacher—you're her *lover*.

> **Chapter Theme Song:**
> "Subway to Venus,"
> Red Hot
> Chili Peppers

> Men and women tend to be "thermally incompatible." It is a biological fact that at "room temperature," most women are chilly and most men are warm.

414

- For women: Place a red rose on the lawnmower along with a note: "I appreciate the work you do. And I'll demonstrate just *how much* I appreciate you when you're done with the lawn—so hurry!"
- For men: Float a flower in the kitchen sink along with a note: "Have I told you lately how much I appreciate you? Well I do. I'm warming up a bottle of massage oil just for you. So hurry!"

Men Are (Not) from Mars*

415 Love is not gender-specific. Therefore, *romance* is not gender-specific. Nearly every idea in this book applies to *both* men and women, even

*Mars, mythologically, was the god of *war*, not the god of *masculinity*.

though I sometimes say "her" and other times "his." Don't forget that deep down, we all want the same things in life. Men and women have different *styles*—not different *needs*.

416 Note: Things have changed since the 1950s—men like flowers, too. My last survey indicates that 74 percent of American men would feel comfortable receiving flowers and would appreciate the gesture.

417 The next time you're tempted to fall into using simple gender stereotypes, think about *The Odd Couple.* Felix and Oscar are both "regular guys"—but they're as different as night and day! Their differences arise from their individual, *personalities,* not from their *gender.*

The same applies to you and your partner. Not all women are emotional, intuitive, and communicative. Not all men are logical, aggressive, and practical. While generalizations are generally true, it's *also* true that it's the quirks and idiosyncrasies—the qualities that make people unique—that we fall in love with.

A very useful exercise is to talk together about *how* and *why* you first fell in love with each other. The challenge is to answer very, very specifically. You'll notice that the qualities most people identify are rarely gender-specific ("His eyes." "Her sense of humor." "The way he smells." "His solid values." "We both *love* the same books.")

People with A+ Relationships tend to stay in touch with these qualities in themselves and support those qualities in their partners.

Proof that men are from Earth:
1. A man wrote *Romeo and Juliet.*
2. A man wrote *The Bridges of Madison County.*
3. Fred Astaire was a man.
4. There is an organization called the Order of the Manly Men. They hold a good-natured Manly Man Festival in Roslyn, Washington complete with a Manliest Vehicle Contest and Manliest Tool Belt Competition. Founder R.M. "Bob" Crane is the self-proclaimed "manliest florist in the United States," according to *The Wall Street Journal.*

Women Are (Not) from Venus*

418 Robin shares this story: "The most romantic gift my husband ever gave me was a pair of needle-nose pliers.

*Venus, mythologically, was the goddess of love, not the goddess of femininity.

"You see, my family draws names for Christmas gifts, and my wish list always includes tools—I just like to *fix* things—but nobody ever gives me any! The year I didn't get the needle-nose pliers I requested, I happened to mention to my husband, Mark, that it bothered me that my family didn't take me seriously.

"When December arrived and we were short on cash, Mark and I decided not to give each other any gifts. Celebrating Christmas with Mark's family, I found a tiny wrapped gift from my husband under the tree. His family simply didn't understand why a pair of pliers would bring tears of happiness to my eyes!"

419 Be aware of the differences in men's and women's styles of communicating, *but don't over-emphasize them.* If you focus on the gap, you'll overlook the bridges!

• Bridge #1: The fact that underneath all our differences in style, men and women all want the same things: to be loved, cared for, respected, and appreciated; to have a place of safety and security where we can be ourselves, grow, experiment, and mature.

"Men are from Earth. Women are from Earth. Deal with it."
—George Carlin

- Bridge #2: Romance itself. Romance is a bridge between the sexes, as it is the expression of love. Romance is a language that uses words, gestures, and tokens to communicate the subtle, multifaceted, and complicated feelings of love.

Tuning In

420 "Tune in" to romantic opportunities. They're all around you. *Listen* for them. Watch for them. Raise your awareness of how you actually "screen out" ideas, resources, tips, and opportunities that you could use to enhance your relationship. For example, observe how you read newspapers and magazines. First,

> "Tune in" to romantic ideas on TV, ads, billboards, in store windows, newspapers, magazines, articles, bookstores, card shops, and catalogs.

notice the kinds of items that automatically catch your eye. Then go back, slow down, and notice what you've skimmed over. Train yourself to notice potentially romantic items. You can eventually pass this task on to your subconscious mind—and the process can become rather automatic.

421 Lots of romantic ideas will appear if you focus on your partner's "orientation." An orientation isn't really a "hobby"— it's more an intense interest or generalized passion. It's something that tends to occupy his or her mind, time, and interest. (Someone who is really *into* his Irish heritage isn't exactly practicing a *hobby,* but his "Irishness" is a great focus for you when thinking up romantic ideas for him.) Here are a variety of orientations expressed by Romance Class participants:

- Cats
- Dogs
- Hometown
- College
- Comics
- Lingerie
- Shopping

- Specific sports
- Specific actors
- Clothes
- Music, classical
- Music, specific type
- Music, specific artist
- WW II

- Ethnic heritage
- Puzzles
- Golf
- Science fiction
- Do-it-yourself
- Food!

Do you know what your lover's orientation is? Does he or she know *yours?*

Fine Tuning

422 Everyone has a sense of humor (even accountants!) But the question is, what *kind* of sense of humor? What tickles his or her funny bone? Robin Williams? Rosie O'Donnell? David Letterman? Jay Leno? Paula Poundstone? Monty Python? Abbott and Costello? The Three Stooges? Intellectual humor? Slapstick? Visual humor? Puns? Stand-up comedy? Funny movies? *Saturday Night Live*? Romantic comedies?

The reason that practical jokes are more often cruel than funny is that they're based on the *joker's* sense of humor, and not on the sense of humor of the *victim*. Be *really careful* when pulling practical jokes on your partner!

Take your partner's specific sense of humor into account when you plan dates, buy gifts, and choose movies.

423
- You know that her favorite color is *blue*. But do you know what *shade* of blue? *Sky* blue? *Navy* blue? *Teal* blue? *Turquoise* blue? *Powder* blue? Blue-*green*?
- You know that his favorite TV show is *Star Trek*. But do you know if he prefers the original series, *The Next Generation*, *Deep Space Nine*, or *Voyager*? Also, do you know his favorite episode? His favorite character?
- You know that she *loves* chocolate. But does she prefer *dark* chocolate or *milk* chocolate? Does she have a favorite candy bar? Does she have one (or two) favorite brands?
- Coke or Pepsi? Diet or classic? Decaf or regular?
- McDonald's or Burger King or Wendy's or KFC?

424

- Do you know your partner well enough to make a *perfect* cup of coffee for him or her? How much cream and sugar?
- Do you know your partner well enough to order coffee for him or her at Starbucks? Regular coffee? Decaf? Café mocha? Café latte? Espresso? Double espresso? Cappuccino? Light roast? Dark roast?

Ordinary is what *everyone* does—like renting a movie for Friday night.

Fine tune your romantic gesture: Let's say your partner is a Barbra Streisand fan. Here's the line-up for your "Weekend-Long Barbra Streisand Film Festival":

Funny Girl
Funny Lady
The Way We Were
The Owl and the Pussycat
Yentl
What's Up Doc?
Prince of Tides
A Star is Born

Starstruck!

425 If you'd like to spend a romantic summer night making wishes on falling stars, mark the second week in August on your calendar. The earth passes through the Perseids Meteor Belt around August 12th every year, which usually results in *spectacular* shows for two to three nights. (You may want to plan an evening of stargazing for the 12th, without telling her about the Perseids. She'll be amazed when about a hundred stars per hour streak across the sky!)

> A great idea for *dreamy* romantics.

426 Speaking of falling stars—those that make it all the way to earth are called meteorites. You can buy small meteorites at some rock and gem shops. Have a custom piece of jewelry created to showcase your falling star.

> A great idea for *science fiction* fans! Also great for coming through on your promise to give her "the moon and the stars."

427 If it's the stars of *Broadway* who interest your partner, why not get him a poster from his favorite show? Today's and yesterday's Broadway hits are represented at the Triton Gallery, 630 Ninth Avenue, New York, New York 10036. Call them at 212-765-2472 or 800-626-6674, or visit www.tritongallery.com.

428 If your interest in the stars is more mystical, call Eric Linter, one of the best astrologers in the U.S. While well-versed in the basics of birth charts and astrological predictions, Eric has a dual focus on "spiritually oriented" astrology readings and on "couple dynamics." He prepares individual charts, couple's charts, and special-purpose readings. Many couples ask him for advice on specific dates and times for when to get engaged or married. Call Eric at 617-524-5275.

Chapter Theme Song: "Starry-Eyed Surprise," Paul Oakenfold

Lovestruck!

429 **22 Creative Ways to Celebrate Valentine's Day**

1. Devote yourselves 100 percent to each other on Valentine's Day.
2. Rent a local hotel's Honeymoon Suite.
3. Take the day off from work on Valentine's Day.
4. One day simply isn't enough! Celebrate for a solid week!
5. Buy several boxes of kids' valentines, and flood your partner with them!

Chapter Theme Song: "Love Struck Baby," Stevie Ray Vaughn

6. Give your partner one card every hour on the hour.

7. Make a batch of heart-shaped cookies.

8. Make a giant Valentine card on the back of a travel poster—

9. And have vacation travel tickets (to that location) taped to the poster.

10. Plan a solid day's worth of romantic music.

11. Stay at a local bed & breakfast.

12. Send ten Valentine's Day cards.

13. Send a hundred Valentine's Day cards!

14. Spend the entire day watching romantic movies.

15. Give your modern gal a piece of antique jewelry.

16. Bake a heart-shaped cake—

17. And decorate it with red frosting and heart-shaped sprinkles.

18. Spend every Valentine's Day together—no matter what.

19. Send a Valentine's Day card each day for a week.

20. Send a Valentine's Day card each day for a month.

21. Find the best "Lovers' Package" at a local hotel.

22. Spend the entire day in bed together.

"Love the heart that hurts you, but never hurt the heart that loves you."

—Vipin Sharma

I'm in the Mood for Love

430 Create special "signals" to let your lover know you're in the mood for love. Herewith, some ideas from creative Romance Class participants:

- Have "your song" playing when he returns home from work.
- Play anything by Billie Holiday on the stereo.
- For men: Casually say, "I think I'll shave tonight..."
- One couple has "His" and "Hers" Japanese kimonos. The interested party changes into his or her robe...and if the other is interested too, he or she changes, also.
- One couple has a special pillow that says "TONIGHT" on one side, and "NOT TONIGHT" on the other side.

Chapter
Theme Song:
"Mood,"
Chante Moore

431 Some couples have created signals or gestures for use in *public,* all of which mean "Let's blow this joint, rush home, and make love together!"

- Holding hands and giving three quick squeezes.
- A code word, such as using the word red several times in a row.
- A code phrase, such as, "Is it *hot* in here, or it just me?"

"To be loved for what one is, is the greatest exception. The great majority love in others only what they lend him, their own selves, their version of him."

—Goethe

- Hum "your song" in her ear.
- Scratch your left ear with your right hand.

432 Create a bouquet of "Long Stem Panties" for her. Buy a dozen red, pink, and white panties; buy some plastic roses; remove the plastic buds and replace them with the rolled-up panties.

I'm in the Mood for Chocolate

433 A lifelong passion for chocolate inspired one couple in the Romance Class to embark on a round-the-world search for the Ultimate Chocolate. They actually arrange their vacations so they can visit all of the major chocolate manufacturers in various countries! Now *that's* fanatical!
- Visit the Nestlé chocolate factory in Broc, Switzerland. Call 41-21-924-2111, or visit www.nestle.com.
- The Chocolate Train takes you on a delicious tour to several Swiss chocolate factories. Call them at 888-382-RAIL.
- Or stay closer to home: Visit Chocolate World at the Hershey Chocolate factory in Hershey, Pennsylvania. Call 717-534-4900, or visit www.hersheys.com/chocolateworld.

Best Chocolate-Related Book Title (non-fiction): *Death by Chocolate: The Last Word on a Consuming Passion,* by Marcel Desaulniers

434 People hold wine-tasting parties, right? So why not hold a *chocolate-tasting* party? Invite your best friends, ask them to bring samples of their favorite chocolates, and create a formal methodology for judging the qualities of the finest chocolate. Conduct blind taste comparisons; rank each chocolate for its aroma, texture, sweetness, depth, initial taste, aftertaste, combination of ingredients, etc.

Best Chocolate-Related Book Title (fiction): *Bittersweet Journey: A Modestly Erotic Novel of Love, Longing, and Chocolate*, by Enid Futterman

435

- *The Book of Chocolate,* by Jeanne Bourin, John Feltwell, Nathalie Bailleux, Pierre Labanne, and Odile Perraud
- *Chocolate Obsession,* by Michael Recchiuti and Fran Gage
- *The Art of Chocolate,* by Elaine Gonzalez
- *Pure Chocolate,* by Fran Bigelow and Helene Siegel
- *ChocolateChocolate,* by Lisa Yockelson

The Gospel According to Godek

436 Romantic gestures have no ulterior motive. Their only purpose is to express love and appreciation; to show that you've been thinking of your partner; to bring love alive in the world.

This is a goal to *strive for*, but one that we rarely achieve perfectly. That's okay. Don't worry about it. Love isn't about *perfection*, it's about *love*. And romance isn't about perfection either; it, too, is simply about love.

437 When it comes to *love*—the emotional side of relation-ships—men and women are much more *alike* than we are *different*.

When it comes to *sex*—now *here's* where most of the differences kick in!

You see, humans are a complex mixture of physical and psychological attributes. The more you move down the physical/sexual end of the scale, the more pronounced the *differences* between men and women are. The more you move up the psychological/emotional end of the scale, the more *similar* men and women are.

Love is *simple* but it's not *easy*.

438
- Romance is an art, not a science.
- Love is a cooperative sport, not a competitive sport.
- Romance is not a business. There's no bottom line.
- Love is not a battle. "War" metaphors are harmful to your health.

The Gospel According to Godek (Revisited)

439

- You can lose yourself in love without losing your individuality.
- You can compromise without compromising *yourself*.
- You can change without losing your uniqueness.
- You can grow without growing apart.
- You can give without losing *anything*.
- You can open up without being judged.
- You can disagree without arguing.
- You can feel without losing control.
- You *can* keep the passion alive in a long-term relationship.
- You can be mature without losing the child inside of you.
- You can only be *truly known* in an intimate, long-term relationship.

• • •

- You cannot be known unless your open your heart.
- You cannot love without being vulnerable.
- You cannot be intimate without taking a risk.
- You cannot share feelings in a non-supportive environment.
- You cannot enter a relationship demanding a guarantee.
- You cannot be interdependent unless you're first independent.
- You cannot be controlling and spontaneous at the same time.
- You cannot live without making mistakes.

You can be *insanely* romantic and still be yourself.

- You cannot realize your dreams if you don't have well-defined goals.
- You cannot grow unless you learn from your mistakes.
- You cannot forgive another until you've forgiven yourself first.
- You cannot heal a broken heart until you risk it again.

• • •

- You have the power to choose how your feelings affect you.
- You have the ability to alter your reality with your beliefs.
- You have all the talents and capabilities to fulfill your purpose.

Getting Down to Business

440 Mark *all* significant dates in your appointment book or business calendar. Note: You and your partner may not consider the same occasions to be "significant." Make sure you *think like your partner* when you mark these dates.

- ❏ His or her birthday
- ❏ Your anniversary
- ❏ Valentine's Day
- ❏ First day of each season
- ❏ A "mystery date"
- ❏ Dinner dates
- ❏ Major vacations
- ❏ Three-day weekends
- ❏ Kids' birthdays
- ❏ Pseudo-holidays that he or she likes
- ❏ Favorite rock star's birthday
- ❏ Favorite movie star's birthday

And here's the key to staying on top of things so these dates don't "sneak up" on you: Write reminders to yourself in your calendar *two weeks in advance* of each date to remind yourself to send a card, buy a gift, or make reservations.

441 Another way to ensure that you get those greeting cards, notes, and gifts out on time is to get a three-ring binder with twelve pocket dividers. Label them with the months, and insert relevant items into each pocket. Attach a "Master List" of significant dates to the inside cover. This way, you'll be prepared well in advance of every event that comes along.

- Insert greeting cards, notes, poems, articles, reminders to yourself, ads, catalog pages, etc.
- Make sure *every* pocket has stuff in it—especially for those months that include no "official" anniversaries or holidays. Make up your own holidays and reasons for celebrating!

442 Delegate more at work. Come home at a reasonable hour!

443 Place a flower in his briefcase. Maybe a dozen. Just because.

Funny Business

444 Write wacky notes, memos and things, based on your profession:

- Teacher: Write a report card.
- Lawyer: Write out a motion.
- Trucker: Make a packing slip.
- Executive: Write a business plan.
- Doctor: Write a prescription.
- Secretary: Write a memo.
- Salesman: Place an order.
- Policeman: Write a ticket.
- Anyone: Write a resume.
- Your profession: (____)

445 Call your lover on the phone. Make up a love song on the spot and sing it to her! Make up a tune, make up the words—and just keep singing! (You'll generate laughter as well as appreciation!)

446 Don't let your serious business executive fool you: Most of them love to "play" at their desks. Executive "desk toys" make great gifts. Note: There are several categories of desk toys. Which kind does your partner like?

- Wind-up toys
- Cartoon characters
- Nostalgic items
- Prestige items
- Toy cars and trucks
- Electronic gizmos

- Sports memorabilia
- Puzzles
- Hobby-related items
- Things that move or swivel
- Things to fiddle with

Resources (I)

447a

- The Celebration Fantastic (weddings & other): 800-235-3272, www.celebrationfantastic.com
- Figi's Gift Catalog (you name it!) 715-384-6101, www.figis.com
- For Counsel (for lawyers!): 800-637-0098, www.forcounsel.com
- Golf House (duffers' gifts): 800-336-4446, www.usgapubs.usga.org

And before you buy any jewelry, become an educated buyer. Visit www.jic.org.

- Into the Wind (kites 'n stuff): 800-541-0314, www.intothewind.com
- Levenger (reader's tools): 800-667-8034, www.levenger.com
- Littleton Coin Company (¢): 800-258-4645, www.littletoncoin.com
- Museum of Fine Arts, Boston (artsy): 617-369-3575, www.mfa.org
- The Nature Store (cool & natural): 800-345-1638, www.thenaturestore.com
- Neiman Marcus (clothing & related): 800-825-8000, www.neimanmarcus.com
- Norm Thompson (all kinds of stuff): 800-547-1160, www.normthompson.com
- The Paragon (miscellany): 800-343-3095, www.theparagon.com
- The San Francisco Music Box Company: 800-227-2190, www.sfmusicbox.com
- Cellini Fine Gifts (unique stuff): 888-323-6068, www.cellinifinegifts.com

Get this book before you buy a diamond: *How to Buy a Diamond: Insider Secrets for Getting Your Money's Worth*, by Fred Cuellar.

Resources (II)

447b

- The Sharper Image (techie & cool stuff): 800-344-4444, www.sharperimage.com
- Signals (great gifts): 800-669-9696, www.signals.com
- The Smithsonian (curious items): 800-322-0344, www.smithsonianstore.com
- Stave Puzzles (jigsaw puzzles): 802-295-5200, www.stave.com
- Sundance (Western & rustic): 800-422-2770, www.sundancecatalog.com
- Vermont Teddy Bear Co. (hand-made!): 800-829-BEAR, www.vermontteddybear.com
- Victorian Papers (elegant papers): 800-700-2035, www.victoriantradingco.com
- Williams-Sonoma (cooking tools): 800-541-2233, www.williamssonoma.com
- Rockler Woodworking and Hardware (practical tools): 800-279-4441, www.rockler.com
- S&S Worldwide Games (games & puzzles): 800-888-0987, www.ssww.com
- White Flower Farm (great flowering plants): 800-503-9624, www.whiteflowerfarm.com
- Calyx & Corolla (exotic flowers): 800-800-7788, www.calyxandcorolla.com
- Smith & Hawken (gardening stuff): 800-776-3336, www.smithandhawken.com
- Harry & David (gourmet food): 800-345-5655, www.harryanddavid.com

Sundance was founded by Robert Redford, one of the best romantic stars of all time.

Resources (III)

448 Bridal magazines are great resources for finding romantic vacation destinations. (If you think that honeymoons are just for newlyweds, you're missing some great romantic opportunities!) Pick up a copy of *Brides, Modern Bride, Elegant Bride, Today's Bride, Bride & Groom*, or *Bridal Guide*.

Catalogs are great resources. Not only for specific gifts, but also for ideas and concepts you can implement on your own.

449 Resources around town: Call 'em, ask 'em questions. Send for their catalogs and brochures.

- Adult education programs
- Convention & Visitors Bureaus
- Dance studios
- Music studios
- Cooking schools
- Local amateur theaters
- Museums
- Nightclubs
- Golf courses
- Tennis clubs
- City Hall
- Recreation Department
- The Parks Department
- Bookstores
- Concert halls
- The YMCA and YWCA
- Comedy clubs

450 She loves flowers. He planted a flower garden "to keep the bloom on our love." The challenge, of course, is that most flowers only bloom for a few weeks of the year. Following fifteen years of many different combinations of flowers, he finally found the perfect resource, *Birthflowers of the Landscape,* by Linton Wright McKnight. This book lists *thousands* of flowers and when they bloom.

For the scientifically minded, shop for gifts at:

The American Museum of Natural History, New York City: 212-769-5100, or visit www.amnh.org

The Smithsonian Institution, Washington, D.C. 202-633-1000, or visit www.si.edu

Resources (IV)

451 For researching music for your music lover: *Rolling Stone* magazine's web site is a great resource with lots of song clips, videos, profiles of 85,000 artists, and more. Visit www.rollingstone.com.

452 Looking for a movie for your lover, or movies by a particular director or actor, or movie reviews, or background info on a particular flick? Visit the Internet Movie Database at www.imdb.com.

453 A great resource for old magazines (great for birthday or anniversary gifts!) is the Avenue Victor Hugo Bookstore, in Boston, Massachusetts. Call 781-871-1787, or visit www.avenue victorhugobooks.com.

454 If you'd be interested in "a connoisseur's worldwide guide to peaceful and unspoiled places," then you should subscribe to Andrew Harper's *Hideaway Report,* a monthly newsletter devoted to upscale travel. For more info, visit www.andrewharper.com. The Report's 2007 list of Hideaways of the Year included:
- Poetry Inn, in Napa, California: a beautiful inn nestled in the heart of California's wine country. Call 707-944-0646, or visit www.poetryinn.com
- Les Mars Hotel, in Healdsberg, California: a luxurious, family-owned and operated European hotel. Call 877-431-1700, or visit www.les marshotel.com.

Do you know a couple with an A+ Relationship? They can be a great romantic resource for you.

Slightly Outrageous

455 Visit a karaoke bar and surprise your lover by getting up and singing "your song" to him or her.

456 Overdo something. Don't hold back. Go for it! Give it everything you've got. Be creative. Be wild. Be expressive.
- Does he love M&M's? Fill a one-gallon glass jar with them for him.
- Make love every day for a week. (For a month!?)
- Take your lover on a *surprise* two-week vacation to Paris.
- Call her from work, *every-hour-on-the-hour,* just to say "I love you."
- Send a birthday message via *skywriting!*

457 Go skinny-dipping: in the ocean, in a pond, in a lake, in a river, in a creek, in your pool, in the neighbor's pool!

458 Fill an entire packet of Post-It Notes with romantic sentiments:
- Write twenty-five *sexy* notes.
- Write sixteen *romantic* ideas.
- Write thirty-one *silly* notes.
- Write seven *romantic* song lyrics.
- Write twelve *suggestive* suggestions.
- Wright nine *intriguing* questions.

   Now stick the whole pack of romantic Post-It Notes throughout the house. Or stick up three new notes per day for several weeks!

Be outrageous!
Do something
unexpected.
Overdo something.

Quite Outrageous

459 Gals: Hire a limousine to pick up your husband at the airport upon his return from a business trip. Send the driver into the terminal to locate and help your husband. Be waiting in the back seat of the limo...dressed in your finest lingerie, sipping champagne, and listening to a recording of *Heart String,* by Earl Klugh.

460 How about a balloon adventure—over Switzerland? (Or France. Or Italy. Or Austria.) Call Buddy Bombard's Europe at 800-862-8537, or visit www.buddybombard.com.

And once you get hooked on ballooning, you'll want to know about "In the Air: The Ultimate Catalog for Balloon Enthusiasts"! Call 800-583-8038, or visit www.intheaironline.com

"Outrageous" is giving her ten pounds of Hershey's kisses. "*Quite* outrageous" is filling the bathtub with Hershey's Kisses.

• • •

"Outrageous" is getting Super Bowl tickets for your sports fan. "*Quite* outrageous" is getting seats on the fifty-yard line.

• • •

"Outrageous" is a balloon bouquet delivered to his office. "*Quite* outrageous" is a hot-air balloon vacation over Switzerland.

461 Kidnap her! Blindfold her. Drive her around town until she's thoroughly lost. Then reveal your destination: her favorite restaurant, or maybe a romantic inn.

462 You want more time for love in your life? Shoot your TV.
TV is a black hole that sucks time into it. Have you ever noticed how you're drawn toward a television set when it's on—*even when you're not particularly interested in what's on?* The average American watches about four hours of TV per day.

Slightly Naughty

463 Fill the back seat of your car with pillows. Go for a little drive in the country. Use your imagination.

Musical accompaniment: "Take Me in the Backseat," by The Donnas.

464 *Talk Dirty to Me: An Intimate Philosophy of Sex,* by Sallie Tisdale, is a thought-provoking book on a subject that embarrasses many people. Tisdale observes that our society is publicly lascivious yet Puritanical at heart. "We're vicariously living out, in a public way, sexual permissiveness—because we don't have one-to-one, intimate, mature conversations about sex." A little "talking dirty" might just be a good thing.

465
• How about staging a personal Lingerie Fashion Show for him?
• Or how about creating a Lingerie Fashion Show *videotape* for him?!

466
Gals: Buy some specially selected items of *cheap* lingerie—so he can literally *rip* them off your body!

467
Buy these items of clothing in matching colors: a necktie and silk boxer shorts for *him,* and a bra and panty outfit for *her.* Make a relationship rule that whenever one of you wears your items, your partner must wear his or her matching items. Guaranteed to keep your partner envisioning you all day long!

"*Slightly* naughty" is a garter belt and stockings.
"*Quite* naughty" is a *black* garter belt, matching black bra and panties, black *seamed* stockings and *three-inch* spike heels.

• • •

"*Slightly* naughty" is the movie *The Forty-Year-Old Virgin.*
"*Quite* naughty" is the movie *Secretary.*

• • •

"*Slightly* naughty" is sharing your sexual fantasies with each other.
"*Quite* naughty" is role playing and acting out your sexual fantasies together.

Quite Naughty

468 Join the Mile High Club.

469 Make love in other unusual places, too: cars, trains, beaches, pools, boats, ponds/lakes/oceans, store dressing rooms, libraries, elevators, bathtubs, fire escapes, porches, rooftops, tree houses, boardrooms, saunas, airplanes, kitchen tables, and hot tubs.

> Fly the friendly skies!

470
- One couple in the Romance Class confided that they have a tradition of making love at every wedding reception they attend!
- Another couple keeps a U.S. map in their den with pins marking the many places where they've made love!

471
- Gals: Perform a personal striptease for him. You might be spontaneous about it or you might choreograph and practice your routine. Note: Some stripteases emphasize the *strip* part, while others emphasize the *tease* part. You choose!

If you want a little inspiration—and some choreography—for performing a personal striptease for your lover: Check out the movie 9½

> Best songs to accompany a striptease:
> "Private Dancer," by Tina Turner
> "Naughty Girl" by Beyoncé

Weeks, and fast-forward to 1:18:20 into the film. Take notes, practice, and you're sure to get a rise out of your guy.

- Guys: Does the word "Chippendale" mean anything to you? And for additional inspiration, watch the movie *The Full Monty.* Grab your black bow tie, grab your top hat, drop your inhibitions and drop your pants!

Shopping for Dummies

472 When window-shopping together, pay close attention to items that she *really likes.* Sneak back later and get them for her. (Store them in your "Gift Closet" for use at your discretion.)

473 Get professional help. No, no, I don't mean a *psychiatrist*—I mean hire a *personal shopper.* He or she can help you run those errands and pick up those gifts that you always seem to forget about. Set a budget, provide your personal shopper with some key information about your partner, then set him or her loose in the mall!

Get help!

474 Around your town are all the stores you'll need to inspire and satisfy your romantic urges. Try browsing in each of these types of shops with nothing specifically in mind...and see what romantic possibilities jump out at you. See a list of ideas on the following page.

- Bookstores
- Used bookstores
- Card shops
- Stationery stores
- Toy stores

- Lingerie shops
- Second-hand shops
- School supply stores
- Nostalgia shops
- Sporting goods shops

- Music stores
- Paper stores
- Dress boutiques
- Hotel gift shops
- Video stores

475 Get to know the owner and manager of her favorite clothing boutique. Ask them to inform you of new arrivals that they feel your lover will love. (This is an easy way to get surprise gifts that are guaranteed to please her.)

Advanced Shopping Strategies

476 While out shopping with her: If she's trying on an outfit she *adores* (or that *you* find sexy)—pay for it quickly while she's still in the dressing room. (A good reason to carry *cash* on these little outings.) Return to the dressing room with a pair of scissors, cut off the price tags, and announce that she can wear the outfit out of the store. Watch her jaw drop. Then watch her leap into your arms.

477 Go shopping with no specific task, and no specific goal in mind. *Let the gift find you.*

Introduce the practice of "Zen Shopping."

478 Always be in a "gift-buying mode." I don't mean that you should be shopping *all the time*—but that you should be prepared to buy a great gift whenever you happen upon one. If you have this mindset, you'll usually have birthday and anniversary gifts already purchased long before you need them.

479 Sign up for a Bridal Gift Registry and then go "fantasy shopping." Do this even if—*especially if*—you're already married! Here's what you do: Before going into the department store remove your wedding rings and prepare to pretend you're single. Filling out the registry form together will be fun and will probably reveal

> This tip will give your partner ideas for future gifts for you!

some surprises about each other. Then browse throughout the store and discuss items that you *wish* you could get as gifts. In other words, pretend that money is no object. Do you want that expensive crystal vase? *Put it on your list!*

Note: If you hold a formal rededication wedding ceremony, you just might *really* get some of these dream gifts!

Words of Love / Shakespeare's

480 Use these elegant words on a homemade Valentine card this year:

> *Doubt thou the stars are fire;*
> *Doubt that the sun doth move*
> *Doubt truth to be a liar*
> *But never doubt I love.*

—Hamlet

Write this sonnet on a scroll. Add your own note, something like, "I can't write this poetically, but I *can* love you this passionately."

Sonnet 29

> *When, in disgrace with fortune and men's eyes,*
> *I all alone beweep my outcast state,*
> *And trouble deaf heaven with my bootless cries,*
> *And look upon myself and curse my fate,*
> *Wishing me like to one more rich in hope,*
> *Featured like him, like him with friends possessed,*
> *Desiring this man's art and that man's scope,*
> *With what I most enjoy contented least:*
> *Yet in these thoughts myself almost despising,*
> *Haply I think on thee, and then my state,*
> *Like to the lark at break of day arising*
> *From sullen earth, sings hymns at heaven's gate;*
> > *For thy sweet love remembered such wealth brings*
> > *That then I scorn to change my state with kings.*

Or how about some "verbal foreplay"?

Use these words to accompany a jewelry gift:

> *Win her with gifts, if she respects not words,*
> *Dumb jewels often in their silent kind*
> *More than quick words do move a woman's mind.*

> —*Two Gentlemen of Verona*

> *Grace on my lips; and if these hills be dry,*
> *Stray lower, where the pleasant fountains lie.*

> —*Venus and Adonis*

World-Class romantic date: Go see the play *Romeo and Juliet.* And it wouldn't hurt to rent one of the many film versions of *Romeo and Juliet.*

Words of Love/Poetic

481a

To see how the power of *eloquent words* can affect the course of romance, see the movie *Roxanne*, starring Steve Martin.

Indeed this very love which is my boast,
And which, when rising up from breast to brow,
Doth crown me with a ruby large enow
To draw men's eyes and prove the inner cost,—
This love even, all my worth, to the uttermost,
I should not love withal, unless that thou
Hadst set me an example, shown me how,
When first thine earnest eyes with mine were crossed
And love called love. And thus, I cannot speak
Of love even, as a good thing of my own:
Thy soul hath snatched up mine all faint and weak,
And placed it by thee on a golden throne,—
And that I love (O soul, we must be meek!)
Is by thee only, whom I love alone.

—Elizabeth Barrett Browning

481b

A great marriage is a love poem with two authors.

O, lift me from the grass!
I die, I faint, I fail!
Let thy love in kisses rain
On my lips and eyelids pale.
My cheek is cold and white, alas!
My heart beats loud and fast:
Oh! press it close to thine again,
Where it will break at last!

—Lord Byron, last stanza of
"The Indian Serenade"

481c Memorize her favorite poem, or the lyrics to her favorite love song. Recite it at private times, or while making love.

"And think not you can guide the course of love. For love, if it finds you worthy, shall guide your course."
—Kahlil Gibran

Words of Love / Your Words

482 Write your own words of love. Here are some ideas to get you started:

- List "Ten Reasons I Fell in Love With You."
- List "Ten Reasons I *Still* Love You."
- List "Ten Ways You Turn Me On."
- List "Ten Reasons You Should Stick With Me."
- List "Ten Reasons You Should Marry Me."

You can use these ideas for scrolls or cards or frame-able items for many romantic occasions.

483 Keep a journal. Every day or so, write down your thoughts about your partner, about your relationship, about your lives together. Some days you'll just jot a quick "I love you"—other days you may be inspired to write page after page. Do this for an entire year. Then present it to her on your anniversary or her birthday.

484 Write your *own* version of Elizabeth Barrett Browning's famous poem "How do I love thee, let me count the ways..."

485 Place an ad in the Personals column of your local newspaper. Let your lover know why he or she is so special. Write it in "code," possibly using your private pet name for her. This is a great opportunity to exercise your creativity and express your feelings in just a few clever words.

- When the ad appears, circle it and leave it on the kitchen table when you leave for work.
- Or call him at work on the day the ad appears, and tell him there's a secret message for him on a certain page of the morning newspaper.

Words of Love/the Ancients

486 "To be able to say how much you love is to love but little."
—Petrarch

"One word frees us all of the weight and pain of life.
That word is Love."
—Sophocles

"Take away leisure and Cupid's bow is broken."
—Ovid

"The anger of lovers renews the strength of love."
—Pubilius Syrus

"Love conquers all things; let us too surrender to Love."
—Virgil

"The happiness of your life depends on the
quality of your thoughts."
—Marcus Antonius

"Because of a great love, one is courageous."
—Lao Tzu

"Love is a grave
mental disease."
—Plato

"The more a man knows,
the more he forgives."
—Confucius

"Union gives strength."
—Aesop

"The madness of love is the greatest of heaven's blessings."
—Plato

"When male and female combine, all things achieve harmony."
—Tao Te Ching

"From their eyelids as they glanced dripped love."
—Hesiod

"Love is all we have, the only way that each can help the other."
—Euripides

"My love for you is mixed throughout my body."
—Ancient Egyptian Love Song

Memorize This List

487a

1. Favorite color
2. Lucky number
3. Favorite flower
4. Favorite author
5. Favorite book (fiction)
6. Favorite book (non-fiction)
7. Favorite fairy tale
8. Favorite children's book
9. Favorite Bible passage

Chapter
Theme Song:
"My Favorite Thing,"
Silverchair

10. Favorite saying
11. Favorite proverb
12. Favorite poem
13. Favorite poet
14. Favorite song
15. Favorite singer
16. Favorite musical band
17. Favorite kind of music
18. Favorite dance tune
19. Favorite romantic song
20. Favorite slow dance tune
21. Favorite rock 'n roll song
22. Favorite ballad
23. Favorite country song
24. Favorite Gospel song
25. Favorite jazz number
26. Favorite R&B tune
27. Favorite songwriter
28. Favorite magazine
29. Favorite meal
30. Favorite food
31. Favorite vegetable
32. Favorite fruit
33. Favorite cookie
34. Favorite ice cream
35. Favorite kind of chocolate
36. Favorite snack food
37. Favorite restaurant (expensive)
38. Favorite restaurant (frugal)
39. Favorite fast food joint
40. Favorite TV show (current)
41. Favorite TV show (old)

42. Favorite comedian
43. Favorite actor (living)
44. Favorite actor (of any era)
45. Favorite actress (living)
46. Favorite actress (of any era)
47. Favorite movie of all time
48. Favorite adventure movie
49. Favorite erotic movie
50. Favorite romantic comedy
51. Favorite comedy film
52. Favorite action movie
53. Favorite Broadway play
54. Favorite musical
55. Favorite show tune
56. Favorite breed of dog
57. Favorite breed of cat
58. Favorite animal
59. Favorite comic strip
60. Favorite comic character
61. Favorite TV cartoon
62. Favorite TV cartoon character
63. Favorite artist
64. Favorite style of artwork
65. Favorite painting
66. Favorite sculpture
67. Favorite hero/heroine
68. Role model (actual person)
69. Role model (fictional)
70. Favorite athlete
71. Favorite sport (to watch)
72. Favorite sport (to play)

Exploring these topics will help you get to know your partner's likes and dislikes a little bit better. Discussing these things will bring you closer together. And knowing these things will also help you express your love more effectively and buy more appropriate gifts.

You should know these things about your lover!

Memorize This List, Too

73. Favorite Olympic sport
74. Favorite sports teams
75. Favorite board game
76. Favorite foreplay activity (to receive)
77. Favorite foreplay activity (to perform)
78. Favorite lovemaking position
79. Favorite sexy outfit (for partner)
80. Favorite sexy outfit (for self)
81. Favorite erotic fantasy
82. Favorite time of day to make love
83. Favorite place on body to be touched erotically
84. Favorite music to make love to
85. Favorite season
86. Favorite time of day
87. Favorite holiday
88. Favorite hobby
89. Favorite type of jewelry
90. Preferred jewelry metal (silver, gold, or platinum?)
91. Preferred style of clothing (for self)
92. Preferred style of clothing (for partner)
93. Favorite designer
94. Favorite erotic clothing (for self)
95. Favorite erotic clothing (for partner)
96. Dream vacation spot
97. Favorite vacation activity
98. Favorite city

99. Favorite foreign country
100. Favorite wine
101. Favorite champagne
102. Favorite beer
103. Favorite soft drink
104. Favorite way to spend a lazy afternoon
105. Favorite room in your home
106. Favorite perfume
107. Favorite cologne
108. Favorite brand of make-up
109. Favorite aroma
110. Favorite fictional character
111. Favorite historical personality
112. Best gift ever received
113. Favorite way to relax
114. Favorite way to get energized
115. Favorite store
116. Favorite side of the bed
117. Favorite TV sitcom
118. Favorite TV drama
119. Favorite joke
120. Favorite classical composer
121. Favorite symphony
122. Favorite opera
123. Favorite album/CD
124. Favorite car (make & year)
125. Favorite color for a car
126. Favorite gemstone
127. Favorite day of the week
128. Favorite month of the year

Togetherness

488 Invite her to accompany you on your next business trip. (All work and no play makes hubby a bore.)

489 Read the Sunday newspaper in bed together. Read the Sunday comics aloud (use appropriate voices).

490 Explore together: auctions, flea markets, second-hand stores, garage sales, and rummage sales. They're great places to find "Trinket Gifts," little surprises and gag gifts.

491 Cook a meal *together*.

492 Go into a bookstore together. Buy each other two books:
- One that you know your *partner* will like.
- And one that *you* want your partner to read.

493 Sit down together on the first day of every month and review your calendars. Make your romantic plans *first,* and *then* fit your other meetings, appointments, and commitments into your schedule. Couples who have an A+ Relationship keep their love life a number one priority.

Chapter Theme Song: "We Belong Together," Mariah Carey

Familiarity does *not* "breed contempt"— it's boredom and lack of creativity that breed contempt.

Dependence isn't healthy in a love relationship. It leads to co-dependency.

Independence doesn't work well, either. What's the point of being a *couple* if your main goal is to be *independent*?

Interdependence is the goal that people in A+ relationships aim for.

Twogetherness

494 Some Things that Come in "Twos"

- Bicycles built-for-two
- Double sleeping bags
- Two-seater sports cars
- A Chinese pu-pu platter for two
- Mozart's Sonata in D Major for Two Pianos, K. 448
- Two-person kayaks
- Two-for-the-price-of-one specials at stores
- Two-for-the-price-of-one specials at restaurants
- Duets: "Endless Love," by Luther Vandross and Mariah Carey
- Loveseats

Chapter Theme Song:
"Party for Two,"
Shania Twain

495 Many couples have "His" and "Hers" matching towels. With a little creative romantic thinking, here's what you can come up with:

- "His" and "Hers" matching silk pajamas
- "His" and "Hers" bottles of red and white wine
- "His" and "Hers" matching motorcycles

Some *more* things that come in "twos":

Stravinsky's Concerto for Two Pianos
Singing songs in two-part harmony
Doubles solitaire
Wedding rings
Double beds
See-saws
Double-scoop ice cream cones
Two-person hot tubs

- "His" and "Hers" matching T-shirts
- "His" and "Hers" overnight bags (have packed at all times)
- "His" and "Hers" matching coffee mugs
- "His" and "Hers" jack-o-lanterns at Halloween
- "His" and "Hers" rocking chairs
- "His" and "Hers" bicycles
- "His" and "Hers" mobile telephones
- "His" and "Hers" Porsches (millionaires need love, too)
- "His" and "Hers" VW Bugs (love for the rest of us)
- "His" and "Hers" tennis rackets
- "His" and "Hers" matching heart-shaped tattoos!
- "His" and "Hers" Christmas tree ornaments
- "His" and "Hers" matching beach towels

Two

496 There are two kinds of people in the world: *Detail People* and *Overview People.*

Detail People focus on the little things; they notice details. Overview People focus on the big picture; they see general trends. Neither is right or wrong, these are simply character tendencies.

It will be much easier for you to pull romantic surprises if you're a Detail Person and your partner is an Overview Person. Detail People are good at covering their trail, paying attention to the little things, and acting "normal." The overview partner won't even notice any little slips. If *you're* the Overview Person, you'll need to be extra careful when planning surprises. Those detail-oriented partners will notice every unusual phone call, every little change in your schedule, and that mischievous look on your face!

497

There are two kinds of people in the world:
Object People and *Experience People*.

Object People see love symbolized in gifts, in *things*: roses, jewelry, socket wrench sets. Experience People see love expressed in time spent together, in *experiences*: dinner, movies, bowling. Neither is better than the other, they're just personal preferences. And, interestingly, neither preference is related to gender.

Why do you need to know this? Because if your partner is an Object Person, and you take her to the best restaurant in town and drop $200 on an elegant *experience*, she'll still be expecting a *gift* at the end of the evening! She's not being selfish, she's simply being herself.

Object People love items that have special *meaning*. Experience People love activities that create special *memories*.

Tip: Don't argue about it. Neither of you will *ever* change the other!

There are two kinds of people in this world: High Maintenance People—and Low Maintenance People. (For further insights into this concept see the movie *When Harry Met Sally*.)

There are two kinds of people in this world: People Who Will Spend Hours to Find That Three Cents Needed to Balance the Checkbook—and People Who Will Round Off to the Nearest Hundred Dollars Just to be Done With It.

Two (II)

498 There are two kinds of people in the world:
Left-Brained People and *Right-Brained People.*

Left-Brained People tend to be logical and analytical. Right-Brained People tend to be emotional and intuitive. The current cultural stereotype is that men are logical and women are emotional. This is often—but not nearly always—true. Studies show that this generalization is true for about 60 percent of people. The important lesson for lovers is to treat your partner as an *individual,* not as a stereotype.

499 There are two kinds of people in the world:

People Who Sleep With the Windows *Open,* and People Who Sleep With the Windows *Closed.*

The serious point here is this: It's not about being *right* or *wrong.* It's about working things through, compromising, appreciating each other's quirks, and laughing a lot. (And on the practical side, an electric blanket with *dual controls* just might be a relationship-saving gift!)

There are two kinds of people in the world: People With One Left Foot and One Right Foot, and People With Two Left Feet. Note: The dancers and the non-dancers always marry each other. Nobody knows why.

5OO There are two kinds of people in the world:

Morning People and *Night People.*

Morning People leap out of bed at daybreak and are raring to go, then they close up shop by 8 p.m. Night People are just getting warmed up by sundown, do their best work after midnight, then sleep until noon. Don't take Morning People on late night dates—they'll doze off. Brisk morning walks and elegant breakfasts are more their style.

Don't serve Night People breakfast in bed. They shine at dinner parties. They love late-night movies and midnight lovemaking.

> There are two kinds of people in the world: Dog People and Cat People. Don't trifle with either kind!

The 99 Best Love Songs of the Twentieth (and Twenty-First) Centuries (#'s 1-25)

500a

1. "You Are So Beautiful (To Me)," Joe Cocker
2. "At Last," Etta James
3. "Something," The Beatles
4. "My Heart Will Go On," Celine Dion
5. "Endless Love," Diana Ross & Lionel Richie
6. "Everything," Lifehouse
7. "Colour My World," Chicago
8. "From This Moment On," Shania Twain
9. "Unchained Melody," The Righteous Brothers
10. "Amazed," Lonestar
11. "Crazy for You," Madonna
12. "Just the Way You Are," Billy Joel
13. "The One I Love," Frank Sinatra
14. "Come Away With Me," Norah Jones
15. "Through the Years," Kenny Rogers
16. "Breathe," Faith Hill
17. "Unforgettable," Nat King Cole
18. "I Will Always Love You," Whitney Houston
19. "Hero," Enrique Iglesias
20. "We Belong Together," Mariah Carey
21. "(I've Had) The Time of My Life," Bill Medley & Jennifer Warnes
22. "My Eyes Adored You," Frankie Valli
23. "All My Life," K-Ci and Jojo
24. "I Won't Last a Day Without You," Paul Williams
25. "I Honestly Love You," Olivia Newton-John

What are *your* Top Ten love songs?

FYI: Frank Sinatra said that the *best love song ever written* was "Something," by The Beatles.

The 99 Best Love Songs of the Twentieth (and Twenty-First) Centuries (#'s 26–50)

500b

26. "Up Where We Belong," Joe Cocker & Jennifer Warnes
27. "Fields of Gold," Sting
28. "We've Got Tonight," Kenny Rogers & Sheena Easton
29. "Let's Talk About Love," Celine Dion
30. "All I Want Is You," U2
31. "Ain't No Mountain High Enough," Diana Ross & The Supremes
32. "Goin' Out of My Head/Can't Take My Eyes Off You," The Lettermen
33. "If I Fell," The Beatles
34. "My Valentine," Martina McBride
35. "Somewhere My Love," Frank Sinatra
36. "The Dance," Garth Brooks
37. "In Your Eyes," Peter Gabriel
38. "A Sorta Fairytale," Tori Amos
39. "Unchained Melody," Rodney McDowell
40. "Can't Help Falling in Love," Elvis Presl
41. "All My Loving," The Beatles
42. "A Moment Like This," Kelly Clarkson
43. "You and I," Eddie Rabbitt & Crystal Gayle
44. "Devoted To You," Everly Brothers
45. "Love Will Find Its Way to You," Reba McEntire
46. "For the First Time," Kenny Loggins
47. "When a Man Loves a Woman," Percy Sledge
48. "Islands in the Stream," Kenny Rogers & Dolly Parton
49. "Blessed," Christina Aguilera
50. "Embraceable You" from the musical *Crazy for You.*

The 99 Best Love Songs of the Twentieth (and Twenty-First) Centuries (#'s 51-75)

500c

51. "Babe," Styx
52. "Your Everything," Keith Urban
53. "You've Got a Way," Shania Twain
54. "The Right Thing To Do," Carly Simon
55. "I Want You, I Need You, I Love You," Elvis Presley
56. "Comfort Me," Tim McGraw
57. "I'll Be There for You," Bon Jovi
58. "It Had to Be You," Harry Connick Jr.
59. "All You Wanted," Michelle Branch
60. "Longer," Dan Fogelberg
61. "Missing You Now," Michael Bolton
62. "My Girl," Temptations
63. "Nights In White Satin," The Moody Blues
64. "Truly Madly Deeply," Savage Garden
65. "Straight from the Heart," Bryan Adams
66. "Suddenly," Olivia Newton-John & Cliff Richard
67. "If You Asked Me To," Celine Dion
68. "The Wedding Song," Peter, Paul & Mary
69. "Time In A Bottle," Jim Croce
70. "Escape," Enrique Iglesias
71. "Back to You," John Mayer
72. "You Are The Sunshine of My Life," Stevie Wonder
73. "I Could Not Ask For More," Edwin McCain
74. "Dreams," The Cranberries
75. "You're the First, the Last, My Everything," Barry White

Is "your song" on this list?

The 99 Best Love Songs of the Twentieth (and Twenty-First) Centuries (#'s 76–99)

500d

76. "(Everything I Do) I Do It For You," Bryan Adams
77. "Coming Around Again," Carly Simon
78. "Music of My Heart," 'NSYNC
79. "Flame in Your Eyes," Alabama
80. "Head Over Heels," Tears for Fears
81. "I Knew I Loved You," Savage Garden
82. "How Sweet It Is (To Be Loved By You)," James Taylor
83. "I Go Crazy," Paul Davis
84. "I Just Want to be Your Everything," Andy Gibb
85. "We've Only Just Begun," The Carpenters
86. "I'm Your Angel," R. Kelly and Celine Dion
87. "You Send Me," Sam Cooke
88. "Last Dance," Brian McKnight
89. "A Whole New World," Peabo Bryson & Regina Belle
90. "Reunited," Peaches & Herb
91. "Say You'll Be Mine," Christopher Cross
92. "I Need Your Love Tonight," Elvis Presley
93. "You Sang to Me," Marc Anthony
94. "Everlasting Love," Howard Jones
95. "(They Long To Be) Close To You," The Carpenters
96. "I Love You," Sarah McLachlan
97. "This Heart of Mine," Judy Garland
98. "Wonderwall," Oasis
99. "Love Is a Many-Splendored Thing," Four Aces

What love song do you think deserves to be number *one hundred?!* Let me know via www.1001waystobe romantic.com.

Songs to Help Express Your Feelings

500e

Friendship & Appreciation
- "Anytime You Need a Friend," Mariah Carey
- "Crash and Burn," Savage Garden
- "My Friend," Annie Palmer
- "I'll Back You Up," Dave Matthews Band
- "I'll Stand By You," The Pretenders

Falling in Love
- "When I Fall in Love," Celine Dion & Clive Griffin
- "Dreaming of You," Selena
- "For the First Time," Kenny Loggins
- "Falling in Love," Howie Day
- "Fallin'," Alicia Keys

New Love
- "We've Only Just Begun," The Carpenters
- "Save the Best for Last," Vanessa Williams
- "Sweet Surrender," Sarah McLachlan
- "The First Time Ever I Saw Your Face," Roberta Flack
- "All My Loving," The Beatles

Love & Joy
- "Everything," Lifehouse
- "It Had to Be You," Harry Connick Jr.
- "Let's Hang On," The Four Seasons
- "Love Me Do," The Beatles
- "The Way You Do the Things You Do," Temptations
- "What a Wonderful World," Louis Armstrong

Gentle & Sweet
- "All Right," Christopher Cross
- "Before Your Love," Kelly Clarkson
- "My Love," Paul McCartney & Wings
- "Strange Magic," Electric Light Orchestra
- "Because of Love," Janet Jackson
- "(They Long To Be) Close To You," The Carpenters

Songs to Help Express Your Feelings

500f

Love & Tenderness
- "Always On My Mind," Willie Nelson
- "First Time Ever I Saw Your Face," Roberta Flack
- "Be Without You," Mary J. Blige
- "In My World," The Moody Blues
- "Truly Madly Deeply," Savage Garden
- "Longer," Dan Fogelberg
- "Evergreen," (from *A Star Is Born*), Barbra Streisand
- "Still," Commodores

Intense Love & Infatuation
- "Can't Take My Eyes Off You," Frankie Valli
- "Do the Walls Come Down," Carly Simon
- "Every Breath You Take," The Police
- "At the Stars," Better Than Ezra
- "Possession," Sarah McLachlan
- "I Fall to Pieces," Patsy Cline
- "I Will Always Love You," Whitney Houston
- "If I Ain't Got You," Alicia Keys

- "When a Man Loves a Woman," Percy Sledge
- "(Your Love Has Lifted Me) Higher and Higher," Rita Coolidge

Loneliness & Missing You
- "So Far Away," Carole King
- "I Miss You," Incubus
- "Here Without You," 3 Doors Down
- "Missing You," Mary J. Blige
- "Remember When It Rained," Josh Groban
- "Wish You Were Here," Incubus
- "You've Lost That Lovin' Feeling," Daryl Hall & John Oates

Songs to Help Express Your Feelings

500g

Longing & Yearning

- "Without You," Badfinger
- "Ain't No Sunshine," Bill Withers
- "Just Wanna Be With You," Enrique Iglesias
- "Closer to Believing," Emerson Lake & Palmer
- "How Can I Tell You," Cat Stevens
- "I Need You," America
- "If Ever You're in My Arms Again" Peabo Bryson
- "If I Can't Have You," Yvonne Elliman
- "Can't Live Without You," Scorpions
- "Until the Night," Billy Joel
- "Watching and Waiting," The Moody Blues
- "Without You," Silverchair
- "You Take My Breath Away," Queen

Forgive Me/Don't Leave Me!

- "Baby Come Back," Player
- "Sorry," Daughtry
- "Hard to Say I'm Sorry," Chicago
- "Forgive Me," Evanescence
- "One More Night," Phil Collins
- "Please Forgive Me," David Gray

Fun & Whimsical

- "Can't You Hear My Heartbeat," Herman's Hermits
- "Crazy Little Thing Called Love," Queen
- "My Love," Justin Timberlake
- "Hello Goodbye," The Beatles
- "Ice Cream," Sarah McLachlan
- "If I Had a Million Dollars," Barenaked Ladies
- "I'm Gonna Be (500 Miles)," Proclaimers
- "Let's Call the Whole Thing Off," Fred Astaire and Ginger Rogers
- "Your Body Is a Wonderland," John Mayer
- "Silly Love Songs," Paul McCartney and Wings
- "When I'm Sixty-Four," The Beatles

Songs to Help Express Your Feelings

500h

Devotion & Commitment
- "Ain't No Mountain High Enough," Diana Ross
- "An Everlasting Love," Andy Gibb
- "I Do (Cherish You)," 98 Degrees
- "Hopelessly Devoted to You," Olivia Newton-John
- "Love of My Life," Santana and Dave Matthews
- "I'll Cover You," from the Broadway musical *Rent*
- "From This Moment On," Shania Twain
- "Love of My Life," Abba
- "The Right Thing To Do," Carly Simon
- "Say You'll Be Mine," Christopher Cross
- "You're My Everything," The Temptations

Adoration
- "Cherish," The Association
- "Adore You," Nikki Hassman
- "I Just Want to be Your Everything," Andy Gibb

- "Hero," Enrique Iglesias
- "My Love," Paul McCartney & Wings
- "Wind Beneath My Wings," Bette Midler

Anniversaries & Celebrations
- "Always and Forever," Heatwave
- "The Anniversary Song," Richard Tucker
- "A Celebration," U2
- "Holiday," Madonna
- "More Today Than Yesterday," Spiral Staircase
- "Our Love Is Here to Stay," Harry Connick, Jr.

Poignant
- "Takes My Breath Away," Tuck and Patti
- "All I Want Is You," U2
- "Truly," Lionel Richie
- "Without You," from the Broadway musical *Rent*

Songs to Help You Express Your Feelings

5001

Suggestive
- "In the Mood," Glenn Miller
- "Lay Lady Lay" Bob Dylan
- "Light My Candle," from the Broadway musical *Rent*
- "Makin' Whoopee!" Eddie Cantor
- "Waiting for Tonight," Jennifer Lopez
- "So Deep Within You," The Moody Blues
- "We've Got Tonight," Kenny Rogers & Sheena Easton

Desire & Sexual Attraction
- "Afternoon Delight," Starland Vocal Band
- "Feel Like Makin' Love," Bad Company
- "I'll Make Love to You," Boyz II Men
- "Desire," U2
- "I Really Want You," James Blunt
- "Turn Me On," Norah Jones
- "In Your Eyes," Peter Gabriel
- "Slave to Love," Bryan Ferry
- "The Sweetest Sin," Jessica Simpson

Hot Passion
- "I'll Make Love to You," Boyz II Men
- "Deeper and Deeper," Madonna
- "Let's Do It Again," TLC
- "Hot Stuff," Donna Summer
- "I Do What I Do," John Taylor
- "If," Janet Jackson
- "Kiss You All Over," Exile
- "Hold Me, Thrill Me, Kiss Me, Kill Me," U2
- "Make Me Lose Control," Eric Carmen
- "Touch Me (I Want Your Body)," Samantha Fox

Songs to Help Express Your Feelings

500j

Country Love Songs

- "Blue," LeAnn Rimes
- "Amazed," Lonestar
- "Forever and For Always," Shania Twain
- "Everything I Love," Alan Jackson
- "Flame in Your Eyes," Alabama
- "He Stopped Loving Her Today," George Jones
- "How Forever Feels," Kenny Chesney
- "I'll Always Love You," Dolly Parton
- "Let's Make Love," Tim McGraw & Faith Hill
- "Cowboy Take Me Away," Dixie Chicks
- "Love Me Like You Used To," Tanya Tucker
- "Love Will Find Its Way to You," Reba McEntire
- "Your Everything," Keith Urban
- "She's in Love with the Boy," Trisha Yearwood
- "The Dance," Garth Brooks
- "This Night Won't Last Forever," Sawyer Brown
- "We Danced," Brad Paisley
- "Unchained Melody," Rodney McDowell
- "Breathe," Faith Hill

Love Songs that Put Women on a Pedestal

- "Island of Life," Jon Anderson & Kitaro
- "Lady," Kenny Rogers
- "Oh, Pretty Woman," Roy Orbison
- "She's a Lady," Tom Jones
- "Three Times a Lady," The Commodores
- "When A Man Loves A Woman," Percy Sledge

Best Love Song Duets

500k

- "A Whole New World," Peabo Bryson & Regina Belle
- "Ain't No Mountain High Enough," Marvin Gaye & Tammi Terrell
- "Ain't Nothing Like the Real Thing," Marvin Gaye & Tammi Terrell
- "All My Life," Linda Ronstadt & Aaron Neville
- "My Boo," Alicia Keys & Usher
- "Beauty and the Beast," Celine Dion & Peabo Bryson
- "Can't We Try," Dan Hill & Vonda Sheppard
- "The Closer I Get to You," Roberta Flack & Donny Hathaway
- "Cruisin'," Gwyneth Paltrow & Huey Lewis
- "I Can't Help It," Andy Gibb & Olivia Newton-John
- "I Finally Found Someone," Bryan Adams and Barbra Streisand
- "I Got You Babe," Sonny & Cher
- "I Just Can't Stop Loving You," Michael Jackson & Siedah Garrett
- "I Knew You Were Waiting (For Me)," Aretha Franklin & George Michael
- "I Like Your Kind of Love," Andy Williams & Peggy Powers
- "Islands in the Stream," Kenny Rogers & Dolly Parton
- "Leather and Lace," Stevie Nicks & Don Henley
- "Broken," Amy Lee & Seether
- "Mockingbird," Carly Simon & James Taylor
- "The Next Time I Fall," Peter Cetera & Amy Grant
- "One Man Woman/One Woman Man," Paul Anka & Odia Coates
- "Put a Little Love in Your Heart," Annie Lennox & Al Green
- "Set the Night to Music," Roberta Flack & Maxi Priest
- "Somewhere Out There," Linda Ronstadt & James Ingram
- "Then Came You," Dionne Warwick & the Spinners
- "Tonight, I Celebrate My Love," Peabo Bryson & Roberta Flack
- "I'm Your Angel," Celine Dion & R. Kelly
- "What Kind of Fool," Barbra Streisand & Barry Gibb

- "Where is the Love," Roberta Flack & Donny Hathaway
- "Love Is," Vanessa Williams & Brian McKnight
- "You're All I Need to Get By," Marvin Gaye & Tammi Terrell

A few *more* romantic duets:

- "With You I'm Born Again," Billy Preston & Syreeta
- "You and I," Eddie Rabbitt & Crystal Gayle
- "Close Your Eyes," Peaches & Herb
- "Somethin' Stupid," Nancy Sinatra & Frank Sinatra
- "Suddenly," Olivia Newton-John & Cliff Richard
- "Your Precious Love," Marvin Gaye & Tammi Terrell
- "Surrender to Me," Ann Wilson & Robin Zander

Best Broadway Love Song

5001

- "Almost Like Being in Love" from *Brigadoon*
- "Can't Help Loving Dat Man" from *Showboat*
- "Ten Minutes Ago," from *Cinderella*
- "Embraceable You" from *Crazy for You*
- "I Could Be Happy With You," from *The Boyfriend*
- "I Could Have Danced All Night" from *My Fair Lady*
- "I Have Dreamed," from *The King and I*
- "I Wanna Be Loved By You" from *Good Boy*
- "I'm in Love with a Wonderful Guy" from *South Pacific*
- "I've Never Been in Love Before," from *Guys & Dolls*
- "If I Loved You" from *Carousel*
- "Love, Look Away," from *Flower Drum Song*
- "Love Song," from *Pippin*
- "Me and My Girl," from *Me and My Girl*
- "My Heart Is So Full of You," from *The Most Happy Fella*
- "On the Street Where You Live" from *My Fair Lady*
- "People" from *Funny Girl*
- "People Will Say We're in Love" from *Oklahoma*
- "Love Makes the World Go 'Round," from *Carnival*
- "So in Love" from *Kiss Me Kate*
- "They Say It's Wonderful," from *Annie Get Your Gun*
- "This Can't be Love" from *The Boys from Syracuse*
- "'Til There Was You," from the *The Music Man*
- "Wishing You Were Somehow Here Again," from *The Phantom of the Opera*
- "Try to Remember" from *The Fantastics*
- "What I Did for Love," from *A Chorus Line*
- "Wonderful Guy," from *South Pacific*
- "You're the Top," from *Anything Goes*

Best Romantic Movies & Best Romantic Movie Couples

500m

The Most Romantic Movies of All Time

- As Good as it Gets
- The Bodyguard
- Breakfast at Tiffany's
- Casablanca
- Dirty Dancing
- Doctor Zhivago
- Flashdance
- From Here to Eternity
- Ghost
- Gone with the Wind
- Memoirs of a Geisha
- The Notebook
- The Princess Bride
- Roman Holiday
- Shakespeare in Love
- Somewhere in Time
- Titanic
- Top Gun
- Untamed Heart
- The Way We Were
- When Harry Met Sally

Movies Starring the All-Time Great Romantic Couples

- Red Dust (Gable & Harlow)
- Sleepless in Seattle (Ryan & Hanks)
- Flying Down to Rio (Astaire & Rogers)
- Top Hat (Astaire & Rogers)
- Maytime (MacDonald & Eddy)
- Sweethearts (MacDonald & Eddy)
- Love Finds Andy Hardy (Garland & Rooney)
- Pretty Woman (Gere & Roberts)
- To Have and Have Not (Bogart & Bacall)
- Fire Over England (Leigh & Olivier)
- Cleopatra (Taylor & Burton)
- The Long, Hot Summer (Newman & Woodward)
- Woman of the Year (Hepburn & Tracy)

Who are your favorite on-screen lovers?

What are your favorite flicks?

Best Romantic Comedies

500n

- 10
- The 40-Year-Old Virgin
- A Touch of Class
- All Night Long
- Along Came Polly
- Annie Hall
- Arthur
- Best Friends
- Blind Date
- Blume in Love
- Bridget Jones's Diary
- Bridget Jones: The Edge of Reason
- Cactus Flower
- Continental Divide
- Crocodile Dundee
- Cross My Heart
- The Cutting Edge
- Fever Pitch
- Forget Paris
- Frankie and Johnny
- Garden State
- Groundhog Day
- House Calls
- Housesitter
- Love Actually

- Modern Romance
- Mr. Jones
- My Best Friend's Wedding
- My Big Fat Greek Wedding
- Notting Hill
- Overboard
- The Owl and the Pussycat
- Pillow Talk
- Play It Again, Sam
- The Princess Bride
- Quackser Fortune Has a Cousin in the Bronx
- Reuben, Reuben
- Risky Business
- Runaway Bride
- Shallow Hal
- Shirley Valentine
- Silver Streak
- Something's Gotta Give
- Starting Over
- The Sure Thing
- That Touch of Mink
- Tootsie
- Who Am I This Time?
- You've Got Mail

Great Date Movies

5000

- *40 Days and 40 Nights*
- *50 First Dates*
- *About a Boy*
- *America's Sweethearts*
- *Angel Eyes*
- *Aladdin*
- *Algiers*
- *American Pie* (trilogy)
- *The American President*
- *Anna Karenina*
- *A Place in the Sun*
- *Basic Instinct*
- *Beauty and the Beast*
- *Braveheart*
- *Breakfast at Tiffany's*
- *The Break-Up*
- *Butch Cassidy and the Sundance Kid*
- *Camelot*
- *Can't Hardly Wait*
- *Carlito's Way*
- *Chapter Two*
- *Circle of Friends*
- *Color of Night*
- *Dances with Wolves*
- *Dance with Me*
- *Dark Victory*
- *Don Juan DeMarco*
- *Down to Earth*

- *Empire Records*
- *The English Patient*
- *Ever After*
- *The Family Stone*
- *Forces of Nature*
- *Four Weddings and a Funeral*
- *French Kiss*
- *Gigi*
- *Great Expectations* (Paltrow & Hawke)
- *Here on Earth*
- *The Holiday*
- *Holiday Inn*
- *How to Lose a Guy in 10 Days*
- *It Could Happen to You*
- *Kate and Leopold*
- *Keeping the Faith*
- *The Lake House*
- *Legends of the Fall*
- *Like Water for Chocolate*

What movie most closely resembles your personal love story?

(More) Great Date Movies

500p

- Lonesome Dove
- The Long Hot Summer
- Lovers—A True Story
- Maid in Manhattan
- Message in a Bottle
- Mickey Blue Eyes
- Moonstruck
- Mr. Skeffington
- Music and Lyrics
- Never Been Kissed
- 9 ½ Weeks
- Nine Months
- The Notebook
- Oklahoma!
- On Golden Pond
- One Fine Day
- Only You
- Out of Africa
- Phenomenon
- Picture Perfect
- Pretty Woman
- Reality Bites
- Return to Me
- Rumor Has It
- Sabrina (with Julia Ormand & Harrison Ford)
- Saturday Night Fever
- Scent of a Woman
- Seems Like Old Times

- Serendipity
- She's All That
- The Shop Around the Corner
- Sleepless in Seattle
- Sliding Doors
- Speechless
- Splendor in the Grass
- Star Wars
- The Story of Us
- Sweet Home Alabama
- The Thornbirds
- The Wedding Singer
- The Truth about Cats and Dogs
- Two Weeks Notice
- A Walk to Remember
- The Wedding Date
- The Wedding Planner
- What Women Want
- While You Were Sleeping
- Why Do Fools Fall in Love?

"Love conquers all"—even war—in Hollywood: in 1999 the Oscar for Best Picture went to *Shakespeare in Love*, not to *Saving Private Ryan*.

Gift Ideas (I)

501 Get her something that she's always wanted to have, but always held back on...because it was too expensive, too impractical, too weird, or too self-indulgent.

502 Music boxes! Find them in gift shops, or get a cool catalog from The San Francisco Music Box Company. Call 800-227-2190 or visit www.sfmusicbox.com. Their music boxes are beautiful, and they have hundreds of songs to choose from.

503
- The gift: A bottle of "Passion" cologne.
- The activity: A night of passion.
- The background music: "Passion," by Rod Stewart.

- The gift: Costume jewelry.
- The note: "The diamond is *fake*—but the love is *real.*"
- The song: "Diamond Girl," by Seals & Crofts.

- The gift: A potted cactus.
- The note: "I'm stuck on you."
- The song: "Stuck on You," by Lionel Richie.

504 Doesn't he deserve a trophy for being the "World's Best Lover"? Doesn't she merit a loving cup to celebrate her latest accomplishment?

What's the difference between a "gift" and a "present"? See index listing to find out.

Trophy shops have a wealth of ideas waiting for you. Just think of the romantic possibilities of plaques, medals, ribbons, nameplates, certificates, and banners. And they all can be personalized, engraved, lettered, or monogrammed.

Gift Ideas (II)

505 Romantic songs and romantic movies go together:

- Get the song "Some Enchanted Evening," by Jay & the Americans—
- And rent the movie *South Pacific,* featuring the song.
- Or—surprise your partner with tickets to the musical.

"Love looks not with the eyes, but with the mind; And therefore is winged Cupid painted blind."
—William Shakespeare

• • •

- Get the song "Summer Nights," by John Travolta & Olivia Newton-John—
- And rent the movie *Grease,* featuring the song.
- Or—surprise your partner with tickets to the musical.

506 Give her a *variety* of jewelry:

- Rings
- Bracelets
- Necklaces
- Earrings
- Watches
- Pins
- Ankle bracelets
- Toe rings
- Hair accessories
- Belly button rings

Gift Giving for Dummies

507 *Don't buy practical items for gifts.* Appliances are wonderful, but *don't give them as gifts for birthdays, anniversaries, or for any event that is in any way a romantic occasion!* (A friend learned this lesson the hard way. For their very first Christmas together, he gave his wife...an electric broom. She still tells the story, thirty-seven years later.

> Exceptions to the "No Practical Gifts" Rule:
> 1) Gourmet kitchen utensils for cooks.
> 2) Garden implements for gardeners.
> 3) Tools for handymen (or women).

508 Don't forget about charm bracelets. They bring good memories alive, and they provide a built-in gift idea for any occasion.

509 Gifts for *her:* anything from Crabtree and Evelyn. Take my word for it. Visit a nearby bath shop, or find a Crabtree and Evelyn boutique, or call them at 800-CRABTREE, or visit www.crabtree-evelyn.com.

510 He was a golf fanatic. She was a chocoholic. She gave him a Ping putter with this inscription engraved on the shaft:

> *"I love you more than chocolate."*

He gave her a dozen boxes of chocolate golf balls. The enclosed note read:

> *"I love you more than golf."*

Discuss with your lover the chapter "Memorize This List." It will inspire many great gift ideas.

Gift Wrapping for Dummies

511 Creative gift wrapping:
• Use Sunday comics for wrapping paper.
• Use cartons of Ben & Jerry's Ice Cream for boxes.
• Use *real flowers* instead of bows.

512 Be prepared to *gift-wrap* your gifts. Remember: The *presentation* is nearly as important as the gift itself. You do a great disservice to your-self as well as to your partner when you're too casual about how you prepare and offer your gifts and presents. Nicely wrapped gifts have *twice* the impact as those that are poorly presented. Thus, have extra wrapping paper, bows, ribbon and boxes around at all times.

> Wrap all her gifts in her favorite color.

513 Wrap your anniversary gift in wedding paper.

514 Buy *several* heart-shaped boxes of Valentine chocolates. Dump out the chocolates and *save the boxes* for later in the year. (Note: It is nearly *impossible* to buy heart-shaped boxes at any time of the year other than early February.) Use these fancy heart-shaped boxes for wrap-ping birthday gifts and anniversary surprises.

> "No one has ever become poor by giving."
> —Anne Frank

Television

515 When it comes to TV, less is more. Now, I don't expect you to reduce your TV watching to zero. (Heaven forbid!) But here's a realistic approach to reducing your TV habit and freeing up some significant time for yourself and your partner:

- Pick three shows that you often watch but which you could easily do without. Cut them out altogether.
- Don't watch *any* reruns!
- If you watch the news, do chores at the same time. The news doesn't need your full attention, and this kind of multi-tasking will further save you time.
- Never watch anything while it's being broadcast. Tape all the shows you want to watch on your VCR or DVR. First, this allows you to zap out the commercials, saving you about eleven minutes per hour of TV-viewing time. And second, this gives you control over *when* you watch TV.

> Definition of a "Quickie": Making love during a commercial break.

516 Are you tired of running to the video store for your fix of romantic movies? Why not simply watch the romantic classics on Romance Classics TV? (From the AMC/American Movie Classic people.)

> Create a romantic surprise based on your lover's favorite TV show!

517 Make a "Mission Impossible" voice recording.

- "Your assignment, should you choose to accept it…is to meet a handsome, dark-haired stranger for a romantic dinner at the elegant Posh Café, tomorrow evening at 7 p.m. I suggest you take on the role of a mysterious and ravishing beauty…"
- Leave the voice recorder with a note, "Play me."

Radio

518 Call a local radio station and request a special love song to be dedicated to your partner. Make sure she's listening!

519 Schedule a weekly Saturday evening date to visit Lake Wobegon together, by listening to America's most romantic humorist and storyteller, Garrison Keillor. Tune in for two hours to *A Prairie Home Companion* on your local public radio station. Listen to the live podcast at www.prairiehome.publicradio.org.

520 If your partner loves to sing in the shower or sing along while the radio blares in the car, here's a great gift for him or her: Karaoke software electronically removes virtually all of a lead vocal from a stereo record, cassette, or CD, while leaving the background music. Visit www.mtu.com to purchase vocal elimination software.

To help you create a soundtrack to your own personal love affair, bring home some new music once a month:

January: *Power of Love*, Luther Vandross
February: *Come Away with Me*, Norah Jones
March: *Forever Friends*, Justo Almario
April: *Distant Fields*, Gary Lamb
May: *No Name Face*, Lifehouse

521 Many people have told me that their best romantic memories are car related. We all drove to and from our dates with the radio on. We all went parking on Lovers Lane with the radio providing mood music.

Re-connect with those romantic memories by creating a custom CD of music that was popular during your dating years.

* Insert the CD in her car stereo. Set it so the first song begins as soon as she turns on the ignition. (What a great surprise!)

* Or go for a leisurely ride in the country and listen to the CD together. (What a great, nostalgic date!)

June: *Livin' Inside Your Love*, George Benson
July: *Sun Singer,* Paul Winter
August: *The Emancipation of Mimi*, Mariah Carey
September: *Heart String*, Earl Klugh
October: *Openings*, William Ellwood
November: *Ten Summoner's Tales*, Sting
December: *Something of Time*, Nightnoise

1-800-ROMANCE

522

- 800-762-6677—for balloon-o-grams
- 800-543-1949—for a romantic trip on a Mississippi riverboat
- 800-CRABTREE—for great bath accessories
- 800-214-9463—for wine with custom labels
- 800-444-3356—to have a custom romance novel written
- 800-SANDALS—for couples-only Caribbean vacations
- 800-MARRIAGE—for *Marriage* magazine
- 800-919-3990—for Brisa Music
- 800-322-0344—for gifts from The Smithsonian
- 800-829-BEAR—for the Vermont Teddy Bear Co.
- 800-LOVEBOAT—for Princess Cruise Line
- 800-888-0987—for games and puzzles
- 877-322-1200—for Harry & David gourmet foods
- 800-367-0343—to attend a Marriage Encounter weekend
- 800-3-STOOGE—for Three Stooges stuff
- 800-423-9494—for lingerie
- 800-888-8200—for *more* lingerie
- 800-323-9525—for *still more* lingerie
- 800-FARE-OFF—for the *Travel Smart* newsletter
- 800-233-4499—for worldwide adventure travel
- 800-JIGSAWS—for very cool jigsaw puzzles
- 800-637-0098—for gifts for lawyers
- 800-862-8537—for hot air balloon adventures in Europe
- 800-FLOWERS—for flowers

Chapter
Theme Song:
"Call You,"
Reel Big Fish

www.romance.com

523

- www.jic.org—to learn how to choose *quality* jewelry
- www.1800flowers.com—for flowers
- www.proflowers.com—for flowers
- www.threestooges.com—for—*nyuk, nyuk, nyuk*—Stooge stuff!
- www.eroticprints.org—for info on The Erotic Print Society
- www.perfumania.com—for a *huge* selection of perfumes
- www.victoriassecret.com—for lingerie
- www.cdnow.com—for music CDs
- www.virginmega.com—for music CDs
- www.godiva.com—for world-class chocolates
- www.sharperimage.com—for all kinds of cool and techie stuff
- www.imdb.com—for The Internet Movie Database
- www.isbn.nu—for hard-to-find books
- www.addall.com—for out-of-print books
- www.abebooks.com—for used books
- www.yournovel.com—for a custom romance novel
- www.creativeworksstudios.net—to have a song custom written
- www.landsend.com—for outdoorsy/casual clothes
- www.ebay.com—for all kinds of things being auctioned
- www.bestfares.com—for an international travel club
- www.luxurylink.com—for auctions of high-end vacations
- www.innfinder.com—for bed and breakfasts
- www.bedandbreakfast.com—for more B&Bs
- www.virtualflorist.com—to send virtual bouquets and messages
- www.travelocity.com—for discount travel arrangements
- www.hotels.com—for discounted hotel rates

Concepts (I)

524 Do you know the difference between the "urgent" and the "important"?

Mixing them up causes us to lose sight of our true priorities and the really important things in our lives.

The *urgent* is what demands your attention *right now:* deadlines, details, and short-term priorities. It may be what's important to you, but more often it reflects the priorities of *others.*

The *important* is what reflects *your* priorities and values. It is more long-term in nature and therefore easier to defer.

Love is *important*—car troubles are *urgent.* Beware of the *urgent* eclipsing the *important* in your life!

> *Major* concept.

525 A "relationship" is an entity. It is a living, growing thing. This isn't just a poetic metaphor; I mean it literally. A *relationship* is something new that is created when two separate people decide to become a couple. The relationship is connected to and related to each individual, but it is still separate from the individuals involved. (There's *you,* there's *me,* and there's this mysterious, indefinable, invisible-yet-very-real thing that we call *us.*) And just as each individual person needs time, attention and care, so does the relationship.

526 Beware of the phenomenon of "Relationship Entropy"—the tendency of relationships to become more diffuse if not cared for and nurtured; the tendency for once-close lovers to drift apart if both of them don't work at it on a consistent basis. (File under "Better Relationships Through Physics Concepts.")

Are you stuck in a "romantic stalemate"—where each partner is holding back, waiting for the other to make the first move? Consider this: Making the first move isn't giving in—rather, it's the more assertive, more loving, and more risky thing to do. (Doesn't look like a sign of weakness to me!)

Concepts (II)

527 *Occasional* romance is "nice," but it's limited. *Romance-over-time* is what it's *really* all about. Why? Because consistency of romantic effort reflects your commitment to your partner. Because it shows that he or she is a top priority in your life.

528 Romantic love consists of a triad of passion, commitment, and intimacy. Let's take a quick look at how these ingredients combine and recombine at different stages in a relationship.

Passion usually takes the lead during dating. Commitment may be nonexistent, and intimacy is just a potential. As the relationship progresses, commitment and intimacy twist and turn around one another, building a framework for further relationship growth. Spurred on by passion, commitment often turns serious, and marriage results. Newlywed passion usually carries the relationship for a year or two, while commitment is assumed, and intimacy builds. When the inevitable challenges and temptations arise, it is hoped that the commitment is strong enough, and the intimacy deep enough, to sustain the relationship. Passion, commitment, and intimacy all come under fire from a variety of outside sources: jobs, friends, money issues, children, etc. Some of the challenges come from *internal* sources: insecurity, lack of self-esteem, fear, immaturity, lack of experience, etc.

Rate your own and each other's levels of passion, romance, and commitment on a scale of 1 to 10. Figure out which areas need the most improvement and *get to work!*

The combined strength of the passion/commitment/intimacy will determine the fate of the relationship. If commitment is strong but passion weak, the couple will "hang in there" but will not be particularly happy. If passion and commitment are strong but intimacy is weak, the couple will stay together but fail to grow. The happiest couples are able to achieve a *dynamic balance* of passion, commitment and intimacy.

Feminine/organic metaphor:
Making romantic gestures is like watering
the flower of your relationship. Don't let it wilt!

• • •

Masculine/mechanical metaphor:
Romance is like working on your car. Imagine this: You just got your dream car—a new red Ferrari F50. You fill it with gas, wax it up—and that's all you need to do in order to keep driving it for the next twenty years, right? *Wrong!* Relationships work the same way. They need to be fueled, tuned up, tinkered with, and polished regularly.

Erotica (I)

529 In case you were wondering (and I *know* how you think): The most *sexually suggestive flower* is the Hibiscus. (And because I know how curious you are, Calla Lilies come in a close second.)

530 Bob used to tease his wife, Tricia, saying she was "pretty as a playmate." She was flattered, but said she was too shy to be a *playmate*—but perhaps she'd be his *pin-up girl.* So Bob began calling her his "Pin-Up Girl." It was just a private little thing until...Tricia hired a local artist to paint a pin-up portrait of *her,* in the Vargas airbrush style from the 1940s. She surprised Bob with it on his fortieth birthday. To say that he was "surprised and pleased and amazed and thrilled" is an understatement!

531 Create an "Erotic Fantasy Jar." On fifty little squares of paper describe some fantasies. Make some subtly erotic, make some blatantly sexy, make some for him, make some for her, make some quickies, make some long and luxurious, make some visual, make some auditory, make some tasty, make some favorites, make some surprises.

Once a week you take turns picking an idea out of the jar.

Chapter
Theme Song:
"Sexual Revolution,"
Macy Gray

"Love is its own aphrodisiac and is the main ingredient for lasting sex."
—Mort Katz

532 Don't leave lovemaking until just before sleeping! Why is it so often the last item on the list? (Why do so many people have their priorities so screwed up? How could those silly household chores possibly be more important than being intimate with your lover?)

Osculate!
Often.

Erotica (II)

533 One man in the Romance Class told us how an accidental wine spill resulted in an erotic tradition celebrated regularly with his wife. She'd spilled a glass of wine on her new silk blouse. Instead of being upset, she thought about it for a second, grabbed *his* wine glass, emptied it down the front of her blouse, and said, "If you want it, come and get it!" (They've since graduated to cordials!)

534 Do you *know* what your partner finds erotic? Or do you *assume* you know? Do you figure she likes what your *last* girlfriend enjoyed? Do you think he's just like the guy described in last month's *Cosmo*? Do you believe everything you read in *Penthouse Letters*?

• Talk about what each of you considers erotic.
• Set your inhibitions and judgments aside.
• Describe what you experience as sexy and erotic.
• Be open to new ways of looking at sexuality.

535 When choosing erotic movies, it may be helpful to remember that men and women often have different definitions of "erotic." Women like the smoldering passion of *The Bridges of Madison County* or *Like Water for Chocolate*. For men, you can pretty much sum up their taste in erotic movies in two words: "Nude blonde." Think of the erotic thrillers *Basic Instinct* or *Body Double*.

Gals—
Pose on a bed of black silk sheets wearing white silk lingerie. Pose on a bed of white silk sheets wearing black silk lingerie.

536 Drip honey on various parts of your lover's body. Lick it off. (Wine and cordials work nicely, too.)

Happy Birthday! (I)

537 Send her a birthday card *every day for a month* preceding her birthday.

538 Find and record a bunch of "birthday" and "age-related" songs for him or her. Like "You Say It's Your Birthday" from the Beatles' "White Album." I've conducted a little musical research on your behalf, and here's what I've come up with:
- "Happy Birthday," Stevie Wonder
- "Happy Birthday," New Kids on the Block
- "Happy Birthday," Altered Images
- "Happy Birthday to You," Bing Crosby
- "Happy Birthday to You," Eddy Howard
- "Happy Birthday to You," Sunsetters
- "Young At Heart," Frank Sinatra
- "I Wish I Were 18 Again," George Burns
- "When I'm Sixty-Four," The Beatles

If your lover is turning thirty, give him or her the soundtrack from the movie *13 Going on 30*. Then use the music as the soundtrack for the birthday party.

539 Original magazines from the week or month of his or her birth date make great birthday gifts. (If, of course, your partner isn't overly sensitive about his or her age!) Try a local used bookstore.

540 If your partner is sensitive about his or her age, but you still want to find some way to celebrate, here's a solution: Count blessings instead of years. You could make lists on scrolls of things that the two of you are thankful for. You could focus on a different blessing at each celebration. You could take turns creating the list. You could celebrate several times a year.

Fun and insightful: *Love Cards; What Your Birthday Reveals About You & Your Personal Relationship*, by Robert Cramp.

Happy Birthday! (II)

541 Use *sparklers* instead of candles on his birthday cake.

542 Get him an actual newspaper from the day he was born! The Historic Newspaper Archives has newspapers from more than fifty U.S. cities, including *The New York Times*, *The Wall Street Journal* and *The Los Angeles Times*. These are authentic, well-preserved editions of the entire original newspapers. Call 800-221-3221, or visit www.historicnewspaper.com.

Chapter Theme Song: "Birthday," Destiny's Child

543 A basic romantic concept: Birthday cards. Some twists:
- Send a card a day for a week, a month.
- Send as many cards as the number of years in his age.
- Send twenty-five cards—all on the same day.
- Hide cards in his briefcase, in the refrigerator.
- Create your own birthday cards.
- Make them simple, with crayons or markers.
- Make them elaborate, created on your computer.
- Write a birthday greeting on a cake—or on a pizza.
- Make a poster-sized card.
- Rent a billboard: Create a HUGE birthday card.
- Have the message written in beautiful calligraphy.

If you're not satisfied with celebrating birthdays just *once* a year, you can always celebrate *half-birthdays* every six months!

544 Convince her boss to call her at home at six o'clock in the morning on the morning of her birthday—to give her the day off!

Money Makes the World Go 'Round

545 "How can I be romantic when money's tight?" many guys ask me.

Actually, a shortage of money can be a *good thing* when it comes to romance. Why? Because it forces you to be more creative, to give more of yourself, to spend time instead of money. Love never dies because of lack of money, but it *often* dies because of boredom and neglect.

Chapter Theme Song: "Money Money Money," Abba

546
• A gift certificate to Tiffany's.
• A one-hour shopping spree with no budget limit!
• Dinner at every five-star restaurant in America.

547 Speaking of money... Did you know that you can write a check on *anything*? As long as you include all the important numbers on the item, it's legal, and the bank has to cash it!
• One guy presented his wife with a check written on a mattress!
• Another wrote a check on a pair of panties.

548 It was nearly midnight on a hot August night. They were watching TV together. Stu nudged his wife gently and whispered, "Let's make love outside on the back porch." "Not tonight! What if the kids hear us?" Peggy exclaimed. "C'mon, honey," he said, "Look, I'll give you a *hundred dollars* if you do!" he grinned wickedly. "Stop teasing!" she chided. He opened his wallet and waved a fistful of twenties at her. She hesitated. She smiled. She grabbed the money and headed for the porch.

Love Makes the World Go 'Round

549 The "Romance Credit Card" is a cool concept created by a couple in one of my Romance Classes. Here's how it works:

You create your own "bank" which issues two types of credit: money and time. On a quarterly basis the bank's officers (the two of you) meet to establish your credit limits. When money is tight, issue more *time*. When time is tight, make more *money* available.

Design, laminate, and carry in your wallets the Romance Credit Card. It's a reminder that you have an obligation to spend time and money on your relationship on a regular basis. (Some couples keep their credit card balances on a chart on the refrigerator.)

> Love may make the world go 'round, but it's *romantic love* that makes the ride worthwhile.

550 Cynthia and Robert were sharing their answers for the "Memorize This List" chapter in this book. When Robert asked Cynthia what her favorite color was, she answered, "The rainbow." This might have stumped a lesser man, but being a creative romantic, here are some of the rainbow-related gifts Robert has given her:

- A crystal prism
- A poster showing a beautiful landscape with a rainbow overhead
- Many kaleidoscopes
- A box of Crayola Crayons (the big, 64-crayon box)
- A trip to Niagara Falls, where rainbows can be seen in the mist (Robert is currently looking for a used spectrometer from a school or laboratory for Cynthia's next birthday.)

Do It Outside

551 Watch a sunset together. It's a great way to change gears at the end of the day. It will slow you down and help you get reconnected with each other.

You may want to conduct some research to find the very best location from which to watch the sun set in your area. It might be an obvious hill, or it might be a subtle slope that you've never noticed before. Or it might be the roof of a building.

Chapter
Theme Song:
"Anytime, Anyplace,"
Janet Jackson

552 Go hiking. Go tobogganing! Go to a ballgame. Go to a state park. Go to an outdoor public garden. Go to an outdoor concert. Go on a picnic. Go for a ride in the country. Go for a walk. Go for it!

553 (Make love in your backyard at midnight.)

554 Go camping! Borrow friends' equipment for starters. If you enjoy it, buy your own stuff. (Make sure you include a *double* sleeping bag on your equipment list.)

"Love is like a mountain, hard to climb, but once you get to the top the view is beautiful."
—Daniel Monroe Tuttle

555 When's the last time you played miniature golf? Go match your skill and have a good time.

Do It in Public

556 Do you praise her in public? When's the last time you told someone else how lucky you feel to have this woman in your life? Complimenting her in front of someone else will make her feel extra special.

557 Whisper sweet nothings in her ear while out in public.

- Whisper compliments; call her by her pet name.
- Whisper *shocking* comments and outright lewd suggestions! (The more formal the gathering, the more outrageous or suggestive your whispered messages should be. The juxtaposition of a stuffy event with the whispered raw passion of your feelings for her should add a little spark to the entire evening!)

558 Do you remember what teenagers used to call "PDAs"— Public Displays of Affection? Are you out of the habit of showing affection for your partner in public? Hold hands. Rest your hand on his shoulder. Entwine your arm with hers.

Chapter
Theme Song:
"In Public," Kelis
(Warning: Very
naughty!)

Just Do It!

559 Have you ever dreamed of taking off with your partner for a fun-filled *four week* vacation touring all of Europe—but you only get *two weeks* paid vacation? Bummer.

Here's what you do: Go *anyway*. Don't let yourself be constrained by your employer's tightwad two-week vacation policy! Simply take an additional two weeks off *without pay*. I know that this is a radical thing for most people to *think* about, much less *do*—but I urge you to consider it. Create a savings plan that will allow you to do this. It might take a year, it might take five. But it will be well worth it!

560 Sally used to complain that Jack never complimented her. After pondering this, Jack realized, "It's not that I don't *love* you, or that I don't have nice things to say. It's just that I never think to say them *on my own*." With that insight, he instituted "Dial-A-Compliment" just for her. Sally could call him any time of the day or night and receive a spontaneous and heartfelt compliment!

Chapter Theme Song: "Do It," Nelly Furtado

Which ten ideas in this book do you think your lover would love most? Don't simply jot them down somewhere—write them directly into your appointment calendar, and schedule time to perform the gestures or buy the gifts.

561 Romantics are always "dating."

"Dating" is a *mindset* as much as it is an activity for singles. Married people who continue "dating" their spouses are among the happiest people in the world.

* Don't just go out to a movie on Saturday, like always. Call her from work on Wednesday and *formally* ask her out on a date.
* Many people with A+ Relationships have told me that they hold "date nights" on a weekly basis.

Just a Little Bit Naughty

562 *Exhibitionism for the Shy.* What an enticing book title! What a cool concept! This awesome book demonstrates how to turn sexual modesty to your erotic advantage! As author Carol Queen says, "To discover a new world of erotic experience, you don't have to shed your inhibitions—you just have to exploit them creatively." This book is a serious exploration and guide book. (No sleazy pictures. In fact, no pictures at all!) In bookstores or call 800-289-8423, or visit www.goodvibes.com.

Chapter
Theme Song:
"Naughty Girl,"
Beyoncé

563 For women only: When you're dressed up and out together, secretly hand him your panties under the table. Watch his expression.

I'll be shocked if he's not *absolutely delighted!*

564 If your lover's not shy, you might want to try nude sunbathing. Its many practitioners praise the sense of freedom, healthfulness, and back-to-nature benefits of baring it all in public.

- *Free Beaches,* a guide to nude beaches located around the world is available from The Naturist Society. Call 800-886-7230, write P.O. Box 132, Oshkosh, Wisconsin 54903, or visit www.naturistsociety.com.

- Call the American Association for Nude Recreation at 800-TRY-NUDE, 1703 North Main Street, Suite E, Kissimmee, Florida 34744, or visit www.aanr.com.

565 The Erotic Print Society sells classic and contemporary limited-edition prints, books, and gifts. At www.eroticprints.org. Or at EPS, 54 New Street, Worcester, WR1 2DL, United Kingdom. Or call (0) 800-026 2524.

The Gift of Time

566 Your partner wants more of *you*, not more "stuff"!

Once every two months give her an entire day of your time. She gets total control over how to use that time. Now, ask her for the same, during the alternate months.

> Just *imagine* the possibilities.

567
- You can *save* time by shopping via catalog.
- You can *reorganize* time by "chore-shifting."
- You can *create time* by "doubling up" on activities.
- You can *use time better* by buying a book on time-management.
- You can *release time* by hiring a housecleaning service.
- You can *make time* by adjusting your sleeping habits.
- You can *appreciate* time by simplifying your life.
- You can *find* time by planning better.

568 "Double-up" on activities. Combine various activities and you'll find more time to be together:
- Meet for lunch. (You have to eat anyway, right?!)
- Eat dinner and watch a romantic movie on video.
- Do chores together: Go grocery shopping, take the car to the shop.

> "How we spend our days is, of course, how we spend our lives."
> —Annie Dillard

569 Two hours of peace and quiet: *possibly the best gift you could ever give someone!*

Time for Love

570 Don't go grocery shopping on *Friday night!* Don't do laundry on *Saturday morning!* Those are *valuable times*—times you could be spending *together.*

Practice "chore-shifting."

* Find ways to shift chores to more efficient times.
* Do two chores at the same time.
* Do chores *together:* Doubling the person-power more than doubles the efficiency!

> **Chapter Theme Song:**
> "Time for Love,"
> Air Supply

571 Once a week: Bring home Chinese take-out, or have pizza delivered. Streamline your dinner hour—then use the time you saved *romantically.*

> Domino's to the rescue!

572 Learn to appreciate time; learn to redefine time; learn to put more love into the time you have. Read this book, it's fabulous: *Time and the Art of Living,* by Robert Grudin.

* Review your calendars and commitments together. Plan "dates."
* Plan surprises well in advance.
* Always have your "Gift Closet" well stocked.

573 Make time in the morning to make love. Get up an hour early!

For Singles Only (I)

574 You've been dating a while, you're considering "getting serious," but you're not sure that he's really everything you're looking for. How do you evaluate the relationship? With this simple formula:

$$70\% + spark = Go\ for\ it!$$

In other words, if this person has at least 70% of the qualities you want your ideal partner to have, plus you have "spark" (passion and romance; you're soul mates; you "click")—go for it! You *know* you're not going to get 100% (there ain't no Prince Charming!)—but you'd better not settle for less than 50%!

575 Listen for "Pings."

And what are Pings? They're any action or habit your partner has that *you just know you couldn't live with for the rest of your life.* For example:

- You're in the car, scanning radio stations for some classical music. You cringe when you hear "Stayin' Alive," but she squeals "Oh, I *love* the Bee Gees!" (*Ping!*)

> What's a "Ping"??

- He told you to prepare for a "special night out" because he's got "box seat tickets." Expecting to attend the symphony and dine at the Posh Café, you spend hours getting ready, and dress in your classiest outfit. He shows up in jeans with two tickets to the Red Sox game. (*Ping!!*)

Note: One person's Ping may be another person's cherished quirk. Pings are relative things!

For Singles Only (II)

576 Guys: When giving jewelry, never, never, *never* package it in a ring box, unless it's an engagement ring. You're probably totally unaware of it, but those little square boxes spell one thing to women: M-A-R-R-I-A-G-E. Ask the jeweler to give you a different kind of box, or present the piece in a creative way. Why ask for trouble?

577

- If you've talked about maybe moving in together, and you decide you want to go for it, place your apartment key in a gift box, wrap it up and give it to her.
- Or—mail it to her with a note: "You already own the key to my heart...now I want you to have *this* key."

578 Advice for the guys:
- How to *catch* her: Learn to dance.
- How to *keep* her: Learn to cook.

> If you don't believe me, guys, go ask some women.

579 Mail her a copy of your business resume instead of a greeting card. Attach a note: "I'd like you to get to know me better." (Other fun stuff to send: A grammar school report card. A photo of yourself as a baby.)

For Marrieds Only (I)

580 On a Saturday afternoon, nonchalantly say to your partner, "If I had it to do all over again, I'd marry you *again*. As a matter of fact, let's do just that!" Then grab him or her and run down to your local church (where you've already planned things with the pastor), and hold a quick little rededication ceremony. Surprise! (You may want to use the song "Let's Get Married Again," by John Conlee.)

Chapter Theme Song: "Husbands and Wives," Neil Diamond

581 Guys: On your wedding anniversary, re-create her wedding bouquet. Since you probably don't know a chrysanthemum from poison ivy, show one of your wedding photos to your florist.

If this doesn't bring tears to her eyes, nothing will!

582 Dig out your wedding album. Have a new eight-by-ten-inch print made of the best photo of your bride. Wrap it up and give it to *yourself* for your birthday or for Christmas.

583

Read *The Case for Marriage*, by Maggie Gallagher and Linda Waite.

- Have your wedding invitation professionally framed. Keep it on your nightstand.
- For your tenth, twentieth, and thirtieth wedding anniversaries, create a formal invitation to your spouse to join you for another *ten* years of marriage.

For Marrieds Only (II)

584
- In the middle of a party or other social event, turn to her and whisper, "You're the *best.*"
- While walking down the street together, turn to her and whisper, "I'm glad I married you."
- While driving somewhere together, turn to her and say, "I can't imagine my life without you in it."

"All weddings are similar, but every marriage is different."
—John Berger

585
Make an artistic collage of photos and memorabilia from your wedding.

586
Carry a copy of your wedding license in your wallet, right next to your driver's license.

Attend a Marriage Encounter weekend. Call 800-795-5683, or visit www.wwme.org.

• • •

Join the Association for Couples in Marriage Enrichment. Call 336-724-1526 or 800-634-8325.

587
Songs that celebrate love and marriage. Make a tape for an anniversary, a birthday, or just to celebrate your love next Tuesday.
- "Love & Marriage" Frank Sinatra
- "I Married an Angel," George Siravo
- "Marriage Made in Heaven," Bob Crewe

- "Be My Wife," David Bowie
- "Happily Married Man," Duane Allman
- "Husbands & Wives," Neil Diamond
- "Longer," Dan Fogelberg
- "Make My Life with You," Oak Ridge Boys
- "Marriage," Ted Nugent
- "Never My Love," The Association
- "You'll Accomp'ny Me," Bob Seger and the Silver Bullet Band

---

Merry Christmas

588

- A gift-a-day for the twelve Days of Christmas.
- Or—go *all out*...

On the first day of Christmas, my true love gave to me—
  A red rose in a bud vase.

On the second day of Christmas, my true love gave to me—
  Two bottles of champagne.

On the third day of Christmas, my true love gave to me—
  Three French kisses.

On the fourth day of Christmas, my true love gave to me—
  Four nights of dancing.

On the fifth day of Christmas, my true love gave to me—
  Five golden rings!

On the sixth day of Christmas, my true love gave to me—
  Six bubble baths.

On the seventh day of Christmas, my true love gave to me—
  Seven movie passes.

On the eighth day of Christmas, my true love gave to me—

Eight Beanie Babies.

On the ninth day of Christmas, my true love gave to me—

Nine romance coupons for back rubs.

On the tenth day of Christmas, my true love gave to me—

Ten shares of Microsoft stock.

On the eleventh day of Christmas, my true love gave to me—

Eleven heart-shaped balloons.

On the twelfth day of Christmas, my true love gave to me—

Twelve CDs by The Beatles.

Some Christmas tree ornament ideas: Create a garland of one-dollar bills taped together. Take the CD discs out of their cases and hang them on the tree as shiny ornaments.

589 One woman came to her marriage with a vast collection of very special Christmas tree ornaments. Her husband jumped on the bandwagon, and they now have a ritual "Search for This Year's Special Ornament."

More Christmas tree ornament ideas: Have a relevant, holiday-oriented comic strip laminated, and hang it on the tree. Have a favorite poem or quote written in calligraphy, and turn it into an inspirational ornament.

Happy Hanukkah

590 In celebration of the "Festival of Lights":
- Light your home with hundreds of candles.
- Choose a menorah that holds special meaning for your partner.
- Write a poem about how he or she is the "light of your life."

591 Celebrate the eight days of Hanukkah:

Day 1: Give a gift that reflects your religious beliefs.

Day 2: Give a gift of one hour of your time.

Day 3: Give a gift that celebrates the number of years you've been together.

Day 4: Give a gift you've made by hand.

Day 5: Give a gift that acknowledges a private joke between the two of you.

Day 6: Give a gift that the two of you can share.

Day 7: Give a gift of music.

Day 8: Give an artistic gift.

592 Buy four dreidels. We're going to change the traditional children's game into a new *romantic* game. On each dreidel remove the traditional Hebrew letters *nun, gimel, he,* and *shin*—and replace them with:
- M, Y, U, F—which stand for *Me, You, Us* and *Family.*
- N, T, W, M—which stand for *Now, Today,* this *Week,* this *Month.*
- D, M, P, C—which stand for *Dinner, Movie, Picnic, Concert.*
- *You* decide how to label this one.

An (im)modest suggestion for a Hanukkah gift: the book *Kosher Sex: A Recipe for Passion and Intimacy,* by Rabbi Schmuley Boteach.

Here's how you play: Taking turns, one person spins one dreidel on each night of Hanukkah. The M-Y-U-F dreidel directs you to do something loving that focuses on whichever person the dreidel indicates.

Happy Anniversary

593 Identify that *one pivotal event* that brought the two of you together. Celebrate that event every year.

What brought the two of you together? Fate? Karma? Cupid? Cosmic coincidence?

594 Most couples celebrate their anniversary once a year. That's a nice, romantic thing to do.

A *few* couples celebrate their anniversary once a month. That's perhaps a little much, but it's very sweet, don't you think?

Chapter Theme Song:
"Anniversary,"
The Cure

Then one day in a Romance Class I met a couple who claimed they'd celebrated 10,958 anniversaries! As they appeared to be in their mid-forties, I was politely skeptical—until they explained: They were married on August 25th—which is often written as 8/25. They translated that to 8:25 and were thus inspired to celebrate their anniversary *every day* at 8:25. And, of course (they explained matter-of-factly), it was obvious that they had to celebrate *twice* a day: first at 8:25 in the morning, and then *again* at 8:25 in the evening. (And I thought *I* was romantic!)

595 On their first wedding anniversary Michael sent Pamela a very romantic card. Pamela saved it and mailed it *back* to Michael on their *second* anniversary. Michael saved the card and mailed it back to Pamela on their *third* anniversary. This impromptu tradition began in 1949—and continues to this day. ("The cost of first-class postage is now more than the original cost of the card!" Pamela recently observed with a smile.)

Happy Birthday

596 Declare your lover's "Birthday *Month*," and do something special every day for the thirty days preceding THE day.

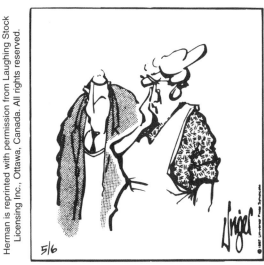

"What a coincidence! You forgot my birthday and I forgot how to cook."

597 How about a video celebration of the year he was born? You can get a thirty-minute DVD newsreel, featuring world events, news, personalities, styles, and major events from the year of your partner's birth (for the years 1929 through 1969). Cool, huh? Such a deal at only $14.95. Call FlickBack Media at 800-541-3533, or visit www.flickback.com.

Custom-Made

598 When you want to present your lover with some loving words rendered in artistic, beautiful, wonderful, elegant, fabulous calligraphy— call Maria Thomas, the most talented "artist of words" in America.

Call Marilyn Haverkate at The Frame & Art Gallery: 864-967-3182, or visit www.lettersalive.com.

599 Jim Rickert, "The Songsmith," will write and record original songs for you. The romantic possibilities are tremendous!

• The quickest and least expensive option is to choose one of his original melodies from a catalog of styles (rock, ballad, country, folk, reggae); then fill out a questionnaire that will allow him to customize the song with names, dates, and personal references. Just $52.

• He can also write new lyrics for you, or set your words to music. This service starts at $87.

• He can also compose entirely new music from scratch for you, and record it simply or elaborately. From $175.

Normal turn-around time is only a few weeks. Call Jim at 617-471-8800, or write to The Creative Works, 49 Centre Street, Quincy, Massachusetts 02169, or visit www.creativeworksstudios.net.

> One of the Top Ten Coolest Ideas: Have an original song written and recorded for your lover.

600 If your lover is also a wine lover, why not surprise him or her with a great California wine bottled with custom labels? Be creative with words or artwork, and create a one-of-a-kind gift for your lover. Call Windsor Vineyards at 800-289-9463, in Tiburon, California, or visit www.windsorvineyards.com.

One-of-a-Kind

601 If she's a one-of-a-kind woman, why not present her with a one-of-a-kind piece of jewelry? Hire a jewelry designer, establish a budget, describe her personality and style and some of your own ideas for the piece, and

> If you aren't married yet, have her *design her own engagement ring!* Visit www.adiamondisforever.com.

let the designer give you some sketches. Then have your unique gift created for her, and present it to her with a flourish.

602 The reason why a dozen roses is so popular is because it works for virtually *everyone*. Roses are a great start—but how about creating a truly *personalized* bouquet?
• A bouquet of pencils—for a teacher, writer, or journalist.
• A bouquet of wrenches—for a handyman.
• A bouquet of kitchen utensils—for a gourmet cook.
• A bouquet of Big Mac coupons for your junk food junkie.

603 Would you like your life to read like a romance novel? Well now it *can!* You can get a romance novel customized with you and your lover as the hero and heroine. Seven titles are available, including *Another Day in Paradise* and *Love's Bounty.* Each book will include more than twenty personal details about the two of you. Only $49.95. Call Your Novel at 800-444-3356, or visit www.yournovel.com.

604 Have a one-of-a-kind jigsaw puzzle created for your puzzle-lover. You might create a special message or propose marriage with one! Call the folks at J.C. Ayer & Co. at 781-639-8162, or visit www.ayerpuzzles.com.

Do-It-Yourself

605 Do-it-yourself: custom-made Chinese fortune cookies! Buy a batch of them at a local Chinese/Oriental grocery store (or get some from your favorite Chinese restaurant). Pull out their fortunes with a pair of tweezers, and insert your own fortunes! From silly to sexy, from playful to profound, you decide!

> "Creativity is the sudde[n] cessation of stupidity."
> —Edwin La[nd]

606 Make your own custom greeting cards. (Those store-bought cards are fine—I have a drawer full of them. But homemade cards are extra special.) You don't have to be artistic, just heartfelt. (Remember, she's with you not because you're Picasso, but because you're *you*.)
• Crayons and construction paper are just fine for this project.
• Create a giant, poster-sized greeting card!
• Design something cool with a graphics program on your computer.

607 What do you do with old greeting cards from your honey? You don't just toss them away, do you?! *Heaven forbid!* True romantics...

> The more of *yourself* that you put into your gifts and gestures, the more they'll be appreciated.

• Display them on mantles and tables.
• Set them on their desks at work.
• Have them mounted and framed.
• Put them in a scrapbook.
• Toss 'em in a file—to use in some creative way in the future.
• Paste 'em on a collage.
• And one crazy couple in my Romance Class actually wallpapered an entire room in their house with greeting cards!

Hide-and-Seek

608 Some hiding places for little love notes, Post-Its, and small gifts:

- Under the pillow
- In the glove compartment
- In the medicine cabinet
- In the refrigerator
- Inside a book she's reading
- In her checkbook
- In his shirt pocket
- In her wallet

- In his briefcase
- In her purse
- In a pizza box
- Under his dinner plate
- In his sock drawer
- In his daily planner
- In the trunk of her car
- In his eyeglasses case

609 *Truly mischievous* romantics go to great lengths to hide gifts and notes. Herewith are some suggestions from the more off-the-wall students of my Romance Classes:

> You'll have as much fun as your partner will.

- Carefully open various product packages, insert the item, and carefully reseal the package. Favorite targets include cereal boxes, soup cans, ice cream cartons, bags of M&M's, candy bars, soda cans, and, of course, boxes of Cracker Jacks!

> "Love isn't blind; it just only sees what matters."
> —William Curry

- Notes have appeared frozen in ice cubes, floating in punch bowls, hidden among bouquets and tied to balloons.
- Little gifts have been delivered via Federal Express.

610

Want some suggestions for notes, gifts, and trinkets to hide? Again, from Romance Class participants:

- Friendship rings
- Earrings
- Comic strips
- Hockey tickets

- Love Coupons
- Invitations to dinner
- Theater tickets
- Valentine conversation hearts

Creativity Exercises

611a

1. Give it a twist:
   Start with something basic, then give it a creative twist.
2. Change your routine:
   Shaking up your routine often leads to new ideas.
3. Consider every crazy idea that pops into your head:
   You won't use them all, but the process expands your thinking.
4. Give yourself a deadline:
   Sometimes working under pressure works!
5. Learn from your mistakes:
   Mistakes aren't really mistakes if they lead you somewhere useful.
6. Go with your strengths:
   Do what comes naturally, go with the flow.
7. Go counter to your natural strengths:
   Try something different.
8. Tap into your unconscious mind:
   There's a lot going on beneath the surface.
9. Challenge the assumptions:

Don't assume you know it all!

10. Imagine how someone else would do it:
    How would Einstein create new ideas? Mozart? Walt Disney?

11. Use different "models" of thinking:
    Think organically; think like a cat; think like a millionaire.

12. Reframe the question:
    The question might be, "How can I be more loving?" Or it might be, "How can I be more spontaneous?"

13. Listen to your intuition/sixth sense/inner voice:
    Whatever you choose to call it, use it!

Exercising Your Creativity

611b

14. Admit that you're dissatisfied with the *status quo:*
    It will inspire you to find solutions.

15. Don't go it alone:
    Brainstorm romantic ideas with a group of friends.

16. Use random ideas to stimulate different avenues of thinking:
    Don't get locked into one mode of thinking!

17. Change your perspective:
    1) See the big picture, or 2) Look at the *details.*

18. Borrow (then customize) ideas:
    Borrow ideas from movies, books, products, other couples.

19. Face your fears:
    What's holding you back from being more creative? More loving? More spontaneous? More fun-loving?

280 • 1001 WAYS TO BE ROMANTIC

20. Draw pictures, doodle, make diagrams:
    Use the visual, graphic side of your brain.
21. Try on a different persona:
    Think like a kid; think like a member of the
    opposite sex; think like your partner.
22. Withhold judgment:
    Generate lots and *lots* of ideas before you begin
    evaluating.
23. Have fun:
    Don't take it so seriously, play with ideas, be
    wacky.

> Start with a
> classic romantic
> idea then "give
> it a twist."

Go Away!

612 Even if you're not newly-weds—especially if you're not newly-weds—visit www.world-party.com. It's the online guide to festivals and parties all over the world.

> Rekindle the way you felt as newlyweds by reserving the honeymoon suite at a hotel or resort. Be sure to put the "Do Not Disturb" sign to good use!

613 Combine your interest in bicycling with your passion for wine! Tour the California wine country by bike. Pedal at your own pace, and stop at as many as thirty-five wineries. These two firms offer five-day guided bicycle tours through the Napa Valley and Sonoma County:
• Backroads Bicycle Touring, 800-462-2848, and www.backroads.com
• Vermont Bicycle Touring, 800-245-3868, and www.vbt.com

614
• Tour a vineyard. Or two.
• Visit a vineyard in *every state* that produces wine—all forty-two of them!

615 A plain old vacation is not the same thing as a "second honey-moon"! There's a feeling of magic and romance around a second honeymoon. How do you create one?

> What's the difference between a *vacation* and a *honeymoon?*

You start planning about a year in advance (so the anticipation builds). You buy her a stack of bride maga-zines (that's where all the honeymoon destination ads are). You send travel brochures to him in the mail (with your personal notes and com-ments written in). You buy special clothes. If you do this *right*, it'll really spice up your life—for a year or more!

Bon Voyage!

616 When vacationing together, always take along a couple of little surprise gifts. It's inexpensive, gives you something to look forward to, lets you gift-wrap ahead of time, and allows you to surprise your lover at a moment's notice.

617 All kinds of travel tips and current information are available from special newsletters about specific destinations and topics. Here are two:

- *La Belle France: The Sophisticated Guide to France*
  An eight-page monthly newsletter. A yearly subscription is $98. Call 800-225-7825 or visit www.lbfrance.com.
- *Golf Odyssey: The Guide for Discriminating Golfers.* Twelve issues a year at just $97. Call 800-550-2286 or visit www.golfodyssey.com/newsletter.html.

618 Imagine your own "Fantasy Vacation." What's your lover's idea of the Perfect, Ultimate, Wonderful, Fantasy Vacation? Let your imaginations run wild. Keep the dream alive over the years by collecting brochures, posters and books on your Fantasy Vacation location.

With the proper planning, a little creativity, a little time, a realistic savings plan and true dedication to your vision, you can make your Fantasy Vacation come true.

"A man travels the world over in search of what he needs and returns home to find it."

—George Moore

Cars

619 Fill his car with balloons. Red ones.

620 When was the last time you went out *parking*? (For most of us, it was way back in high school.)

Rediscover the sexual rush, the thrill of being caught, the just-plain *fun* of parking! Find the local "Lovers Lane" in your town, fill the back seat of your car with pillows, and make a date for late Friday night!

621 Hang a pair of your panties on his rearview mirror.

622 Hide little one-line notes all over his car: on the sun visor, in the glove compartment, in the ash tray, in the trunk, under the hood, on the mirror, on the seat belt.

623 Wash and vacuum her car until it sparkles like new.

FYI: It takes 217 balloons to fill a Honda Accord.

Go for a drive in a classic VW "Love Bug."

Sports

624 Sports fans *love* sports memorabilia. Pennants, posters, T-shirts and caps from favorite teams, signed photographs and signed balls—all make great gifts. And of course, there's always season tickets!

"OKAY, LORETTA, I'LL SHARE MY FEELINGS... I WANT TO WATCH THE BALLGAME."

The Lockhorns, Copyright © 1994 by Hoest Enterprises, Inc. Reprinted with permission of King Features Syndicate.

625 For your baseball fanatic: Have a local graphic artist create a custom baseball card featuring your partner. Write your own humorous "Vital Statistics," have his or her photo scanned in, and paste it onto cardboard. (Present it to your partner by slipping it carefully into an "unopened" package of baseball cards!)

626 While he's watching sports on TV, bring him peanuts and popcorn, beer and ice cream bars. When it comes to sports fanatics, the only reasonable philosophy to adopt is, "If you can't beat 'em, join 'em!"

Dining In

627 Choose a bottle of wine for its romantic label. I recently bought a bottle of Il Cuore Cabernet Sauvignon 1996. The label is a colorful, geometric rendering of heart shapes. The back label explains: "The original artwork for Il Cuore was created by Dan Rizzie, whose bold cubistic works are in the permanent collections of both The Metropolitan Museum and The Museum of Modern Art in New York." The label also explains that Il Cuore is Italian for "the heart." Thanks to Aficionado Cellars in Graton, Sonoma County, California. Call 888-751-WINE, or visit www.aficionadocellars.com.

> Slow down! Every meal doesn't need to be "romantic," but every meal *can* be an opportunity to talk and connect.

628 It's romantic—but commonplace—to eat dinner by candlelight. So here's a change of pace: Eat *breakfast* by candlelight.

629 Prepare *love food* for your partner on special occasions or when he or she needs a boost. Love food is "comfort food" served with an extra helping of love. Comfort food is a highly individual thing. It might be hot oatmeal with brown sugar, served late at night. It might be a cup of hot cocoa served on a cold winter afternoon. It might be two scoops of Ben & Jerry's ice cream. Does your lover know what your comfort food is? Do you know his or hers?

630 Make a toast to one another every time you hold a wine glass. Make eye contact. Take turns making the toast. Whisper it.

Dining Out

631 Did you know that there are *two* kinds of romantic restaurants?
1. The elegant/active/often-with-great-views restaurant.
2. The small/dark/cozy-with-tiny-tables restaurant.
Which kind of restaurant does she prefer? Don't take her to one when she's crazy about the *other*.

632 Arrange to have a small gift delivered to your table during dinner. Picture an elegantly wrapped box presented on a silver tray.

Other patrons will think you're newlyweds!

633 Arrange to have a dozen red roses delivered to your table.

634 Hire a musician to serenade your lover at your table. Have him play one of her very favorite romantic songs.

635 Get a menu from his favorite restaurant. Turn it into a "Certificate Good for One Romantic Dinner." Mail it to him at work.

Play "footsie" under the table at an elegant restaurant.

636 Sunday brunch! Check the Sunday newspaper for restaurant listings. Ask your friends for their favorite spots.

By the Number

637

- Send 20 stuffed animals to her on her 20th birthday.
- Send 30 red roses to him on his 30th birthday.
- Send 40 reasons why you love her on her 40th birthday.
- Send 50 classic love songs to him on his 50th birthday.
- Send 60 greeting cards to her on her 60th birthday.
- Send 70 sunflowers to him on his 70th birthday.
- Send 80 love quotes to her on her 80th birthday.
- Send 90 balloons to him on his 90th birthday.
- Send 100 Hershey's Kisses to her on her 100th birthday.

638

- Send him one birthday card for each year of his age—send them *one a day for as long as it takes.*
- Send him one birthday card for each year of his age—send them *all at one time!*

639

- Does he *love* Beethoven? Get him recordings of all 9 symphonies.
- If it's Mozart he loves, you'll have to buy 41 symphonies.
- And if it's Haydn he loves, you're *really* in trouble, because Haydn composed an incredible 108 symphonies!

> Variations on a Theme: Present those 9 Beethoven symphonies with 9 red roses, 9 balloons, and 9 little love notes.

By the Book

640 Wouldn't it be cool to *publish a book for her*?! Perhaps a book of poems you've written for her. Maybe a collection of love letters. Maybe it's a book of memories the two of you have shared. Maybe it's a fictional story based on your life together. (Maybe it's an *erotic* novel!)

Armed with any computer and PageMaker or Quark software, anyone can write and design a professional-looking book. Next, design a cover (maybe hire a professional graphic designer) then call a local printer and have one copy printed up. If it's a Memory Book for your twenty-fifth wedding anniversary, or a big fiftieth Birthday Book, you may want to have copies printed for everyone who attends your party.

641 Read aloud to one another. It's a wonderful, quiet way to share time and a story. (Think of the comfort and closeness you create when reading aloud to a child.) Some favorite read-aloud books from Romance Class participants include:

- *Illusions,* by Richard Bach
- *The Lord of the Rings,* by J.R.R. Tolkien
- *The Prophet,* by Kahlil Gibran

> Reading some good *erotic* literature aloud might be defined as "foreplay."

642 Of *course* there's www.amazon.com and www.barnesandnoble.com. But additional web resources for popular books and harder-to-find books include: www.isbn.nu; www.addall.com; www.powells.com; www.fatbrain.com. And a resource that lets you search the inventories of thousands of used bookstores is www.bibliofind.com.

Engaging Ideas

643 One guy in the Romance Class was inspired to present his girlfriend with one red rose...*that had a diamond ring hidden inside the unopened bud.* The rose sat on her desk for two days, where she admired it and smelled it often, before it bloomed, revealing the ring! (She nearly fainted.)

> **Chapter Theme Song:**
> "Marry Me,"
> Amanda Marshall

644 And then there's always the classic "Diamond-Ring-in-the-Box-of-Cracker-Jacks" trick.

> **FYI**
> The ancient Romans believed that diamonds were splinters from falling stars with which Eros's arrows were tipped. The ancient Greeks believed that diamonds were the tears of the gods.

645 Apply for the job of "Husband"! Write an "Engagement Resume" outlining your "goals," your desirable qualities, your qualifications and relevant experience.

646 *Engagement Rings for Men!* Why should *women* be the only ones to get engagement rings??

From a modern woman's point of view: Engagement rings are public statements that you're "spoken for" or "taken." Why should *he* be running around "free"?

From a man's point of view: You just dropped several thousand dollars on a diamond—

> A call for equal rights (for men)!

wouldn't you like her to put her money where her mouth is, too?

Will You Marry Me?

647 Here are some of the more cre-
ative and unusual ways that some Romance
Class participants have gotten engaged:
- Skywriting proposals
- Sky banner proposals
- Custom jigsaw puzzle proposals
- Videotaped proposals
- Proposals on billboards
- Proposals inside custom-made Chinese fortune
  cookies
- Audiotaped proposals
- Telegrammed proposals
- Using lit candles to spell out "Will you marry me?"
- Painting the proposal on the roof, then taking her flying!

**Chapter
Theme Song:**
"Will You Marry
Me?" Paula Abdul

648 A touch of class for men: Send a clever telegram to her
parents, asking their permission to marry their daughter.

649 Some couples consult
astrologers for the best dates and
times to get engaged. (Couldn't
hurt. Might help.)

Astrology?! Hey, don't
knock it! With a 51%
divorce rate, we need all
the help we can get!

650 Gals: Make a photocopy
of your hand and new engagement ring. Attach a note saying "I've
got a piece of the rock." Mail it to him to show your appreciation.

651 She received an unexpected gift for no special occasion. A beautifully wrapped box from Tiffany's. She opened it to find a sterling silver tray—engraved with "Sally, will you marry me?"

Winner, Quirkiest Proposal Award: He gift-wrapped a stack of twelve bridal magazines and said to her, "You're going to need these!"

Marriage Matters

652 One husband in the Romance Class always introduces his wife in this manner: "...And I'd like you to meet my *bride*, Alice." (Alice, his sixty-four-year-old wife of forty years, always blushes.)

653 Get a subscription to *Marriage Magazine*, one of America's great little secrets. I find every issue to be both inspiring and practical. Call for a subscription: 800-MARRIAGE, or visit www.marriagemagazine.org.

Chapter Theme Song: "I Will (Take You Forever)," Christopher Cross

654 1. *The Seven Principles for Making Marriage Work*, by John M. Gottman & Nan Silver
2. *How to Improve Your Marriage Without Talking About It*, by Patricia Love, EdD. & Stephen Stosny, Ph.D.

3. *The New Rules of Marriage*, by Terrence Real
4. *Passionate Marriage: Keeping Love and Intimacy Alive in Committed Relationships*, by David Schnarch
5. *7 Stages of Marriage*, by Rita M. DeMaria & Sari Harrar
6. *The Act of Marriage*, by Dr. Tim LaHaye & Beverly LaHaye
7. *Love Between Equals: How Peer Marriage Works*, by P. Schwartz
8. *Marital Myths Revisited*, by Arnold Lazarus
9. *The Mirages of Marriage*, by William Lederer & Don Jackson
10. *Take Back Your Marriage*, by William J. Doherty, Ph.D.

"For two people in a marriage to live together day after day is unquestionably the one miracle that the Vatican has overlooked."

—Bill Cosby

655 Have your wedding vows penned in beautiful calligraphy. Have them framed. Hang them in your living room.

Monogamy—Not Monotony

656 Have you ever noticed that most of the best movie romance occurs between *single* people? Contrary to popular belief, this is not because the romance ends with marriage; it's because it is simply so much easier to catch infatuation on film than it is to catch the depth, meaning, and subtleties of a long-term, A+ Relationship on film.

"In real life, of course, marriage, with its subterranean motifs and trade-offs, is more fascinating and unfathomable, hence more tantalizing, than a score of love affairs. But in movie life, surfaces—faces, in fact—must tell the story, and once those faces become familiar or imply the virtues of endurance rather than the sparks of strangeness, romance loses its necessary tension." From *The New York Times*, "The Love That's Forever: Making Matches," by Molly Haskell.

Chapter Theme Song: "True to You," Kim Wilde

657 Create your own personal "anniversary ritual" that you reenact every year together in a private little ceremony. You might play special music for background; you might light candles; you might read aloud to one another your original wedding vows; you might write a poem every year.

658 Get a large wardrobe box from a local moving company. Wrap the box with wrapping paper in your partner's favorite color and a giant bow. Place the box on your front porch. Hop inside. Have a friend close the lid, finish the wrapping, ring the doorbell, and run.

For a rare treatment of mature love, see the great movie *On Golden Pond.*

(More) Kid Stuff

659 Buy some crayons. If you're right-handed, take a crayon in your left hand. Write a short note to him as if you were in first grade.

660 Wind-up toys are very cool: monsters that walk and shoot sparks, creeping bugs, racing cars, crawling babies, lumbering robots. Use your creativity and wrap a little wind-up toy with a clever note. Call Lilliput at 800-TIN-TOYS, or visit www.lilliputmotorcompany.com.

Go fly a kite!
Ride on a carousel.
Play a board game.
Share your favorite jokes.
Blow bubbles.
Toss a Frisbee.
Watch cloud formations.
Wish on a falling star.

661 Notes to accompany stuffed animals...

• Teddy bears: *"I can't bear being away from you..."*
• Stuffed pigs: *"I'm hog-wild over you!"*
• Stuffed lions: *"I'm roarin' to get you!"*
• Stuffed tigers: *"You're Grrrrrrreat!"*
• Stuffed monkeys: *"Let's monkey around!"*

662

• Visit a playground, swing together, play on the teeter-totter.
• Visit a playground—at midnight, under a full moon, with a bottle of fine champagne.

(More) Funny Stuff

663 Send comics to him or her at work. Work-related, hobby-related, or relationship-related. He'll appreciate the fact that you thought about him.

664

• Present him with a *written bill* for the next dinner you prepare for him: "Jean-Ann's Café: Bill for Services: Salad: 1 kiss. Entree: 8 kisses. Dessert: 3 kisses. Total bill: 12 kisses. (Tipping *is* encouraged.) You may want to take advantage of our Frequent Diner Program. See the manager. Thank you, come again!"

The New Yorker is a great resource for relationship-oriented cartoons.

• Present her with a bill for the next time you change the oil in her car: "John's Garage: Bill for services: 6 quarts of oil: 1 kiss each. Oil filter: 1 kiss. New wiper blades: 3.5 hugs. Labor: 4 kisses. Total bill: 11 kisses. No checks accepted. Note: Special rates for customers who sleep with the mechanic!"

665 Get a favorite comic blown up to poster size. (Head for your local copy shop.) Mount it on cardboard. Send it to her at work or prop it up on the front porch.

666 For your comic strip lover: Check out www.comics.com for info on the Sunday Comic Store.

"We cannot really love anybody with whom we never laugh."
—Agnes Repplier

(More) Cool Stuff

667 Give your lover a bouquet of edible flowers!

- Anise hyssop flowers
- Arugula flowers
- Borage
- Calendula
- Chamomile
- Chive flowers
- Chrysanthemums
- Daisies
- Dandelions
- Day lilies
- Hollyhocks
- Honeysuckle
- Lavender
- Marigolds
- Mustard flowers
- Nasturtium flowers
- Pansies
- Rose petals
- Squash blossoms
- Violets

Float some of these beautiful, edible petals in a glass of your favorite wine or champagne!

668 Musical greeting cards! Yes, open one up and it plays an electronic tune for you. Very cool. Look in card shops and gift stores.

Cool, huh?!

669 You can get a complete lobster feast shipped to you anywhere in the USA! Call Clambakes to Travel, at 800-722-CLAM, or visit www.clambakeco.com.

They'll send you an entire lobster feast including the pots and utensils—air expressed overnight! The traditional New England seafood dinner, for-two includes: two 1-1/4 pound lobsters; 1-1/2 pounds of steamers; a pound of mussels; two ears of fresh corn; four to six red bliss potatoes; two chunks of onion; and two links of sweet Italian sausage.

(More) Concepts

670 *"Time is money."* You've heard it a *thousand* times. A call for efficiency. A time management maxim. An excuse for workaholics.

Well, it's a *lie*. Time is *not* money!

You can *save* money, but you *can't* save time—it's slipping by all the time, regardless of what you do. Also, you can create *more* money—by working harder or longer or

> Time is *not* money.

smarter. But you *can't* create more time. *That's it. Sorry. Nope. No more. No—you can't live on "borrowed time"—it doesn't work that way.*

So I suggest that you *save the money* (perhaps for a big gift or special event)—but *spend the time* now, while you still have it.

671 Romantics do not put their partners first by ignoring their own needs and wants. Rather, they put their *relationship* first, and

> Romantics are *not* martyrs.

they do things that enhance the couple as a whole. You see, self-sacrifice always backfires because it builds resentment in the giver and creates guilt in the receiver. Romantic gestures performed out of love provide benefits to both the giver and the receiver.

672 Your physical surroundings affect your emotional well-being. While many of us would agree with this, the Chinese art of *feng shui* takes it to quite another level. *Feng shui* regards homes, buildings, and rooms as "energy systems" that affect *qi*—our basic life energy. It makes sense to me that we should do everything possible to create personal environments that support our lives and our loves. Here are two books to help you learn more: *Feng Shui Your Life,* by Jayme Barrett and Mary Steenburgen. *Interior Design with Feng Shui,* by Sarah Rossbach and Lin Yun.

(More) Do-It-Yourself

Chapter
Theme Song:

"Handy Man,"
James Taylor

673 Learn to play the guitar just well enough to accompany yourself as you sing a favorite love song. Now serenade her! Responses to the most common excuses for not doing this:

- Excuse: "I'm not musical." Answer: Practice, practice, practice!
- Excuse: "I can't sing." Answer: Then don't! But play an instrumental version of the song on guitar.
- Excuse: "I'd be too embarrassed." Answer: C'mon! Challenge yourself. Stretch yourself.

674 Make a "This Is Your Life" DVD. Interview his friends and family, neighbors, high school teachers, college buddies, fraternity brothers, colleagues and co-workers. This idea is an especially great idea for a special birthday.

675 Make a custom certificate for your lover. You can get blank certificate forms at a stationery or paper store. It doesn't have to be

Convert home videos of him to DVD on a DVD recorder. You can use Windows Movie Maker on your computer to edit videos and add music to make a beautiful *video montage* of your lover!

artistic and perfect; don't forget, *it's the thought that counts!* Here are some certificates that were created by Romance Class participants:

- A certificate "For Putting Up with Me Over the Years"
- An award "For Meritorious Conduct in Bed"
- An acknowledgment of "The World's Best Wife"
- A ribbon "For Hugs & Kisses Above and Beyond the Call of Duty"

(More) Custom-Made

676 Compose an original song for your lover. You may get some help from a local musician, but the essence of the song should be yours.

* Present him or her with the score, rolled into a scroll and tied with a red ribbon.
* Sing the song to him or her.
* Hire a band to perform the song for him or her at a party.

> One-of-a-kind items are among the most cherished gifts.

677 How about a scrapbook to commemorate your relationship? Get out your old photographs, mementos, and love letters, and be sure to have plenty of glue sticks on hand! Your lover will treasure it *forever*.

678 Make a "Commemorative Scroll" to celebrate some special occasion: your lover's birthday, your wedding anniversary, some other special date, or maybe a special *year*.

* Research the major happenings of that date or year. Consider these categories: in the news, quotable quotes, famous people, world events, scientific breakthroughs, advertising and commercials, TV shows, popular music, movies, books, Broadway, sports, art, politics, daily life, religion, miscellany.
* Some resources to help you: *American Chronicle* by Lois & Alan Gordon, *The Timetables of History* by Bernard Grun & Eva Simpson, and *Celebrity Almanac* by Ed Lewis.

This commemorative scroll can be handwritten, designed on computer, or rendered in calligraphy. Tie it with a bow and present it. You may want to make a special presentation of it: Read it aloud to your partner.

(More) Surprises

679 Buy tickets well in advance to the theater, symphony, ball game or concert. Don't tell her what the tickets are for. Simply tell her to mark her calendar. The mystery surrounding the event will be almost as much fun as the event itself. Guaranteed.

680 Surprise her by bringing dinner home from the best restaurant in town.

681 Surprise him by making his favorite homemade dessert.

682 While the two of you are out grocery shopping or running errands together, have a friend deliver a gourmet dinner to your home. Have him or her set the table with your best china, candles, and flowers, and turn the stereo on to play some soft jazz.

Many men understand the fun and romance of presenting an engagement ring as a surprise. How can you surprise her *now*?

683 If the two of you have to be *apart* for a birthday, anniversary, or Christmas: Wrap a new mobile telephone as your gift. Give instructions that the gift must be opened at a *precise time* that you name. Then, call your partner on the new phone *exactly one minute* before it's to be opened, and let the gift ring until he or she unwraps the box and answers the phone. (Note: Make sure you synchronize your watches!)

(More) Flowers

684 One gal in a Romance Class gives her guy *pressed* flowers. She explained that, "*Flat* flowers are more versatile than *real* flowers: You can slip them in between the pages of a book he's reading; you can hide them in his work files; and you can *mail* them!"

685 Give him one giant sunflower. Attach a note: "You are the sunshine of my life." Also attach a copy of Stevie Wonder's song "You Are the Sunshine of My Life."

> Chapter
> Theme Song:
> "Bring Me Flowers,"
> Hope

686 Always ask *specifically* for fresh flowers. A good, fresh rose should last nearly a *week,* while an older one can wilt in less than a day.

687
• Every home needs one elegant crystal vase.
• And a bud vase.
• And it wouldn't hurt to have a special vase for flowers at work.

(More) Romance on a Budget

688 Timing is *everything* when it comes to saving a few bucks. You could save 20 to 50 percent on virtually every gift you buy if you shop smart.
- Hit the stores immediately after Christmas.
- Shop at end-of-the-season sales.
- Look for overstock sales.
- Scan catalogs regularly, looking for deals.

689 Most cities have "City Coupon Books" that include hundreds of discount coupons for restaurants, shops and services. These coupon books usually cost just a few bucks, and can save you *hundreds* of dollars. They're also a good incentive to get the two of you out of the house, and get out of that rut you've been in!

Romantics aren't spendthrifts! (But there is a difference between being *frugal* and being *cheap*.)

FYI, lingerie catalogs often have great end-of-season sales.

690 Rediscover coffeehouses and small clubs. They're an inexpensive and entertaining change of pace. (Folk music never really dies, it just continually ebbs and flows.)

691 "TKTS" in New York City is the place to get half-price tickets for Broadway shows on the day of performances! Located in Times Square and at South Street Seaport, it's the best deal in town. (Be prepared to stand in line—a *long* line. It's a "scene" in itself!)

(More) Bubble Baths

692 Run a bath for her while she's out running errands. Put a candle, a glass of wine, and a bottle of fancy bubble bath on the kitchen table—along with a note saying, "I'll put the groceries away for you. Go relax. You deserve it. I love you."

693 Towel her dry after she showers. S-L-O-W-L-Y.

694 If your lover loves nothing more than a luxurious soak in a steamy, hot, elegant tub, then consider taking him or her on vacation to one of these first-class hotels—where they really understand the romance of baths.

- Post Ranch Inn, Big Sur, California. Picture sunken marble tubs in rooms at the edge of 1,000-foot cliffs overlooking the Pacific Ocean. Call 800-527-2200 or visit www.postranchinn.com.
- Chateau de Bagnols, Bagnols, France. Featuring huge old tubs in Renaissance castle near Lyons. 011-33-4-74-71-4000 or visit www.bagnols.com.
- Park Hyatt Hotel, Tokyo, Japan. Imagine sitting in a deep, hot tub that overlooks the city of Tokyo. Call 81-3-5322-1234 or visit www.tokyo.park.hyatt.com.
- Mandarin Oriental Hotel, San Francisco, California. How's this for luxury with a view? A bathroom on the 48th floor, with floor-to-ceiling windows overlooking the Golden Gate Bridge. Call 415-276-9888 or visit www.mandarinoriental.com/sanfrancisco.

Thinking of You

695 Buy some small, red, heart-shaped stickers and place one on the face of your wristwatch. It's a reminder to think of your lover every time you check the time. If you're like most of us, that's about a thousand times a day!

696 Make a donation to her favorite charity—instead of going on your next expensive date. You can show her that you care about *her—and* at the same time show you care about the whales or the birds or the environment or whatever her favorite cause is.

697 Wonderful insights can be gained by asking each other quirky questions:

1. If you could be a comic strip character, who would you be?
2. If your name were to appear in the dictionary, how would you define yourself?
3. If you could create the perfect job for yourself, what would it be?
4. Who are your heroes? (Fictional and real.)
5. If you had three wishes, what would they be?
6. Could you live for a year in a tent with your partner (without going crazy)?
8. If you could accomplish one crazy stunt that would land you in the *Guinness Book of World Records*, what would it be?
9. Would you rather be really *smart*, or really *good looking*?
10. If you could be a super hero, who would you be?

> Ask yourself what's *important* to your partner—then make gestures that reflect it.

> Tuck a little gift into the inside zippered pocket of her favorite purse.

11. If you were Rick, in the movie *Casablanca,* would you have let Ilsa leave at the end?

12. What one part of your body would you like to change?

Think Different

698 Do something *totally out of character.*
* Always late?—Be on time.
* Not creative?—Think up something original and unexpected!
* Forgetful?—Remember her birthday *every day for a month!*
* Watch TV every night?—Go out to dinner instead.
* Two left feet?—Take dance lessons together!

> Think "different"— and you'll *never* run out of romantic ideas.

699 Are you stuck in a rut? Are you taking each other for granted lately? Try "reframing." Reframe, or redefine, how you see your partner.
* Start thinking of her as *your lover* once again.
* Start treating him as your *best friend*—which he *was,* once upon a time. Remember??

700 Act out different fantasies of meeting for the first time.
* Meet in a bar after work.
* Meet while grocery shopping.
* Meet in line, waiting at the bank.
* Meet over lunch at work.

701 Spend an "all-night" together: Make love, watch videos, go out to an all-night diner, go for a moonlit stroll, make love again, watch old movies on TV, blast the stereo and dance at three in the morning. Then sleep all day the next day to recover.

Choreography

702 "Choreograph" your lovemaking to your favorite music! This may sound artificial and contrived, but several people in my Romance Class have told me that they often do this, although they never thought of it as "choreography."

I don't mean that you plan *every* movement, but rather that you match some favorite music to the general mood and pace of your lovemaking.

- For example, some people like to start slowly and gently, and build to a fast-paced climax. Their musical choreography could look like this: Start with a little George Winston; move to some Al Jarreau; mix in some Glenn Miller; and finish up with Maynard Ferguson.

> This choreography technique is not taught at Arthur Murray!

- Others like to start out fast and passionately, and wind down to a gentle conclusion. Their musical choreography could look like this: Start with the soundtrack from *Nine-1/2 Weeks*; move to the soundtrack from *When Harry Met Sally*; and end with the soundtrack from *Out of Africa*.

• One couple prefers Mozart symphonies. "Beethoven is great music, but too frenetic for our lovemaking," Judy B. explains. "Mozart is great—especially *The Jupiter Symphony*, No. 41. It has four movements, which correspond with our pattern of lovemaking.

  1) "The first movement, *Allegro Vivace*, is strong and passionate, this gets us going. It runs 11:50—good for energetic foreplay.

  2) "The second movement, *Andante Cantabile*, slows the pace, which allows us to talk a little and build the intimacy more. This runs a good 10:53.

  3) "The third movement, *Menuetto: Allegretto*, picks up the speed again, which moves us from quiet intimacy into a more intense passion. This one is quick, at 5:13.

  4) "The last movement, *Molto Allegro*, races to a roaring and passionate conclusion. Just perfect at 8:37."

• What music would *you* use to choreograph your lovemaking?

Creativity

703 Keep a journal. It will benefit you in lots of ways. Many Romance Class participants have observed that creative ideas often flow while they're writing in their journals.

704 George was a bibliophile. He loved browsing in bookstores. On his forty-third birthday he happened to be wandering by his favorite local bookstore—and stopped suddenly on the sidewalk. The window display held hundreds of copies of a book titled: *Happy Birthday, George!* Looking closer he saw that the author was his wife! He ran into the store, where the clerk handed him a copy of the book. George discovered that the *Happy Birthday, George!* book was really a different book with a custom-made book jacket slipped over it.

Guys: Learn a little sleight-of-hand well enough to make her diamond engagement ring "appear" out of thin air!

Shaking his head in wondrous surprise, George turned the book over and read on the back cover: "Happy Birthday, oh wonderful husband of mine! This book is Surprise #1. Surprise #2 is a $100 gift certificate for books. Enjoy! Surprise #3 is waiting patiently to enjoy lunch with you at the Posh Café. Happy Birthday!"

705 Use a thesaurus to help you express your love—and to help you rev up your love letters.

Are you—infatuated, crazy, frantic, frenetic, frenzied, intoxicated, mad—with love for him or her?

- Tell your mate that you—love, adore, admire, cherish, desire, want, need, prize, esteem, idolize, revere, treasure—him or her.

- Describe how you're—crazy about/mad for/nuts about/smitten with/stuck on/sweet on/wild about—your mate.

- Tell your lover that you're—enchanted by/captivated by/enamored of/fond of—him or her.

Cruisin'

706

- Abercrombie & Kent Int'l.: 800-323-7308, www.abercrombiekent.com
- American Canadian Caribbean Line: 800-556-7450, www.accl-smallships.com
- Carnival Cruise Lines: 800-227-6482, www.carnival.com
- Celebrity Cruises: 800-437-3111, www.celebrity cruises.com
- Clipper Cruise Line: 800-456-8100, www.intrav.com
- Club Med Cruises: 800-258-2633, www.clubmed.com
- Costa Cruise Lines: 800-332-6782, www.costacruise.com
- Cunard Line: 800-7-CUNARD, www.cunard.com
- Disney Cruise Line: 800-939-2784, www.disneycruise.com
- Holland America Line: 800-426-0327, www.hollandamerica.com
- Norwegian Cruise Line: 800-327-7030, www.ncl.com
- Princess Cruise Line: 800-PRINCESS, www.princess.com
- Royal Caribbean Int'l.: 800-327-6700, www.royalcaribbean.com
- Star Clippers: 800-442-0551, www.star-clippers.com
  - Windjammer Barefoot Cruises: 800-327-2601, www.windjammer.com
    - Windstar Cruises: 800-258-SAIL, www.windstarcruises.com

Chapter Theme Song:

"Cruisin'," Gwyneth Paltrow & Huey Lewis

Have you ever seen the sun set over the Caribbean from the deck of a cruise ship?

Lovin'

707 Make love in *slow motion.*

708 **Things to Never, Never, *Never* Do While Making Love**

* Never, never, *never* answer the phone.
* Never, never, *never* call her by a former lover's name.
* Never, never, *never* glance at your watch.
* Never, never, *never* interrupt yourselves for a whining pet.
* Encourage open-mindedness, but *never* push too far.
* Never, never, *never* leave too little time.
* Never, never, *never* say anything negative about your partner's body.
* Never, never, *never* criticize his or her technique (but *do* discuss it later).
* Never, never, *never* get into arousal without dealing with birth control first.
* Never, never, *never* criticize your lover in any way.
* Never, never, *never* lose your sense of humor.
* Never, never, *never* talk about work or children in bed.
* Never, never, *never* fake orgasm.
* Never, never, *never* leave the bedroom door unlocked if kids are in the house.

709 Make love by catering to her sexual desires 100 percent—and putting your sexual desires on hold until tomorrow.

Please, Mr. Postman

710 You can get your Valentine card postmarked from one of these romantic cities or towns:

- Valentine, Texas 79854
- Valentine, Nebraska 69201
- Loveland, Colorado 80537
- Loving, New Mexico 88256
- Bridal Veil, Oregon 97010
- Loveland, Ohio 45140

Chapter Theme Song:

"Please Mr. Postman," The Marvelettes

Just put your card, addressed and stamped, inside another envelope addressed to the postmaster of the town of your choice. Attach a note requesting that your Valentine be hand-stamped and mailed.

711 Carry stamps in your wallet at all times. (Preferably several Love Stamps!)

712 The following is part of a "Junk Mail Campaign" that one Romance Class participant created for her husband. She designed it to look like a Publishers Clearinghouse mailing. Clever, huh?

YOU MAY ALREADY BE A WINNER! The Publishers Clearinghouse Lovestakes has chosen *YOU* to be the recipient of AT LEAST 1,000,000 kisses—that's ONE MILLION kisses (and hugs!) Nothing to buy! No coupons to fill out! What do you have to do in order to qualify for ONE

Items to insert inside love letter envelopes: confetti, a lock of your hair, feathers, stickers, heart-shaped paper cut-outs.

MILLION kisses and hugs?!—Just bring home one bottle of champagne this Friday. That's all!

But—if you want to qualify for the BIG BONUS PRIZE of 1,000 nights of passionate lovemaking, you'll have to bring home one red rose per week for the next year. A SMALL PRICE TO PAY, WOULDN'T YOU SAY—FOR 1,000 NIGHTS OF PAS-SIONATE LOVEMAKING!!

This offer expires *tomorrow*—so act *TODAY!*

You've Got Mail*

713 With a nod to America Online... Stay in touch with your lover through e-mail. Always use the latest electronic communications technology to break down the artificial barriers between "work time" and "personal time." Email is great for keeping a conversation going with your partner all day long.

> Treat email as an *extra* method for staying connected. Email doesn't take the place of real love letters via "snail mail."

714

* Type this: colon, close parenthesis :) and you get a smiley face when you look at the page sideways.
  * Type this: semi-colon, hyphen, close parenthesis ;-) —a wink!
  * Type this: colon, hyphen, open parenthesis :-(—a frown.

> Use your lover's pet name as your email password.

These are called emoticons or "smileys," and they're used by frequent emailers to enhance the emotional content of their emailed notes.

715 It's getting easier and easier to send audio files via e-mail. With the proper software your lover will be able to hear your voice as well as read your words. This Technology is especially great if you're in a long distance relationship

*This chapter dedicated to Meg Ryan and Tom Hanks.

716 Create your own custom-made electronic greeting cards. Using PowerPoint or similar software you can use scanned-in pictures and animation to create lively, funny, and entertaining e-cards.

Mindset of a Romantic

717 Romantics have a good sense of humor.
There's no such thing as a "humorless romantic." While the foundation of romance is a serious love, the *nature* of romance is lighthearted.

718 Romantics "work at it."
Yes, relationships require work. But it's not "work" like nine-to-five work. It's more like an artist working on a painting. Painting requires skill, time, effort, planning, frustration, and sweat sometimes—but the work is so

Mindset of a Romantic:
Creative
Quirky
Flexible
Observant
Childlike
Thoughtful
Fun
Wacky
Curious

rewarding that the artist doesn't view it as "work." Working on a loving relationship is like that.

719 Romantics not only *work* at it, they "play at it," too!

Being romantic is a lot of *fun*. (In case you haven't guessed by now!) Being romantic involves your creativity, self-expression, and your passionate spirit. Remember my earlier definition of romance as "adult play"?

720 Romantics live in the moment.

"Carpe diem"—seize the day! Seize the moment. Don't let another ten minutes go by without making some expression of your love for your partner. (Yes, I mean that *literally*. If you're at home reading this, set the book down, saunter over to him or her, and wrap your arms around your lover. If you're out somewhere, call on the phone. Go do it. *Carpe diem*.)

Thinking Like a Romantic

721 Romantics are *magnets* for romantic ideas.

Romantics find romantic ideas *everywhere*.

- Romantics keep an eye on the concerts and shows scheduled to appear in their area.
- Romantics read the newspaper not only for the news, but for romantic opportunities.
- Romantics notice articles *and* ads in newspapers and magazines.

- Romantics save miscellaneous articles for future reference.
- Romantics notice unique gifts when shopping for other things.

722 Romantics are flexible.
- What would *you* do if you'd planned a romantic picnic, and it started raining? One couple held their picnic *in bed!* Another couple grabbed two umbrellas and headed for the park *anyway!*
- If your partner showed up at your office wearing a trench coat *and nothing else*—what would you do?
- Would you be comfortable taking the afternoon off work on the spur of the moment to spend it with your partner?

Idea inspired while eating Alpha-Bits: For each letter of the alphabet, write down three possible romantic gifts or concepts. Use this list for generating romantic ideas.

723 Employing the concept of "Couple-Thinking" will automatically turn anyone into a romantic. Couple-Thinking is a technique in which you *first* think of yourself as a member of a couple, and second as an independent individual. (Men, and our culture in general, put too much emphasis on rugged individualism, and not enough emphasis on relationship-building and connection-making.) Note: I am *NOT* suggesting that you martyr yourself on the altar of Relationship.

Romantics have a portion of their brains assigned to the task of recognizing romantic opportunities when they appear. Other people screen them out.

Love Is...

724 Love is...eliminating *all* interruptions so you can really be alone together. Disconnect the phone; unplug the TV; ship the kids to the neighbors; disconnect the doorbell.

725

- Love is...framing a favorite greeting card she's given you.
- Love is...reading aloud to each other before bed.
- Love is...having a poem delivered to your table at a restaurant.
- Love is...sending a postcard every day that you're away from her.
- Love is...believing in one another.

726

- Romance is the expression of love.
- Romance is the icing on the cake of your relationship.
- Romance is *always* about love, but only *sometimes* about sex.
- Romance is a state of mind.
- Romance is also a state of being.
- Romance is what you *do*. (Love is what you *feel*.)
- Romance is the language of love.

Chapter
Theme Songs:

"I Want to Know What Love Is," Foreigner
"Love Is," Vanessa Williams & Brian McKnight
"Love Is Powerful," Seal
"Love Is a Many Splendored Thing," The Four Aces

Love is...waking her gently with soft caresses and kisses.

"Love Is..."

727

"Love is a little haven of refuge from the world."
—Bertrand Russell

"Love is the fairest flower that blooms in God's garden."
—Anonymous

"Love is a flower and you its only seed."
—Amanda McBroom

"Love is a promise, love is a souvenir, once given never forgotten, never let it disappear."
—John Lennon

"Love is a great beautifier."
—Louisa May Alcott

"Love is, above all, the gift of oneself."
—Jean Anouilh Ardele

"Love is being stupid together."
—Paul Valery

"Love is as much of an object as it is an obsession; everybody wants it, everybody seeks it, but few ever achieve it. Those who do will cherish it, be lost in it, and among all, never...never forget it."
—Curtis Judalet

Love is merely an empty concept unless you bring it alive through action.

"Love is blind."
—Geoffrey Chaucer.

• • •

"Love is blind. That is why he always proceeds by the sense of touch."
—French Proverb

"Love is a chain of love as nature is a chain of life."
—Truman Capote

"Love is patient and kind; love is not jealous or boastful."
—1 Corinthians 13:4

"Love is the triumph of imagination over intelligence."
—H.L. Mencken

"Love is the only sane and satisfactory answer to the problem of human existence."
—Erich Fromm

"Love is something eternal; the aspect may change, but not the essence."
—Vincent Van Gogh

"Love is the final end of the world's history, the Amen of the universe."
—Novalis

Love is patient, Love is kind,
it does not envy;
it does not boast,
it is not proud.
It is not rude, it is not self-seeking,
it is not easily angered,
it keeps no record of wrongs.
Love does not delight in evil
but rejoices with the truth.
It always protects, always trusts,
always hopes, always perseveres.
—1 Corinthians 13:4-7

The Way to a Man's Heart*

728 When in doubt, buy her chocolate. When in doubt, order him pizza.

729 You can spice up *any* meal at home—from gourmet extravaganzas to TV dinners—by adding candlelight and soft music. Don't wait for "special occasions" or weekends to bring out the romance.

730 Get the pizza chef to arrange the pepperoni in the shape of a heart.

> Or—Shape the entire pizza into a heart-shape.
> Or—Cut each and every slice of pepperoni into a tiny heart-shape.
> Or—Use the mushroom toppings to spell out both of your initials.

731 If your lover is a tea lover, get her a subscription to the *Upton Tea Quarterly* newsletter. It includes listings and information on hundreds of varieties of fine loose tea. Write to Upton Tea Imports, 34A Hayden Rowe Street, Hopkinton, Massachusetts 01748. Call 800-234-8327 or visit www.uptontea.com.

732 What's her all-time favorite meal? Learn to make it! Get help from friends, neighbors, or relatives—whatever it takes.

> *Also the way to a *woman's* heart!

733 Create an "At-Home Date": includes dinner and dancing. Formal attire required.

Recipes for Romance

734 Spread whipped cream or chocolate syrup on selected body parts and invite your lover to enjoy dessert.

735 The way to his stomach often involves directions to his favorite restaurant. Do you know his all-time favorite restaurant; favorite diner; favorite fast food joint; favorite fancy restaurant; favorite pizza parlor?

Create a personalized "Wine-of-the-Month Club" for her.

736 Embark on a series of "Restaurant Discoveries": Each week go to a different restaurant within a 100-mile radius of your house. Choose a restaurant "theme" that appeals to both of you.
- You might choose a type of *food:* French, Thai, Mexican, Italian, Chinese, etc.
- You might choose a type of *restaurant:* diners, elegant bistros, casual cafés, pizzerias, etc.

(Not) For Newlyweds Only! *The Newlywed Cookbook*, by Robin Vitetta-Miller

737
- Take a wine-tasting class together.
- Attend wine tastings at local wine shops.
- Host wine-tasting parties for your friends.
- Get a subscription to *The Wine Spectator.* Call 800-752-7799 or visit www.winespectator.com.

Aphrodisiacs

738 You know, of course, that green M&M's are *aphrodisiacs*, don't you? With that as a start...

- Carefully open a one-pound bag of M&M's and empty it out. Refill it entirely with green M&M's. Seal it up so it looks like new.
- Give him a heart-shaped box full of green M&M's.
- Fill his box of Cheerios with green M&M's.

Chapter Theme Song:
"(You're My) Aphrodisiac," Dennis Edwards

739 Someone in every Romance Class asks, "What about *aphrodisiacs*!?"

Wondrous claims have been made about a great variety of foods, from oysters and chocolate to basil and green M&M's. Personally, I feel that it's the *mood and environment* surrounding the presentation of the food that determines the potential amorous conclusion of the evening.

But by all means, try some exotic recipes. (Couldn't hurt—might help!)

And regardless of whether or not certain foods can *chemically* make one more interested in love, you can definitely use food to *psychologically* affect one's mood for love! There's always the scientifically proven "placebo effect," which indicates that the mere *belief* in the power of an agent can bring about the believed-in effect. This means that virtually *any* food could potentially be an aphrodisiac.

740 If you'd like to prepare some real gourmet meals that have real aphrodisiac potential, you must get the book *The New InterCourses: An Aphrodisiac Cookbook,* by Martha Hopkins and Randall Lockridge. This is the most amazing, elegant, and erotic cookbook you've ever seen! The photos *alone* will inspire some fantasy ideas that have never before occurred to you. I *guarantee* it! Visit www.intercourses.com.

Henry Kissinger once said, "Power is the ultimate aphrodisiac." Does that mean only world leaders are leading sexy lives? Not at all! We all have tremendous potential in our *personal* power, the power of *charm,* the power of *romance,* the power of *imagination* and the power of *love.*

(More) Recipes for Romance

741 Picnics. (I checked, and nowhere is it written that you can't have picnics indoors, in the nude, in front of a fireplace, in your office, in bed, on the roof of your apartment building, or at midnight.)

742 Bake a giant chocolate chip cookie for him. (And I mean GIANT—at least two feet in diameter.)

"Blockbuster Recommends" ...the classic film *Tom Jones*. (Watch for the pub scene. Wow!)

743 If you're especially inept in the kitchen, you've got a great opportunity to surprise your partner. *Cook a gourmet meal!* Send your partner out for the afternoon. Enlist the help of a friend who cooks. Prepare your lover's favorite dish. *Voilà!*

744 Create your own special mixed drink and name it after your partner. ("A Peter Colada." "A Catherine Cooler.")

745

- Carefully open a packet of tea. Remove the tea bag and replace it with a little love note. Seal the packet to make it look untouched.
- Create custom "Love Quote Tags" and attach them to the end of the string on each tea bag.

FYI— The most popular soft drink in Brazil, Guarana, is also a recognized and legendary aphrodisiac!

Classic Romance

746 What could be more classic than a fine gold locket with your photo inside? (Maybe a photo of the two of you.)

747 *Revive chivalry.* Women love a real gentleman.

- Open her car door for her. Hold her dinner chair. Help her on with her coat.
- Older women will love the revival of manners.
- Some younger women will need to be encouraged to see these gestures as tokens of respect and affection, and not as messages that men feel women are inferior and helpless.

"We do not need to think alike to love alike."
—Francis David

748 *Go out dancing!* Ballroom dancing is enjoying a resurgence unlike anything since World War II. Glenn Miller, Benny Goodman, and the Big Band sound are once again being heard in dance halls, restaurants, clubs, and church basements throughout the land. Sign up for ballroom dancing lessons; it may be the single best romantic decision you make this decade.

Arthur Murray Dance Studios:
305-445-9645
www.arthurmurray.com

749 Go for a horse-drawn carriage ride through the city—or the country.

Classical Romance

750 My panel of experts has compiled its official list of The Most Romantic Operatic Arias:

- "Deh Vieni, Non Tardar," from *The Marriage of Figaro*
- "Che Gelida Manina," from *La Bohème*
- "Parigi, O Cara," from *La Traviata*
- "Recondita Armonia," from *Tosca*
- "Bimba, Bimba, Non Piangere," from *Madama Butterfly*
- "The Flower Song," from *Carmen*
- "Sì, mi chiamano Mimì," from *La Bohème*
- "Celeste Aïda," from *Aïda*
- "Amor Ti Vieta," from *Fedora*
- "Mon Coeur S'ouvre à Ta Voix," from *Samson and Dalilah*
- "Quando, Rapito In Estasi," from *Lucia di Lammermoor*

Does your partner like the power and passion of Beethoven? Or the beauty and grace of Mozart? Or the depth and elegance of Bach?

751 Most Romantic Piano Concertos (just take my word for it):

- Mozart's Piano Concerto No. 21 in C
- Beethoven's Piano Concerto No. 2 in E flat
- Schumann's Concerto in A Minor for Piano & Orchestra
- Grieg's Concerto in A Minor for Piano & Orchestra

"Tell me who admires and loves you, and I will tell you who you are."
—Charles Augustin Sainte-Beuve

752 Be prepared with a Romantic Music Library. True romantics have everything from Beethoven to The Beatles, from Mozart to Meatloaf; from jazz to rock to country to R&B to folk to acoustic to show tunes.

Classic

753 *Serenade her.* Sing her favorite love song, or "your song" to her. You don't need to have a great voice. Your sincerity will more than make up for your lack of perfect pitch.

* Sing along with The Beatles or Celine Dion on CD.
* Get a good friend to accompany you on guitar.
* If singing truly embarrasses you, hire a local singer/guitar player to serenade her for you.

One of the most romantic film scenes of all time: In *Say Anything*, Lloyd stands outside Diane's window, holding up a boom box playing their song. Reenact this scene for your lover!

754 A true classic is the lazy-Sunday-afternoon-canoe-ride on a calm, beautiful pond, lake or river.

* Version 1: "Just Do It!"—Toss on your jeans and T-shirt, grab a bottle of wine and some cheese, and hop in an old rowboat and *go!*
* Version 2: "Your Sunday Best"—Dress up in your best clothes, pack a great picnic basket, rent a nice canoe, and enjoy!
* Version 3: "A Victorian Afternoon"—Rent costumes! Tails and top hat for him, hoop skirt and parasol for her! Guaranteed to cause a stir at the shore.

755 Write a classic, romantic, passionate, handwritten, heartfelt love letter. Most adults haven't written a love letter since *high school.* (Why not?? Have we lost our youthful idealism, or have we just gotten lazy?) No excuses! Sit down for twenty, maybe thirty minutes, and simply *put your feelings on paper.* Don't try to be eloquent or "poetic." Just be yourself. The effort and intention are more important than the precise words you use.

> One guy in the Romance Class wrote to his wife: "Honey, I love you as much as I love the Super Bowl!" (She cried with relief and happiness.)

Classy

756 Dress up for dinner at home. Tuxedo for him, evening gown for her.

757 Hire a pianist to play during a romantic dinner at home.

758 *Anything* from Tiffany's.

> Save that Tiffany's box! That distinctive "Tiffany's turquoise" box is guaranteed to get your lover's heart racing, *regardless* of what's inside!

759 Take a leisurely stroll through a local park or public garden.

760 Learn calligraphy so you can create *incredible* love letters for him or her.

761 Get a pair of crystal champagne flutes. Use them *often!*

762 Hire a limousine for an elegant evening out.

FYI—
Shakespeare-in-the-Park in New York City's Central Park. Call 212-260-2400 or visit www.publictheater.org.

763 Have dinner-for-two prepared in your home by the best chef in town.

Picture This

764 Have a special photograph blown up to *poster size.* You might choose a wedding photo, or a really funny photo of the two of you.

765
- You do, of course, carry a photo of her in your wallet, *don't you*?
- And you have an eight-by-ten of her on your desk at work, *right*?

"Love, the key that unlocks the bars of impossibility."
—Fikayo Ositelu

766 Tape funny photos of the two of you to the refrigerator door, then add funny cartoon balloons.

767 Turn your drawer of miscellaneous photographs and slides into a "Video Photo Album." Gather your favorite photos, choose some favorite music, and have a local production studio turn them into a keepsake DVD.

Make a life-size cardboard cut-out of yourself; and give the gift of "yourself"!

768 Find your old high school yearbook picture. Add funny captions. Mail it to her. (If yours is as awful as *mine* is, it could be the funniest thing you ever give her!)

769 How about an original, signed photograph of your honey's hero, favorite movie star, sports star, or celebrity?

Picture Perfect

770 Have his portrait painted from a photograph.

771 Capture your memories and the good times... Or, as they say at Kodak, "For the times of your life"—take up photography. Whether you use a sophisticated digital camera or a disposable camera, it'll add fun to your outings, and provide you with scrapbooks full of good memories.

772 You do, of course, have a photo of your wife on your desk, *don't you*?!

- If you don't, here's what I want you to do: Get a nice eight-by-ten photo made, frame it, gift wrap it, and *give it to yourself*. Open it over breakfast with your wife, then take your gift to work with you. You'll leave her with a great memory.
- Note: Place the photo *front-and-center* on your desk, not off to the side. Her smiling face will help you keep your priorities straight when you start to get stressed out over some seemingly important work problem.

"You know you are in love when you see the world in her eyes, and her eyes everywhere in the world."
—David Levesque

Commission a photographer to shoot a formal portrait of the two of you.

773 Spend an entire afternoon together taking instant pictures of each other with a digital camera. One couple simply documented their experience of a dinner date. Another couple spent the afternoon in bed. One couple focused on close-ups, and another couple focused on the artistic settings.

Flower Power

774

- On Monday place a single red rose on the kitchen table. No note. No explanation.
- On Tuesday place one lily on the coffee table.
- On Wednesday place one daisy in the bathroom sink.
- On Thursday place one geranium on his or her pillow.
- On Friday place one forget-me-not in the mailbox.
- On Saturday place one sunflower on the kitchen counter.
- On Sunday present your lover with a *huge* bouquet made specifically with the kinds of flowers you've been giving all week.

Chapter Theme Songs:

"Bed of Roses," Bon Jovi
"Passion Flower," Duke Ellington
"Wildflower," Sheryl Crow

775
My twenty-year survey reveals that 99.9998 percent of all women *love* flowers. Basically, you can't go wrong with flowers. The remaining 0.0002 percent of women have the belief that, "It's wasteful to buy flowers that are simply going to die in a few days." It's not really that they don't *like* flowers, it's that they don't like being *wasteful*. Tip: Get these gals *flowering plants* instead of *cut flowers*.

"Love that is true never grows old."
—Elben Bano

776
Get to know your local florist. Become a "regular"—you'll get better service and fresher flowers!

777 Use a flower as a "private signal." One couple in the Romance Class told us that for years they've used the "Flower-on-the-Pillow" as a signal that they're interested in making love that night. Sounds good to me!

More Power!*

*Thanks to Tim Allen and *Tool Time!*

778 Look, guys, this *ain't* brain surgery! You want more *sex*? Then be more *romantic*. It's as simple as that.

779 If you want your lover to wear lingerie more often, *why do you think that you have the right to slouch around in your ratty boxer shorts or dirty sweat pants?!* Take a hint! Get a nice bathrobe, or silk pajamas, or a lounging jacket, or a Japanese kimono!

Consult *Redbook* monthly for new and exciting ways to spice up your sex life!

780 *Listen* to her! Don't problem-solve; don't give advice; don't agree or disagree. Just *listen*. Validate her. Honor her.

Often, when men think women are looking for *answers*, they're simply looking for *compassion and understanding*.

781 Pick up a copy of *Cosmopolitan* or *Glamour* or *Ms.* or *Redbook* or *Shape* or *Self* or *Vogue* or *Ladies Home Journal.* (How do you expect to know what women are thinking about and talking about if you don't peek at their magazines occasionally?)

Greg & Karyn

782 Most people celebrate "anniversaries." Karyn and I celebrate "Thursdayversaries": We celebrate our first date every week. This provides us with a frequent reminder of our romantic early times, and it gives us a good excuse to celebrate!

Our first date didn't even start out as a "date"—it was a casual business get-together (bestselling author wanting to trade secrets with talented humorist speaker) at my favorite coffee shop, the Pacific Bean, in Pacific Beach, California. We met at 11:30 a.m. When we looked up it was 12 hours later! We'd obviously hit it off. The rest, as they say, is history.

And so...we declared Thursday to be "Our Day," and we celebrate it in some manner every week. If we're in town, we head over to The Pacific Bean, chat over coffee, then walk-and-talk on the beach. [Note: We placed a small brass plaque on "Our Table."] If we're not together, we at least wish each other a happy anniversary.

783 Last year I substituted Karyn's regular Christmas stocking with *real silk stockings.* (Ho-ho-ho!!)

784 I created The *LifeChart* to celebrate Karyn's birthday last year. On poster paper I drew a timeline representing her life—from birth to the present. Along the line are noted events from her life: significant, outrageous, funny and serious. (I interviewed her parents and friends for items that I had no way of knowing.) Parallel timelines indicate a few events from my life, and some world events, for putting her life into perspective. It became an instant heirloom.

• Maybe I'll update it every ten years for our anniversary. That would make a nice ritual, don't you think?

• And then maybe on our fiftieth anniversary I'll have the whole thing rendered in calligraphy. (But will I be able to wait that long??)

Heart & Soul

785 For your next vacation do something different, spiritual, and rejuvenating. Spend a week on a spiritual retreat at a quiet sanctuary or monastery.

• Green Gulch Farm Zen Center, Muir Beach, California. Buddhist workshops and meditation periods in Japanese-style surroundings on the picturesque Pacific coast. Call 415-383-3134 or visit www.sfzc.org.

Chapter Theme Songs:

"Heart and Soul,"
Jan & Dean
"Heart and Soul,"
Huey Lewis &
The News
"Heart and Soul,"
Johnny Maddox
"Heart and Soul,"
The Cleftones

- The Mountain Retreat, Highlands, North Carolina. Atop a breathtaking 4,200-foot peak overlooking the Blue Ridge mountains, you and your lover can experience retreats and workshops hosted by the Unitarian Universalist Association. Call 828-526-5838 or visit www.mountaincenters.org.
- Marie Joseph Spiritual Center, Biddeford, Maine. Followers of all faiths are welcomed by the sisters of the Presentation of Mary to join in daily prayers and experience the peaceful environment on the beautiful Atlantic shore. Call 207-284-5671 or visit www.mariejosephspiritual.org.

786 Read an inspirational passage every morning and evening. Some suggestions for inspirational readings:
- *The Prophet,* by Kahlil Gibran
- *The Bible,* by You-Know-Who
- *A Course In Miracles,* Foundation For Inner Peace
- *Morning Notes,* by Hugh Prather

Moon & Stars

787 Diamond Astrological Pins! Jewelry designer A.G.A. Correa has created an incredible collection of constellation pins. Based on star charts, the pins are not only elegant, they're accurate: Each diamond is proportional to the magnitude of its corresponding star. All of the signs of the Zodiac are available, plus other constellations. Prices vary depending on the number of stars in each constellation and on their magnitude. Prices range from around $1,700 to $5,600. Write to Post Office Box 1, Edgecomb, Maine 04556, call 800-341-0788, or visit www.agacorrea.com.

> Especially for diamond-lovers, sci-fi fans, and astrology nuts!

788 Inspired by the classic romantic song "Fly Me to the Moon," one gal is planning to take her husband to the moon. Literally! She figures that regular commercial flights should be running by the year 2025. Anticipating that the tickets will probably be rather expensive, she put $5,000 into an annuity fund in 1990. Here's her rationale: "We skipped our annual vacation for one year to set this money aside. No big deal. And I figure that $5,000 at a modest return of seven percent per year will yield $53,382 in the year 2025."

> When was the last time you took a quiet, romantic moonlit stroll?

789 You may not be able to give her the moon and the stars, but you can name a star after her! The International Star Registry will provide you with a beautiful certificate that notes the star's coordinates and its new name, plus star maps and stargazing information. Though your star won't be recognized officially by NASA, you both will be able to cherish it forever. At only $54 per star, this makes a great, unique gift for that person you're starry-eyed over. Call the International Star Registry at 800-282-3333, or write to 34523 Wilson Road, Ingleside, Illinois 60041, or visit www.starregistry.com.

Science Fiction

790 If your lover is a Star Wars fanatic, take a vacation in Tunisia, where key scenes from Star Wars (Episodes One and Four) are set, including Luke's homestead and the Cantina. Call TunisUSA for info on their Star Wars tours: 800-474-5500, or visit www.tunisusa.com.

791 Rent all of the *Star Trek* movies and watch them over a weekend. Rent all of the *Star Wars* movies. Rent all of the *Alien* movies. Rent a dozen classic sci-fi movies from the 1950s and 1960s.

Visit Forbidden Planet Bookstore, the greatest sci-fi bookstore in the world. Call 212-473-1576 or browse at 840 Broadway in Manhattan. Visit www.forbiddenplanet.com.

792 Consider a stargazing vacation at the Star Hill Inn, located in Sapello, New Mexico. The Star Hill Inn has been a well-kept secret of amateur astronomers and star-gazers for several years. At 7,200 feet above sea level, and far enough east of Santa Fe to be unaffected by the nighttime glare, the inn caters to its clientele with an observation deck, star maps, and a well-stocked astronomy library. Call 505-429-9998, or visit www.starhillinn.com.

793 If your lover would love to watch a space shuttle (or other rocket) launch, call NASA for timetables and other info (or visit www.nasa.gov):
- 321-867-4636—will get you launch information.
- 321-449-4444—will get you a base pass so you can watch a rocket launch from close up!
- 202-358-0000—will get you NASA Public Information.
- 321-452-2121—will connect you with the Kennedy Space Center.

Trekkers celebrate James T. Kirk's birthday: March 22, 2233 A.D.

Wonderful Weekends

794 Love is timeless. And to *prove* it, cover up all the clocks in your house for the weekend. Turn them to the wall or cover their faces. You'll discover that time seems to pass more leisurely when you don't know exactly what time it is.

795 Surprise your partner with an *unexpected* three-day weekend. Arrange it ahead of time with his or her boss and staff. This may take some time to coordinate just right, but the payoff is well worth it!

Just picture the scene: It's a typical Friday morning. You both get up at your usual time. You shower and get dressed. Over breakfast you turn to your unsuspecting partner and say, "Oh, by the way, we've both got the day off work today. What would you like to do?"

After your partner recovers from the shock—and showers you with kisses and thank-yous—you get to plan the day together. What are you going to do?? Go back to bed and sleep till noon? Go back to bed and make love? Go for a drive? Go shopping? Go out for lunch?

796 The surprise get-away weekend is a romantic classic. Find a quaint bed and breakfast or picturesque inn. Pack bags for both of you, and whisk your partner away upon his or her arrival home from work!

Chapter Theme Song: "Big Weekend," Tom Petty

FYI—The weekend is twenty-nine percent of a week. This is a *lot* of time! Don't waste it doing chores!

797 What if you have a house full of kids? Try the "Distraction Diversion": Rent several of your kids' favorite movies; buy a ten-pound bag of popcorn and a bunch of juice boxes. The kids sit hypnotically in front of the TV while the two of you escape upstairs for some "quality time" together.

Mark Your Calendar

798 Surprise your partner by celebrating some oddball special occasions that you know he or she will appreciate. Create a fun ritual or get a funny little gift to mark the event.

* Cat in the Hat Day is March 2nd.
* International Lefthanders Day is August 13th.
* Trivia Day is January 4th.
* Bad Poetry Day is August 18th.
* Take Your Pants for a Walk Day is July 27th.
* Chicken Soup for the Soul Day is November 12th.

You can find something to celebrate every day of the year in *Celebrate Today*, by John Kremer.

Even natural-born romantics mark our calendars. Sometimes the ole memory slips!

799 Print up a batch of custom business cards, patterned after a doctor's appointment card. Something like this:

Your Next Appointment With Your Wife Is On:

_____

The Evening's Activities Will Begin With:

_____

Continue With:

_____

And Conclude With:

_____

No cancellations. Only one rescheduling is permitted. Proper attire is required.

Fill out several cards: Make one classically romantic, one outrageous, one sexy, one easy, one hard, one inexpensive, one expensive, one time-consuming, one quick, etc. Mail 'em one at a time to your lover.

February 14th

800 *Don't buy roses for Valentine's Day!*
It's common, expected, and expensive. Buy *different* flowers. Flowers in her favorite color. Flowers that match his eyes. Flowers that send a message. Flamboyant flowers. Tiny, delicate flowers. Lots and *lots* of flowers. One single flower.

Chapter Theme Song:
"My Valentine,"
Martina McBride

801 Keep your eyes open for pre-Valentine's Day articles in magazines and newspapers. Rip out the articles, circle the best ideas, and plan accordingly. (And don't forget to *keep those articles for future reference!*)

Rose Is Rose reprinted by permission of United Feature Syndicate, Inc. © 1990.

802 Use kids' valentines: a whole box full of silly puns and clichés, all for just a couple of bucks.

- Mail a boxful of 'em.
- Fill his briefcase full of them.
- Tape them all over her car.
- Fill the sink with them.
- Fill her pillow with them.
- Mail one a day for a month.

Valentine's Day

803 Valentine's Day is *not* the most romantic day of the year. You *still* have to recognize it and act on it—send flowers and/or chocolate and/or cards and/or jewelry and/or perfume and/or romantic gifts—but you *don't* get any extra credit for it,

> Even though you won't get any *extra credit* for remembering Valentine's Day, you will certainly win some bonus points if you go beyond *generic romance.*

guys. Valentine's Day is one of those *Obligatory Romance* days.

804 Turn Valentine's Day into a real holiday: Take the day off work. Then spend the day in bed together. Go to the movies. Go out to dinner. Go dancing. Take a drive. Make love. Go for a stroll.

805
- Mail him a Valentine's Day card. Mail him twenty!
- Make your own, *custom* Valentine card.
- Write your own romantically poetic card.
- Or use some verses from a favorite love song.
- Make a *huge* card. Use colored markers and draw a card on poster paper or on a refrigerator-size cardboard box!
- Send a *musical* greeting card.

Tip: If Valentine's Day falls on a *weekday*, simply shift your personal celebration to the nearest weekend.

806

- Send her a box filled with those Valentine Conversation Heart candies. A BIG box.
- Use Valentine Conversation Heart candies to spell out a romantic message to her. Leave it on the kitchen table or paste it to a piece of construction paper.
- Replace all the Cheerios with Valentine Conversation Hearts.

For Lovers—of Books

807

- Give him a first-edition book by his favorite author.
- Give her a book signed by her favorite author.

808 Write your *own* book!

- A love story (non-fiction)—about the two of you.
- A "Romance" novel—based loosely on the two of you.
- A mystery, a science fiction saga, a Western.
- A picture-book—with photos or sketches of your life together.

Chapter Theme Song:
"Storybook Love," Willy DeVille (from *The Princess Bride*)

809 If he already has that special book in hand, and you'd like to make it even *more* special, you could have it bound in leather for

him. Paperbacks can be made to look like family heirlooms, and old, ratty books can be beautifully restored. Call the Argosy Bookstore at 212-753-4455, or drop in at 116 East 59th Street, New York City 10022. Visit www.argosybooks.com.

810 For fans of Ernest Hemingway:

- Visit the Hemingway Museum in Piggott, Arkansas. Visit www.hemingway.astate.edu.
- Visit Hemingway's birthplace, Oak Park, Illinois. Call 708-848-2222. Visit www.ehfop.org.
- Attend the legendary "Hemingway Look-Alike Contest" at Sloppy Joe's Bar in Key West, Florida, in July. Call 305-296-2388 (ext. 21) or visit www.sloppyjoes.com.

Attend a book signing by his favorite author.
Have the cover of her favorite book made into a poster. Have it framed for her office.
Buy him every book written by his favorite author.
Visit the hometown of, or museum/library dedicated to, her favorite author.
Vacation at locations featured in his favorite books.

Sex—by the Book

811a

Humbly submitted for your perusal, some *erotic fiction:*

- *Erotic Edge: 22 Stories for Couples,* edited by Lonnie Barbach
- *Taboo: Forbidden Fantasies for Lovers,* edited by Violet Blue
- *Little Birds,* by Anaïs Nin
- *Naughty Bedtime Stories,* by Joan Elizabeth Lloyd
- *Tropic of Cancer,* by Henry Miller
- *Tropic of Capricorn,* by Henry Miller
- *Wolf Tales* series, by Kate Douglas
- *Caramel Flava: The eroticanoir.com Anthology,* edited by Zane
- *The Collected Erotica,* edited by Charlotte Hill and William Wallace
- *Herotica: A Collection of Women's Erotic Fiction,* edited by Susie Bright
- See above, also available: *Herotica 2* and *Herotica 3.*

> If you and your partner
> looking for some sexy stories
> set the mood *right now*, re
> some erotic fiction online! T
> following sites should prov
> *plenty* of inspirati
> www.eroticfiction.c
> www.pinkflamingo.c
> www.literotica.c

811b

Modestly submitted for your perusal, some *sexy non-fiction:*

- *The Pop-Up Book of Sex,* by Melcher Media
- *She Comes First,* by Ian Kerner
- *He Comes Next,* by Ian Kerner
- *The Kama Sutra*
- *The Art of Seduction,* by Robert Greene
- *Daily Sex,* by Jane Seddon
- *The Joy of Sex,* by Alex Comfort
- *Sex & The Perfect Lover: Tao, Tantra, & The Kama Sutra,* by Mabel Iam
- *The Sex Bible: The Complete Guide to Sexual Love,* by Susan Crain Bakos
- *The Couples' Guide to Erotic Games,* by Gerald Schoenewolf

Married...with Children

812 Guys: Give your *wife* a gift on your *kids'* birthdays. (Why should the kids get all the gifts? Your *wife* is the one who did all the work!)

813a Sometimes you really need to *escape* from the kids. Time *alone* together is required in order to build intimacy.

- Hang a "DO NOT DISTURB" sign on your bedroom door when you want a little privacy. Enforce this directive strictly! (Teach your rug rats to read "Do not disturb," before "Once upon a time.")
- Declare every Wednesday to be Mom's and Dad's "date night." Just go off by yourselves for a couple of hours. Maybe just take a walk or go out for coffee. It makes a great, rejuvenating break in the middle of the week.

813b Sometimes it's great to *include* your children in your romantic adventures. (How *else* are they going to learn how loving adults are supposed to act?!)

- Take vacations at family-oriented resorts. When there are lots of things for the kids to do, it takes the pressure off you. The kids will have a better time and so will you.

> Chapter
> Theme Song:
> "Eyes of a Child,"
> The Moody Blues

> "Marriage is not a ritual or an end. It is a long, intricate, intimate dance together and nothing matters more than your own sense of balance and your choice of partner."
> —Amy Bloom

- Declare every Thursday to be "family night." Make a special point to have dinner together. Play a board game. Pile onto the couch and watch a movie together. Take a walk together. Read aloud from a favorite book.

Kid Stuff

814 Instead of having the babysitter come in while the two of you go out, *have the babysitter take the kids out—while you two stay home!* Send all of them to a movie—a *double feature.* ("Now, what was it we used to do with all this peace and quiet? *Oh, yes…!*")

815 Send your kids to summer camp. It just might revitalize your marriage unlike any specific romantic gesture *ever* could! Some resources:
- American Camping Association: 800-428-CAMP, www.acacamps.org
- National Camp Association: 800-966-CAMP, www.summercamp.org
- Tips on Trips and Camps Service: 866-222-TIPS, www.tipsontripsandcamps.com

816 Guys: Add Mother's Day to your list of *Obligatory Romance* dates to observe. Mark it on your calendar *now.*

Chapter
Theme Song:
"Young,"
Kenny Chesney

817 Make special "Love Coupons" to help each other deal with the kids:
- An "I'll get up in the middle of the night with the baby" coupon.
- An "It's my turn to stay home with the next sick kid" coupon.
- A coupon for "Five 'taxi trips': Hauling the kids to soccer practice."
- An "I'll cook the kids' dinner" coupon.

> True romantics retain a *childlike* mindset. Therein lies wonder, joy, and a natural, uninhibited way of expressing love.

Rituals of Romance

818 For your next anniversary: Write a short, sweet poem titled, "Another Wonderful Year with You." Then for the following year, write *another* poem (same title). This ritual gives you a built-in gift every year!

For your twenty-fifth or fiftieth anniversary you might collect the poems into a book, or have them all framed, or have them rendered in elegant calligraphy.

> Rituals heighten the meaning of special events in our lives.

819 One couple in the Romance Class told us that they celebrate the changing of the seasons by taking a walk together on the first day of summer, autumn, winter, and spring—*regardless* of the weather.

820 Another couple plants a new rose bush on their anniversary to celebrate another year together.

821 One man brings his wife a cup of tea before bed every night—*whether she wants one or not.*

822
* Write a toast, just for the two of you. Use it whenever having wine.
* Write *two* toasts: One for *private* use, and one for *public* use.
* Write a new toast once a year.
* Write a toast that incorporates lyrics from her favorite love song.

Surprise her with roses from your special garden—*daily!* Put them on her pillow, tape them to the bathroom mirror, arrange them in a vase on the table— the sky is the limit!

Romantic Rituals

823 Some couples have *morning* rituals:
* They spend ten minutes talking in bed before rising.
* They read an affirmation aloud to one another.
* They make a point of kissing before parting.

Chapter Theme Song: "The Things That We Do," Yolanda Adams

824 Some couples have *evening* rituals:
* They go for a walk after dinner together.
* They meditate silently together.
* They take turns every other night giving each other backrubs.

825 And, there are Sunday morning rituals:
* Attending a church service together.
* Reading the Sunday funnies aloud to each other.
* Sunday brunch.

826 My wife and I have a little "car ritual" we've performed for as long as we've known each other: I always open the car door for her (regardless of which one of us is driving), and she always leans over and unlocks my door from the inside. I never really thought of it as a "ritual" until recently. It's just a little thing we *always* do that helps us not take the other for granted.

Buy a wall calendar for your kitchen. Instead of penciling in doctor's appointments and meetings, use it to plan your romantic outings, movie nights, and vacations! The calendar will be a great keepsake to remind you of all the things you have done as a couple.

Oldies but Goodies

827 Romantic inspiration from the famous Burma Shave roadside ads. (Ask a senior citizen to explain it to you.) Hang a series of four brief-and-clever signs in your house.

- WELCOME HOME—LET'S MISBEHAVE—THE KIDS ARE OUT—BURMA SHAVE!
- TO LOVE YOU—ONE NEEDN'T BE BRAVE—JUST KINDA CRAZY—BURMA SHAVE!
- BE MY WIFE!—FULFILL MY DAYS—JUST SAY YES—BURMA SHAVE!

828 Hold your own "Oldies But Goodies" nights at home. Here are some different themes that Romance Class participants have tried:

- *The 1920s:* complete with flapper outfits and jazz.
- *WWII:* complete with military uniforms, USO posters and patriotic music.
- *The 1960s:* love beads, Woodstock, old jeans, and tie-dyed T-shirts!
- *The Victorian Era:* with rented costumes, minuets and horse-drawn carriage rides!

Some Oldies But Goodies:
"I Can't Give You Anything but Love" (1928)
"All of Me" (1931)
"I'm Getting Sentimental Over You" (1932)
"Let's Fall in Love" (1933)
"I'm in the Mood for Love" (1935)
"In the Still of the Night" (1936)
"My Funny Valentine" (1937)

"The time to begin most things is ten years ago."
—Mignon McLaughlin

829 Creating a nostalgic mood will help you remember (then recreate!) those favorite romantic memories. Look for popular music from the 1930s, '40s, '50s and '60s in stores or visit www.cdnow.com to order some great romantic classics.

More Oldies But Goodies:
"Some Like It Hot" (1939)
"You Made Me Love You" (1941)
"People Will Say We're in Love" (1943)
"As Time Goes By" (1943)
"Sentimental Journey" (1945)
"Some Enchanted Evening" (1949)
"Love Is a Many Splendored Thing" (1955)
"Moon River" (1961)

Oldies but Goodies: Movies

830 Hold an at-home "Romantic Oldies But Goodies" movie festival, organized by decade. Great for recreating memories.

Movies from the 1930s
- *Gone With the Wind*
- *Camille*
- *The Awful Truth*
- *Wuthering Heights*
- *The Thin Man*
- *City Lights*

Movies from the 1940s
- *Casablanca*
- *The Shop Around the Corner*
- *Adam's Rib*
- *The Philadelphia Story*
- *Now, Voyager*
- *To Have and Have Not*

Movies from the 1950s
- *The African Queen*
- *Roman Holiday*
- *An Affair to Remember*
- *Sabrina*
- *South Pacific*
- *Pillow Talk*

Movies from the 1960s
- *Doctor Zhivago*
- *Breakfast at Tiffany's*
- *West Side Story*
- *David and Lisa*
- *Splendor in the Grass*
- *Two for the Road*

Movies from the 1970s
- *The Way We Were*
- *Annie Hall*
- *Robin and Marian*
- *Love Story*
- *The Goodbye Girl*
- *Mahogany*

Movies from the 1980s
- *An Officer and a Gentleman*
- *The Princess Bride*
- *When Harry Met Sally*
- *Moonstruck*
- *Say Anything*
- *Dirty Dancing*

Movies from the 1990s
- *Shakespeare in Love*
- *You've Got Mail*
- *Ghost*
- *Titanic*
- *Pretty Woman*
- *Sleepless in Seattle*

Movie Madness

831 Present her with a framed movie poster from her all-time-favorite movie! Vintage or current, romantic, dramatic, or funny! Prices vary depending on availability, size, age, and condition. Call Jerry Ohlinger's Movie Material Store at 212-989-0869 or visit www.moviematerials.com. They have a vast assortment of stuff from the 1930s to the present. Visit their amazing shop at 253 West 35th Street, New York, New York 10011.

832 Or create themes for your At-Home Video Film Festivals. Choose your lover's favorite "type" or genre of movie.

- Comedy
- Science fiction
- Silent films
- Elvis movies
- All of the Pink Panther movies
- All of the Beatles' movies
- All Rocky Balboa movies
- All Woody Allen movies
- James Bond movies
- All of John Wayne's films

833 Don't neglect the many classic film series hosted by local colleges and universities, YMCAs, museums, and classic theaters.

834 And don't forget about drive-ins! They're a great way to inspire some nostalgia and ignite some passion.

What is your partner's favorite movie of all time? (What insights does this reveal about his or her personality?)

Mad About You

835 She hung a thirty-six-inch-wide strip of butcher paper on the wall. She then painted her body with water-based red tempera paint, then struck a pose and pressed her painted body against the paper—creating a very personalized and definitely one-of-a-kind work of art. She let it dry, rolled it up, tied it with a red ribbon, and gave it to her husband for Valentine's Day. He still talks about it to this day.

836 He always did have a tendency to "overdo" things. One year he rented a limousine for her birthday. She enjoyed it so much that the following year he rented the limo *again*...but this time he rented it *for an entire week!* So in addition to their fancy night on the town, she got chauffeured to the supermarket, to the dry cleaner, to church; the kids got chauffeured to school, to soccer practice, to the playground. A memorable experience for one and all!

837 It was Sally's birthday, but her husband David hadn't acknowledged it all day, and Sally's disappointment was starting to turn into anger. Then David asked her to run some errands for him while he went out to play golf, and her heart just sank. She gave up.

Remember when you were "mad about" each other? You *can* recreate that feeling!

While walking dejectedly through the mall she did a double-take at a store mannequin who looked remarkably like David. Then the mannequin *winked* at her. It was David, who stepped out of the store window and kissed her. Dressed in a tuxedo, he led her to the dress department, where he bought her an elegant evening gown. Then, in their formal attire, they went out to the best French restaurant in town.

Great Escapes

838 Don't just "go to the islands"—*rent a private island* for a truly amazing fantasy vacation or honeymoon!
- Turtle Island, Fiji—the location for the film *The Blue Lagoon*. Call 877-288-7853 or visit www.turtlefiji.com.
- Little Palm Island, Florida—an exotic honeymoon hideaway in the Keys. Call 800-343-8567 or visit www.littlepalmisland.com.

839 Visit Liverpool, England, for a "Magical Mystery Tour" of The Beatles' hometown. Walk down Penny Lane, see the Cavern Club, visit the multi-media exhibit, and ponder the Eleanor Rigby statue (dedicated to "All the lonely people.") And, of course, there's The Beatles Shop, which is chock-full of memorabilia and music.

Escape from the mundane. Escape from the clock. Escape from the stress. Escape from the kids. Escape from the Rat Race. Escape from boredom.

840 The romance of the open road...the vacation that never ends...the RV lifestyle! (Some people think that "RV" stands for "Recreational Vehicle." *I* say it stands for "Romantic Vehicle.")

Call 800-327-7778 or visit www.cruiseamerica.com for CruiseAmerica, which rents all makes and sizes of RVs—so you can try different units before buying one.

841 Go for a "mystery drive" in the country. Keep to the back roads and ignore the map. Agree to have lunch at the first charming inn or classic diner you pass. If you stumble onto a quaint bed-and-breakfast, stay the night! (You do, of course, have "His" and "Hers" overnight bags stored in the trunk, don't you?!)

Getting Away from It All

842 The top five "romantic images," from polling thousands of Romance Class participants:
1. Candlelight dinner
2. A classic wedding ceremony
3. Cuddling in front of a roaring fireplace
4. Walking on a beach
5. An ocean cruise

> Some of my most romantic memories involve cruises.

When you're ready to take the ultimate in romantic vacations and you want to book a cruise, my suggestion is to talk to lots of people and see whom they recommend. Norwegian Cruise Line keeps popping up at the top of the list. For destinations, schedules, info on their ships and services: 800-327-7030, www.ncl.com.

843 Before going on vacation, get stacks of brochures, posters, and books about your upcoming destination. Mail them to your partner on a regular basis. It will help build the anticipation for your vacation.

844 Two opposite approaches to spending money on vacations:
• Spend as *little as possible* on accommodations, and *as much as possible* on dining out! Some folks appreciate a great meal more than anything. This approach allows them to indulge without guilt!
• Pamper yourselves with *the most luxurious room* you can find, and save money by *cutting other corners,* like eating frugally and avoiding costly tourist traps. Some folks create a "love nest" out of their vacation room and settle in for a week of loving, reading, cuddling, and relaxing.

Great travel resource: *Modern Bride Honeymoons and Weddings Away,* by Geri Bain.

An Anniversary Gift List

Nobody knows *why* these lists always jump by five-year intervals following number fifteen! (It's up to *you* to fill in the in-between years!)

845 I pose this question in my Romance Classes: "Just who made up this anniversary gift list, anyway?" Well, no one has been able to answer the question definitively, so I figure *my* gift list is as good as anybody's!

Year	Traditional	Modern	Godek's
1	Paper	Clock	Lingerie
2	Cotton	China	Lingerie
3	Leather	Crystal/Glass	Lingerie
4	Fruit/flowers	Appliances	Software
5	Wood	Silver/silverware	Books
6	Candy/iron	Wood	Lingerie
7	Wood/copper	Desk sets	Wine
8	Bronze/pottery	Linens/laces	A cruise
9	Pottery/willow	Leather	CDs
10	Tin/aluminum	Diamond jewelry	Jewelry
11	Steel	Fashion jewelry	Silk
12	Silk/linen	Pearls	Perfume
13	Lace	Textiles/furs	Umbrellas
14	Ivory	Gold jewelry	Lingerie
15	Crystal	Watches	Computers
20	China	Platinum	Champagne
25	Silver	Silver	Jacuzzis
30	Pearl	Diamond/pearl	Diamond

Year	Traditional	Modern	Godek's
35	Coral	Jade	Sculpture
40	Ruby	Ruby	Stocks
45	Sapphire	Sapphire	Emerald
50	Gold	Gold	Rolls Royce
55	Emerald	Emerald	Gold
60	Diamond	Diamond	Paris vacation

A Romantic Basics Checklist

846 Here, in checklist form, are all of the "Romantic Basics." These items are described and expanded upon elsewhere in this book, but here's a quick-and-handy reference page for you.

How would you *personalize* this list?

❏ Roses
❏ Chocolate
❏ Champagne
❏ Lingerie
❏ Love songs
❏ Love poetry
❏ Ballroom dancing
❏ Dinner out
❏ Dinner at home
❏ Formal dates
❏ Love Coupons

❏ Flowers
❏ Perfume
❏ Jewelry
❏ Greeting cards
❏ Love letters
❏ Love notes
❏ Breakfast in bed
❏ Movie at a theater
❏ Movie at home
❏ Little surprises
❏ Handmade cards

- ❏ Classic gold chain
- ❏ Massages
- ❏ Romantic fantasies
- ❏ Sexy fantasies
- ❏ Diamonds
- ❏ Cruises
- ❏ Vacations
- ❏ Honeymoons
- ❏ Birthdays
- ❏ Special holidays
- ❏ Heart-shaped box of candy

- ❏ Candy
- ❏ Candles
- ❏ Having sex
- ❏ Making love
- ❏ Wine
- ❏ Drive-in movies
- ❏ Bed and breakfasts
- ❏ Hotel suites
- ❏ Anniversaries
- ❏ Valentine's Day
- ❏ Crystal champagne flutes

Generating Ideas

847 Set a goal of generating or discovering one new romantic idea each day for a year. (Your commitment will help draw ideas to you.) Keep your notes, articles, comics, ads, and miscellaneous reminders in a shoebox under your bed.

848 Train your subconscious mind to find romantic ideas *for* you. Hey, why should your subconscious mind be doing nothing but daydreaming all day long while the rest of your mind is doing all the work?

"You will find as you look back upon your life that the moments when you have truly lived are the moments when you have done things in the spirit of love."

—Henry Drummond

Scientists say that we only use about 10 percent of our brains: This is a way to boost your brain efficiency to 25 percent or better!

Seriously, you *can* assign a small portion of your brain the task of being constantly on the lookout for romantic ideas. The goal is to retrain your mind to stop *filtering out* those ideas, and start letting them come to the attention of your conscious mind. What starts happening is that romantic articles and gift ideas will start "jumping out at you." Guaranteed.

849 Practice creating "Variations on a Theme" for generating romantic ideas. Start with any idea and build on it, expand it, extend it.

- Start with "greeting cards": Buy one; buy a *hundred!* Make some yourself. Send one-a-day for a week, send one-a-day for a *month!* Frame some cards that she's given you.
- Start with "candy": What's her favorite? Buy ten pounds of it. Fill her shoes with candy; fill her purse, her glove compartment, her pillow. Send it to her at work. Spell out words with it. Create trails throughout the house with it.

You have tremendous, untapped reservoirs of creativity inside!

Romantic Brainstorming

850 Hold a "Romantic Idea Brainstorming Session" with a group of friends. Serve pizza and beer. Hand out pads of paper and markers. Use a large pad on an easel to compile ideas.

The goal is to generate *as many ideas as possible* in one hour: serious and silly, practical and unrealistic, expensive and inexpensive, thoughtful and outrageous, sweet and sexy.

Chapter Theme Song: "Think About It," Will Young

851 Generate romantic ideas using your partner's likes, passions, and favorite things. What's his or her favorite color, favorite author, poet, artist, movie, TV show, song, singer, wine, perfume, restaurant, ice cream, sport, or flower? Use this knowledge as a springboard for creating romantic ideas that you *know* will be unique and special.

852 Tap into the strength of your own personal style and your special talents. Do you have a flair for writing, dancing, building things, organizing, cooking, or drawing? Use these talents and abilities to enhance the romance in your life!

Sit down and take an inventory of your own personal talents, interests, skills, aptitudes, and passions. Write a list. Use it as an idea-generator.

Keep a romantic ideas journal in a secret (but accessible) place. As ideas come to you, be sure to log them!

853 Institute the "Buddy System." Team up with a good friend and act as each other's personal "Romance Coach." Encourage each other, trade ideas, remind each other of important dates, compare notes, and share new discoveries.

A Kick in the Pants

854 Do you take your partner for granted? *Well, stop it!* Taking your partner for granted is not only the death of romance, but could well be the death of your relationship.

I *dare* you to be romantic!

855 Take a risk—be romantic. *I dare you.*
  Being truly romantic is a risky thing to do. I respect this difficulty and at the same time encourage you to leap off the cliff. Being truly romantic involves opening yourself up and revealing your feelings. Let's face it, nobody wants to be burned, and it's hard to risk a broken heart when you've been through a number of relationships.

• But if you're not going to open up to your lover, who else is there?
• And if you're consciously choosing *not* to open up, you might want to ask yourself what you're afraid of, or what you're hiding.
• And if you're not going to be romantic and open up, then what's the point of being in a relationship in the first place?!

856 Change one bad habit. Just *one!* (You'll be helping *yourself* as well as pleasing your partner!) Lose those ten pounds you've been meaning to shed. Stop smoking. Eat more healthfully. Dress better. Exercise more. Listen better. Be more courteous. Slow your pace.

Go for it!

Motivating Your Partner to Be More Romantic

857 The *Nice* **Approach**

Do things that your *partner* will interpret as loving gestures. Do these things *without an attitude,* without expecting anything in return, and without any wise comments.

Most people respond in kind. It might take a week or two, but most people *do* come around. Now don't forget that love is worth working on, and that these things take time.

858 The *Psychological* **Approach**

Don't try to get him to be more romantic to you. Instead, aim at changing his *level of awareness* about the need for more romance/intimacy/communication in your relationship. Successful long-term changes in behavior usually follow a change in awareness. If you start with behavior modification, you'll probably only produce *short-term* results. Some techniques for raising awareness include:

• Simply talking (heart-to-heart)
• Model romantic behavior ("Monkey see, monkey do!")

- Getting like-minded friends to set him straight
- Good psychology/relationship books
- A class or seminar on love and relationships
- Couples counseling

859 The *Give-and-Take* **Approach**

If you have a *really reluctant* partner, I recommend that you play a lighthearted game that I call, "I'll do *this* for you if you'll do *that* for me." You might trade meals, chores, sex, erotic fantasies, back rubs, babysitting, naps, or balancing the checkbook. This simple and fun approach often works to recharge a relationship when the more sophisticated "psychological" approaches fail.

Motivating the Romantically Impaired

860 A major reason why some people aren't romantic is that a lack of it *doesn't affect them.* If you want him to be more romantic, but he's satisfied with the status quo..."Well, tough luck—that's your problem!" he says/thinks.

The solution? Simple: *Make it his problem.* People only really solve problems that they see as *problems that relate to themselves.*

How do you "make it his problem"? Well, you start by telling him up front *what* you want (more romance), and *how* you want it (circle your favorite items in this book!). You need to be specific, positive, and loving in your approach.

It might help both of you to remember that problems (especially *relationship* problems) are actually opportunities in disguise! I've seen couples use this technique to transform frustrating D- Relationships into happy, solid B+ Relationships. (You can do it, too!)

861 Seven Ways to Woo a Workaholic Away from Work

1. Promise your partner the best sex of his or her life—
2. Follow through on your promise!
3. (If you can't beat 'em, join 'em!): Create a business together.
4. Make a "Mission Impossible" audio tape that leads him or her to a mystery date with you.
5. Book a hotel room—within walking distance of his office—and invite him over for an afternoon "meeting."
6. Meet him for lunch; dress very sexy. Then coyly ask him if he'd like another lunch date next week.
7. Have a courier deliver a steamy love letter to her office.

> No, the Romantically Impaired are *not* entitled to use parking spaces for the handicapped.

Attitude Adjustment Section

862 Be spontaneous. Be silly. Lower your inhibitions. Express your love. If you do these things, you'll *automatically* be romantic.

863 Try being totally positive, accepting, supportive and

nonjudgmental for one entire week. No complaining, nagging, preaching, etc. It may change your life!

864

- Loosen your purse strings.
- Loosen your schedule.
- Loosen your tie.
- Loosen your *attitude.*
- Loosen your inhibitions.

> "Is not this the true romantic feeling—not to desire to escape life, but to prevent life from escaping you?"
>
> —Thomas Wolfe

865 Want to keep your marriage fresh and vital? *Live as lovers.* Not just as husband and wife, mother and father, workers and housekeepers, caregivers and bill payers. First and foremost *you are lovers.* Remember that's how you *started* your relationship. You *can* recapture the glow, the passion and the excitement. It's largely a mindset, followed by a few active gestures.

For one week, make this your affirmation, your mantra, your prayer: *Live as lovers.* Post notes to yourselves, remind each other, and practice!

License to Love

866 Create a custom CD or iPod play list of romantic love songs for her.

- Choose a dozen great songs and put them on a CD or iPod.

Drive by his parking lot at work. Attach balloons to the side mirror. Tape streamers to the back windshield. Leave a love note on the front seat.

- Listen to the music together in the car. Sing the solos to her. Sing the harmonies together. Sing the duets at the top of your lungs!

867 Surprise her with a personalized license plate!

Most states charge somewhere between $50 and $100 a year.

	"Code Phrases":
• Her initials	
• Both of your initials	• ILY
• Her birth date	• IMWLD4U
• Your anniversary date	• 4EVER
• Your pet name for her	• UNME

Many of the most popular and common names and phrases are already taken, so you'll have to use a little creativity. Consider these possibilities, and use them to spark your own ideas:

Note: The most populous states usually have the most digits in their license plates, giving the creative copywriter more flexibility. (One innovative man in the Romance Class registered his wife's car in a neighboring state, New York, so he could use seven digits to spell out his wife's name.)

Pun alert!

868

- Jim's wife is a graphic artist. He created for her an "artistic license" that hangs on her office wall.
- Harriet's husband writes poetry in his spare time. For his birthday she created a "poetic license" that he carries proudly in his wallet.

Baby, You Can Drive My Car

Chapter Theme Song:
"(I'm Your) Passenger," Deftones

869 Place a little love note or poem under the driver's side windshield wiper of his or her car.

> True romantics let *nothing* stand in their way: If it's rainy or snowy, place the love note in a Ziploc bag!

870 Other items to put under the windshield wiper:

- A single rose
- A candy bar
- Wildflowers
- A little book
- A poem
- A pizza coupon
- A cartoon
- A Love Coupon
- A short note

871 Buying a new car? Arrange to have it delivered one day *earlier* than she expects it, park it in the driveway, and wait for her to notice it.

> Wrap the car with a big red bow!

872 Write and design a fake traffic ticket; place it under the windshield wiper. Possible violations include:

- Leaving the scene of a love affair
- Speeding down the highway of life
- Driving me crazy

Possible options for making restitution include:

- Taking the judge out to dinner
- Bribing the officer with sexual favors
- One sensual backrub

Little Love Stories (I)

873 She gave him the key to her apartment in a velvet jewelry box. On the card she wrote: "You hold the key to my happiness, and now you hold the key to my home. You've unlocked my heart. Please don't break it."

874 During their seven years of dating he'd given her many flowers. During their long-awaited wedding ceremony she surprised him with a roomful of flowers—the very flowers he had given her. She'd had *every flower he'd ever given her* carefully and lovingly dried or pressed.

Calvin and Hobbes, Copyright © 1987. Reprinted with permission of Universal Press Syndicate.

875 At a farmhouse in Iowa: A wire fence runs along the western side of the Smiths' house. One morning Sara notices hundreds of red ribbons hanging like streamers from the fence. She asks Fred about it, but gets only a mischievous grin in return. Later that day when the wind starts blowing and the ribbons start flapping, Sara sees that they are tied in a pattern that spells out "I LOVE MY SARA."

Little Love Stories (II)

876 Charlie and his girlfriend Randi were aboard Continental Airlines flight 191 from Newark to San Francisco. Shortly after takeoff the pilot made this announcement: "I have an important message for the passenger in seat 3-B. Will you marry the gentleman in seat 3-A? If the answer is yes, press the Call Button for the flight attendant." As Randi burst into tears, Charlie kept saying "Push the button!" When she did, a flight attendant came up with a silver tray, champagne, and the ring!

877 Mary was a Beanie Baby *fanatic.* Her husband, Bob, hired a custom doll-maker to create a "Beanie Bob" for her.

> Bob credits the comic strip Bizarro, by Dan Pirato, for this idea.

878 Tom arrived home from running errands one Saturday morning to find his wife, Susan, gone. His daughter handed him a note from her: "Go to the drug store. See the pharmacist." Even though his first reaction was, "Why? Who's sick?" he went along. What else could he do but follow instructions? When he started up the car, a tape of romantic music started playing. ("Ah, ha! I think something's going on here!") The pharmacist had a card for him: "Happy Anniversary!—Now, head for the liquor store!" A bottle of champagne was waiting for him there, along with *another* note: "Ready to celebrate? Not yet! On to the men's shop first!" A monogrammed shirt was his sur-

> "Love creates an 'us' without destroying a 'me.'"
>
> —Leo Buscaglia

prise there. The note was no longer a surprise: "Almost done! But first, please stop at the grocery store." A picnic basket packed with goodies was ready for him there.

The last note simply had an address on it. It led him to a romantic little bed and breakfast, where Susan was waiting for him. The rest, as they say, is history.

Notes from an A+ Relationship

879 While *everyone* knows that commitment is important in a relationship, only folks with A+ Relationships are *specific* about their commitments. These are the dozen best relationship commitments generated during twenty years of my Romance Classes:

How to spot people who have an A+ Relationship : Look for the sparkle in their eyes.

1. Commit yourselves to your relationship.
2. Commit to spending 10 percent more time together.
3. Commit yourselves to being less judgmental.
4. Commit yourselves to living up to your wedding vows.
5. Commit yourselves to having more fun together.
6. Commit yourselves to practicing your religious beliefs on your partner.
7. Commit yourselves to seeing your partner's negative behaviors as calls for love.

8. Commit to communicating your feelings fully.

9. Commit yourselves to your partner's happiness.

10. Commit yourselves to feeling your feelings of love.

11. Commit yourselves to acting on your feelings of love.

12. Commit yourselves to listening to the voice of love inside you.

880

• Touch your partner—with your eyes.

• Touch your partner—with your words.

• Touch your partner—with gifts and presents.

• Touch your partner—with your thoughts, prayers, and wishes.

• Touch your partner—with your actions.

Did you know—?
Having an A+ Relationship can help you live a longer and healthier life. This is not simply common sense, but has been proven *medically*. See these two books by Dean Ornish, M.D.: *Love & Survival: The Scientific Basis for the Healing Power of Intimacy*, and *Love & Survival: 8 Pathways to Intimacy & Health*

Recipe for an A+ Relationship

881 **Overview**: Recipe takes 2 individuals and turns them into 1 couple.

Background: Gather ingredients over time, and practice cooking for twenty to thirty years.

Ingredients:

1 cup attraction

1 cup compatibility

2 nuts

1 quart honesty (with 2 quarts comparison)

1 pint each of faith, hope, and charity:
    Combine and mix vigorously
        1 dash thoughtfulness
            1 pinch

2 pints cooperation combined with 2 pints compromise

2 quarts forgiveness

2 gallons sense of humor

2 pounds sex (raw)

Plus an endless supply of love, sex, and romance, in the ratio 2:1:3.

Preparation:

Combine all ingredients and stir like crazy. Leave medium lumps. (If too smooth, days will be boring; but if lumps too big, problems will be too big to swallow.) Heat with passion but never bring to a boil!

Spice to your personal taste.

The first two years tend to be spicy. The middle years tend to be nutty. The later years tend to be savory. But they're all *delicious!*

Each day tastes different. *This is normal.* Some days are sweet. Some days are sour. Some days are smooth. Some days are chewy and difficult. Some days are spicy. Some days are hard to swallow. But every day is *exactly what you need,* and the portions are just right for your needs.

Important! Pass down this recipe to your children and to future generations.

Serving:

Yields 50 or more years of marriage.

Divide into 50 years and serve separately.

Sub-divide each year into 365 days; savor each day individually.

Romance Across America

882

• Visit all fifty states—one or two a year for as long as it takes.
• Camp in every national park in the country.
• Then, start on the state parks.

883 Go whitewater rafting! Adventurous folks at these firms will get you started downstream:
• Appalachian Wildwaters:
  800-624-8060, www.awrafts.com
• USA Raft: 800-USA-RAFT, www.usaraft.com
• Rio Grande Adventures: 800-343-1640

884 Bicycle across the United States! The 4,500-mile TransAmerica Bicycle Trail follows side roads and uncrowded state routes through rural America. The trail goes from Yorktown, Virginia to Astoria, Oregon, and takes from fifty to ninety days to complete. For more information, call Adventure Cycling at 800-755-2453 or 406-721-1776, or write P.O. Box 8308, Missoula, Montana 59802, or visit www.adv-cycling.org.

885 Attend one of America's many *hot air balloon festivals*.
- The National Balloon Classic: early August, in Indianola, Iowa. Call 515-961-8415.
- The International Balloon Fiesta: mid-October, in Albuquerque, New Mexico. Call 888-422-7277 or visit www.balloonfiesta.com.

Bonus Spots:
- When you're in Rochester, New York:
  Dine at Café Cupid. (A *stunningly* romantic little place!) 754 East Ridge Road, in Irondequoit. Call 585-342-2640.
  Shop at the coolest gift shop in America, The Parkleigh, 215 Park Avenue in Rochester. Call 800-333-0627, or visit www.parkleigh.com.
- When you're in Springfield, Massachusetts:
  Visit the Titanic Museum (the *ship*, not the movie). Call 413-543-4770, or visit www.titanichistoricalsociety.com.
- When you're in Atlanta, Georgia:
  Take your chatterbox to visit the Bellsouth Telephone Museum. Call 404-986-3289.
- When you're in Fort Wayne, Indiana:
  Visit the butterfly aviary at the Fort Wayne Children's Zoo. Call 260-427-6800, or visit www.kidszoo.com.
- When you're in Phoenix, Arizona:
  Visit the Hall of Flame Museum of Firefighting. Call 602-275-3473 or visit www.hallofflame.org.

Romance Around the World

886 Some recommendations from Romance Class participants:
- The most romantic restaurant in Vienna: Steirereck
- The most romantic restaurant in Amsterdam: De Goudsbloem
- The most romantic restaurant in Rome: "Les Etoiles" Roof Garden
- The most romantic restaurant in Stockholm: Hasselbacken

887
- The most romantic hotel in Paris: L'Hotel
- The most romantic hotel in Vienna: Romischer Kaiser
- The most romantic hotel in Rome: Guesthouse Arco dé Tolomei
- The most romantic hotel in Amsterdam: Pulitzer
- The most romantic hotel in Copenhagen: Skovshoved
- The most romantic hotel in Madrid: Santa Mauro

888 If your lover loves the beach, plan a vacation to one of the great beaches of the world. Choose a beach based on the kind of beach activity he/she likes to indulge in:

A+ for *unspoiled:*
- Barbuda, West Indies
- Kea, Greek Islands

A+ for *lazing:*
- Isla de Cozumel, Mexico
- Molokai, Hawaii
- North Island, New Zealand

A+ for *beachcombing:*
- Mindoro, Philippines
- Sanibel Island, Florida

Bonus Travel Tips:

- Austria: 212-944-6880, www.austriatourism.com
- Belgium: 212-758-8130, www.visitbelgium.com
- England: 800-462-2748, www.visitbritain.com
- Cyprus: 212-683-5280, www.cyprustourism.org
- Denmark: 212-885-9700, www.visitdenmark.com
- Finland: 800-346-4636, 212-885-9700, www.visitfinland.com
- France: 310-271-6665, www.francetourism.com
- Germany: 800-651-7010, www.cometogermany.com
- Greece: 213-626-6696, www.gnto.gr
- Iceland: 212-885-9700, www.icelandtouristboard.com
- Ireland: 800-223-6470, www.discoverireland.com
- Italy: 310-820-0098, www.italiantourism.com
- Netherlands: 888-464-6552, www.us.holland.com
- Norway: 212-885-9700, www.norway.org
- Poland: 201-420-9910, www.polandtour.org
- Portugal: 800-767-8842, www.portugal.org
- Sweden: 212-885-9700, www.visitsweden.com
- Switzerland: 877-794-8037, www.myswitzerland.com

The Right Stuff

889 Psychological experiments have shown that most people can turn a new behavior into a habit in three weeks. *Their* experiments involved *boring* activities like exercising or waking up an hour earlier than usual. *My* suggestion (as you might have guessed) is that you conduct your own experiment in turning romantic behavior into a habit.

> "True love comes quietly, without banners or flashing lights. If you hear bells, get your ears checked."
>
> —Erich Segal

Here's a possible approach to your Experiment In Romance: For three weeks—that's twenty-one straight days—practice these behaviors:

- Say "I love you" to your partner at least five times a day.
- Find at least one romantic idea in the newspaper every day.
- Call your partner from work at least three times a day.
- Reduce your TV-watching by one hour per night. Do something *together* with that time.
- Make love at least twice a week.
- Circle ten ideas in this book that you think your partner would enjoy. Discuss them with him/her.
- Surprise your partner in some *small way* every other day.

Start your "Romance Regimen" today! See *instant* results!

At the end of three weeks you'll be a more romantic person. You may not become Valentino, but you *will* be more aware of the importance of romance in your life, you'll be more in touch with your own feelings of love, and you'll be in closer touch with your lover. Not a bad habit, huh?!

The Write Stuff

890 Some books on love, relationships, men and women, etc.
* *Love and Respect Workbook,* by Emerson Eggerichs & Fritz Ridenour
* *Living, Loving & Learning,* by Leo Buscaglia
* *The New Rules of Marriage,* by Terrence Real
* *Dear Lover: A Woman's Guide to Men, Sex, & Love's Deepest Bliss,* by David Deida
* *Love,* by Leo Buscaglia
* *How to Be an Adult in Relationships,* by David Richo
* *Ten Lessons to Transform Your Marriage,* by John M. Gottman, Ph.D., Julie Schwartz Gottman, Ph.D. & Joan DeClaire
* *Loving Each Other,* by Leo Buscaglia
* *The Truth About Love,* by Dr. Patricia Love
* *Men, Love, & Sex,* by David Zinczenko, Ted Spiker & Stephen Hoye
* *Keeping the Love You Find,* by Harville Hendrix
* *Iron John,* by Robert Bly

891 Some *fun and funny* books about relationships, love and/or sex:
* *Dave Barry's Guide to Marriage and/or Sex,* by Dave Barry
* *Mack Tactics: The Science of Seduction Meets the Art of Hostage Negotiation,* by Christopher Curtis & Rob Wiser
* *Dating, Mating, & Manhandling: The Ornithological Guide to Men,* by Lauren Frances & Konstantin Kakanias
* *Why Did I Marry You, Anyway?* by Arlene Modica Matthews

892 Be prepared: Write it down! Make a list of at least ten little things you know your partner would love. Would she love a massage? Would he love

A Bookstore Coupon

Good for a one-hour shopping spree in the bookstore of your choice.

a special dessert? Would she love to have her car waxed? Would he love a new CD?

Don't put this off until later—write this list by the end of the day today. Then keep this list with you as a reminder. Commit yourself to accomplishing one item per week over the next ten weeks.

Real Men Are Romantic

893 Do something *with* her that you normally hate doing (and do it cheerfully without complaint). Go dress shopping with her; go out to a movie with her; attend the ballet with her; do some gardening with her.

894 Do something *for* her that you hate doing (and do it cheerfully and without complaint). Go grocery shopping, wash the dishes, weed the garden, get up in the middle of the night with the baby.

Proof that Real Men *are* romantic: Clint "Dirty Harry" Eastwood directed and starred in *The Bridges of Madison County,* one of the most romantic movies of all time.

895 Shave on Saturday night.

896 Do you treat your employees better than you treat the woman in your life? A lot of men do. (What *is it* with you guys?!)

Here's a hypothetical role-playing exercise for you: View your lover as a customer, client, or employee. Good managers think of ways to motivate their employees, they don't simply order them around or take them for granted. And salesmen are always considerate of their customers... After all, customers are very important. Well, isn't she just as important?!

"Sure, God made man before woman. But, then again, you always make a rough draft before creating the final masterpiece."
—Anonymous

897 Be *extra* nice to her during her menstrual periods. (Mark the dates on your calendar as a reminder.) And thank heaven that *you* don't have to experience cramps!

Real Women Are Romantic

898 Do you want to give him flowers—but you're concerned that he'll feel uncomfortable because it's not "manly" enough?

- Reconsider your assumptions. A big, burly construction worker in my Romance Class once told me that his girlfriend had sent flowers to him at his work site! After the required good-natured ribbing from the guys, he found that many of them complained that their gals had never sent flowers to *them*!
- Send a variety of flowers—all in his favorite color. (Sixty-two percent of American men say their favorite color is blue). Here are some blue flowers: Forget-Me-Not, Balloon Flower, Catmint, Delphinium, Lobelia, Sea Lavender, Spiderwort, and Virginia Bluebells.

• Present the flowers in a "manly" vase—like a distributor cap or a toolbox. Or how about placing three small roses in the finger holes of his bowling ball?

> Seventy-four percent of American men have *never* received flowers from a woman. Eighty-two percent of them say they would appreciate the gesture.

899 Do something *with* him that you normally hate doing (and do it cheerfully and without complaint). Accompany him fishing, bowling, bird-watching, running, or camping. Or simply watch "the Game" on TV with him.

900 Do something *for* him that you normally hate doing (and do it cheerfully and without complaint). Iron his shirts; wash his car; cook his favorite, hard-to-make dinner; run some errands; perform that little sexy fantasy you know he loves so much.

I highly recommend a thoroughly enchanting and practical book, *The Goddess' Guide to Love*, by Margie Lapanja.

Guy Stuff

901 Guys, I don't *blame* you for being freaked out by the whole Valentine's Day thing. The problem is not with *you*—it's with our screwed-up culture.

The problem, you see, is with Cupid. Cupid represents romantic love, right? Now Cupid is a cute, naked little cherub who flits around and boinks people with his little arrows. *How cute!* So along comes February, and the store windows are full of flitting Cupids and are, of course, swathed in pink and red. What's the problem with this? The problem is that the images are either infantile or feminine.

The ancient Romans understood love better than we do. Cupid was originally the Roman god of romantic love. His mother, Venus, was the goddess of love. So the Romans had both feminine *and* masculine images for the concept of love. Pretty smart, huh? You may also be interested to know that Cupid was an adolescent—not a chubby cherub. (Picture one of those classic marble sculptures: Heroic pose, bulging muscles and a bow big enough to bring down a *bear,* much less two lovers!)

All of which is to say…that there *is* a masculine side to romantic love. It's just that our culture has few good male role models. Our culture also promotes simplistic, stereotypical thinking

Real Men love the *Three Stooges,* right? So get him a gift from the "Soitenly Stooges" catalog! Call 800-3-STOOGES, or visit www.soitenlystooges.com.

Best guy quote from a Romance Class: "I'm not *dumb*—I'm just confused."

("Men are logical, women are emotional,") which makes it doubly difficult for us guys to get in touch with that side of ourselves.

What to do? Well, you could celebrate Valentine's Day in a *masculine* way on *even* years, and celebrate in a *feminine* way on *odd* years. (So, for example, on even years you'd go on a bowling date, give tools for gifts, dine at a pub, and then have sex. Then on odd years you'd stay at a bed and breakfast, give perfume, dine at a French café, make gentle love.)

Gal Stuff

902 Many men would consider this the *Ultimate Gift:* a "Fantasy Photo" of you. You can get a sensual, provocative and stunning "Fantasy Portrait" made of yourself by contacting a photographer who specializes in the growing art form often called "Boudoir Photography."

Many of these photographers are women with a talent for making their subject feel comfortable, and then bringing out the subtle, sexy side of her personality, and capturing it on film. "Lingerie" portraits seem to be most popular, followed by "Fantasy Outfit" shots, "Pin Up Girl" poses and "Playmate/Nude" photography.

> The Classics of romance are fine in the beginning. Then what??

Look for professional studios in your area, check references, or call:

- Fantasy Photography by Daphne, in Arlington, Massachusetts, at 781-641-2100 or www.fantasyphotography.com.
- Lucien Flotte Photography, in New York City, at 212-564-9670.

903 F.M. Shoes.

904 Take a quick look through *Playboy* or *Penthouse*—see for yourself what *men in general* find sexy. Then ask your guy *specifically* what he finds sexy. You might be surprised at what you learn about him! You might also open up the door to more frank discussions about sexuality and sensuality.

Characteristics of True Romantics

905 Romantics are cheerleaders.
Romantics are the biggest fans of their lovers. They provide enthusiastic support, constant encouragement, and unconditional love. (They don't succeed 100 percent of the time, naturally, but they're always in there trying.)

906 Romantics are creative.
Romantics see their relationships as opportunities to express their creativity, as arenas for self-expression, as safe havens for experimenting, and as places for growth.

Guys, kiss her in a special way: Cup your hands and hold her face gently in your hands when you kiss her.

907　Romantics are mind-readers. Those who are tuned in to their lovers—those who *listen really well*—develop a kind of "sixth sense" about what their lovers would love. One of the best things about long-term relationships is that you can develop this sense. And as it develops, your relationship deepens and your intimacy grows.

- What kind of special *gift* do you know would please your partner?
- What little *gesture* do you know would bring a smile to his or her face?
- What special *meal* or *dessert* could you prepare that you know he or she simply loves?
- What has he *really wanted* for a long time, but held back from buying? Get it for him!

Have you *complimented* her lately?
Have you *thanked* him recently?
Have you *encouraged* her lately?
Have you *surprised* him lately?
Have you *acknowledged* her accomplishments?
Have you *marveled* at his talents lately?

Characteristics of Crazy Romantics

908 Slow-dance at a restaurant— *when there's no music playing.* (When one man from the Romance Class did this with his girlfriend, he reported that they were applauded by the other patrons, and given a complimentary bottle of champagne by the management!)

Chapter Theme Song: "Crazy Love," Van Morrison

Don't forget to open the flue!

909 Snuggle up to a roaring fire in the fireplace—in the middle of August.

910 Cool things you could rent from a rental store. Great for theme dates, surprise parties, or fantasies acted out in great detail!
• An automatic bubble machine
• A "fogger" that makes special-effects fog
• Various costumes
• A jukebox
• A Victorian carriage and horse
• A pinball machine

911 On a budget? Create a "Disney World Vacation-At-Home"! Shop at a Disney Store for paraphernalia such as Mickey ears, stuffed animals, wind-up toys, balloons, puppets, and posters. Rent the most romantic Disney movies: *Beauty and the Beast, Lady and the Tramp, The Little Mermaid,* and *Pocahontas.*

Speaking of Love

912 Let other *things* speak for you. Romantics *do not* constantly buy gifts and presents for their partners. But they *do* give "things." Little things. Private things. Goofy things. Meaningful things. Things like comic strips, love quotes, a "perfect" cup of coffee, flowers, greeting cards, penny candy, magazine articles, little toys.

913 Let other *people* speak for you. You don't have to be *eloquent* in order to be *romantic*. You don't have to write great poetry—or even mediocre love letters. And, you don't have to be particularly well-spoken. But you *do* have to express your feelings *somehow*. One great strategy is to *borrow* the romantic words of the great poets, songwriters, and wordsmiths of the world.

Let these people speak for you: William Shakespeare, Billy Joel, Paul McCartney, Charlie Brown, Susan Polis Schutz, Elizabeth Barrett Browning, Kahlil Gibran, Stevie Wonder and, Emily Dickinson.

Chapter Theme Song: "Speaking of Love," Air Supply

"No sooner met but they looked; no sooner looked but they loved; no sooner loved but they sighed; no sooner sighed but they asked one another the reason; no sooner knew the reason but they sought the remedy; and in these degrees have they made a pair of stairs to marriage..."
—William Shakespeare, *As You Like It*

Now, I *don't* suggest that you try to take credit for composing "How do I love thee? Let me count the ways." Your expression isn't diminished in the least when you borrow others' words. Simply add to the note something like, "Stevie Wonder expressed my love for you when he sang 'You Are the Sunshine of My Life.'"

914 Let your *touch* speak for you.
Sometimes words are simply inadequate to express the incredible feelings of love inside of you. At those times a simple touch can express volumes. A caress, a squeeze, a hug. Sometimes the simplest things are *just right.*

Speaking of Romance

915 Guess which major magazine this quote is from:
"...we need romance and sentimentality in our lives...Note that I say 'we need'—*all* of us, men and women, right down to the most macho truck driver or professional mud wrestler. There was a general supposition a couple of decades ago, when women first banded together to seek 'liberation,' that one of the first casualties would be 'romance,' particularly in its more obvious and exploitative forms. Would Betty Friedan really expect a box of chocolates on February 14? Would Kate Millett wait for flowers? Would women, once they had become astronauts, weight lifters, firepersons, and entrepreneurs, and after becoming dependent on the Pill and sisterhood, still crave romance? And was not romance

itself merely another of those many cultural traps that men had perfected for women over the centuries? As anyone could have predicted, romance won out, in fact was never in danger at all."

Where did this item appear? *Cosmo?* Nope. *Glamour?* Nope. *Reader's Digest?* Nope. *Penthouse?* Yup! By Michael Korda.

916 A word to the wise: *Don't equate romance with sex.* Romance is intertwined with both love *and* sex, so there's plenty of opportunity for misunderstandings between lovers.

Romance is *really* love-in-action. But sometimes actions that *look* a lot like romance are used for *seduction.* And sometimes actions that *look* a lot like romance are used for peace offerings. And sometimes actions that *look* a lot like romance are used for barter.

> When it comes to romance, the *passion* is more important than the happy ending. Think:
> *Romeo and Juliet*
> *Titanic*
> *The Notebook*
> *Gone With the Wind*

What's in a Name?

917 Name your boat after her.

918 If her name is April, May, or June, declare the corresponding month "her" month, and do something special for her every day that month. (*Every* woman is "one-in-a-million," but few are "one-in-twelve"!)

919

• What's in a name? Make special use of her name flower if she's a Rose, Daisy, Ivy, Lily, or Iris.

• What's in a nickname? Use Buttercups, Poppies, and Sweet Peas.

• If your pet name for her is Angel: Make angels in the snow; celebrate August 22nd—it's "Be an Angel Day"; visit Los Angeles, the "City of Angels"; record these songs for her: "Angel of the Morning," by Merrilee Rush; "I Married an Angel," by Larry Clinton; "Angel of Mine," by Monica; and "Lips of an Angel," by Hinder.

Her name in a song:
"Jane," Ben Folds Five
"Denise," Fountains of Wayne
"Maria," Green Day
"Joanna," Kool & the Gang
"Kathleen," Willie Nelson
"Tracy," The Cuff Links
His name in a song:
"Ben," Jackson 5
"Daniel," Elton John
"William," The Others
"Jeremy," Pearl Jam
"Rudy," Supertramp

920 Most couples have private "pet names" for one another. Many pet names lend themselves to specific gifts. From some of my Romance Class participants here are some pet names and their corresponding gifts.

- Big Bear: a five-foot-tall teddy bear
- Macho Man: a "muscle T-shirt" and the Village People's CD
- Bunny: bunny motif clothing, posters, figurines
- Sweetie: candies of all kinds
- Cookie: a cookie-a-day, for nine years—so far!
- Tiger: 1) A stuffed "Tigger," 2) Calvin & Hobbes books

If you ever have occasion to discover a new planet or comet, name it after your lover.

The Meaning of a Name

921 Do you know the *significance* of your lover's name? Here are a few samples taken from a "baby name" book:

- Ada is Teutonic for "joyous."
- April is Latin for "open, accepting."
- Barbara is Roman for "mysterious stranger."
- Catherine is Greek, meaning "pure."
- Cheryl is French for "beloved."
- David is Hebrew for "beloved."

Chapter
Theme Song:
"Name,"
Goo Goo Dolls

- Diane is from the Latin Diana, meaning "Goddess of the Moon."
- Dominique is French, meaning "she who belongs to God."
- Erik is Scandinavian for "ever-powerful."
- Frederick is Germanic, meaning "peaceful."
- Gary is Germanic for "spear carrier."
- Gregory is Greek, meaning "vigilant, watchful."
- Helen is Greek for "light."
- Jean derives from Jane, Hebrew for "God is gracious."
- Jennifer is Welsh, for "fair one."
- John is Hebrew for "God is merciful."
- Judy is Hebrew, meaning "admired and praised."
- Kelsey is derived from Gaelic, meaning "female warrior."
- Kevin is Irish for "handsome, gentle, lovable."
- Linda is Spanish, meaning "beautiful."
- Marjorie is derived from Greek, meaning "pearl, precious one."
- Neil is Gaelic, meaning "champion."
- Raymond is Old English for "wise guardian."
- Richard is Old German for "powerful ruler."

I heard a rumor that one couple, inspired by the comic strip "Zits," has legally changed their name to one word, *Tomandsusan.*

Get a book of baby names and discover what your lover's name means. Then use that meaning as a theme for romantic gifts and gestures.
For Linda: Find poems and song that use the word *beautiful.*
For Neil: Play for him "We are the Champions" by Queen.
For Susan: Give her many lilies.

- Sally is Hebrew for "princess."
- Susan is Hebrew for "lily."
- Thomas is Aramaic, meaning "the twin."
- Warren is Germanic for "defender, or protective friend."
- Wendy was invented by J.M. Barrie for the heroine of Peter Pan!

And Now for Something Completely Different*

922 Are you stuck in a boring routine every evening? (Home from work; run some errands; grab some dinner; pay some bills; watch some TV; crawl into bed exhausted.) *Radically change your routine:*

- Meet after work at the local art museum; eat at the café there; spend the evening browsing with the high-brow.
- On a Tuesday night, order a quick pizza for dinner, then head for an early movie.
- Meet at the mall; go window shopping; dine at your favorite fast food joint.

*For your Monty Python fan:
Serve Spam, eggs, Spam, and Spam for breakfast.
Plant some shrubbery.
Promise that you'll never, "Run away!"

923 There's no better way to loosen up than to get in touch with the child inside yourself. That little kid is playful, creative, curious, spontaneous, trusting, and imaginative! Stop being such an adult, and recapture those childlike qualities. Suggested reading:
• *The Tao of Pooh,* by Benjamin Hoff
• *Where the Sidewalk Ends,* by Shel Silverstein
• The *Harry Potter* series, by J.K. Rowling
• *The Stinky Cheese Man and Other Fairly Stupid Tales,* by Jon Scieszka & Lane Smith

924 Is your honey a *Wizard of Oz* fanatic? Well, take her to the Judy Garland Museum and see rare photos, video documentaries, rare recordings, and memorabilia. It hosts a Judy Garland Festival every year, too. The Yellow Brick Road is in Grand Rapids, Minnesota. Call 800-664-JUDY or visit www.judygarlandmuseum.com.

What Is Your Quest?

925 If the two of you decided to undertake a quest to share *one million* kisses over the course of your lives, *how often* would you have to kiss?

Note: For the sake of practicality I'm making these assumptions: You each sleep six hours per night—so you can't kiss during that time. And between work, commuting, and separate chores, you'll spend an additional sixty hours per week apart. Given all that, here's how often you'd have to kiss if you wanted to share 1,000,000 kisses:

- Over ten years you'd have to kiss once every 2.06 minutes.
- Over twenty years you'd have to kiss once every 4.12 minutes.
- Over thirty years you'd have to kiss once every 6.18 minutes.
- Over forty years you'd have to kiss once every 8.24 minutes.
- Over fifty years you'd have to kiss once every 10.3 minutes
- Over sixty years you'd have to kiss once every 12.36 minutes.

Note #1: You're welcome, of course, to bunch your kisses together so that you'll have time to attend to other matters in your life.

Note #2: Sorry, but the judges have ruled that *extra long* kisses still only count as one kiss each. (That goes for French Kisses, too.)

926 If your quest is to fill the house with the wonderful aroma of flowers, be aware that your favorite flowers aren't necessarily the most *fragrant* ones. Create a bouquet of especially fragrant flowers, and your romantic gesture will take on a whole new dimension.

927 Go in search of "The Perfect Pizza." It could take you months or years, and you might gain ten pounds—but if your lover is a pizza *fiend,* it will all be worth it!

Especially *fragrant* flowers:
Freesia
Roses
Casablanca lilies
Rubrum lilies
Stock
Stephanotis
Lilacs
Gardenias
Hyacinths

Getting to Know You

928 Interview his mother, father, siblings, friends, and colleagues—to learn about his unique quirks, likes, dislikes, hobbies, and passions.

929 What's the difference between "sexy" and "sleazy"? What's the difference between "cute" and "coy"? I'll bet *your* definitions differ from your partner's. But you'll never know unless you talk about it.

930
- Play "Show and Tell": Pick a beloved object. Talk about its history and why it's special to you. (An old baseball glove; a doll from childhood; something given to you by a grandparent; a stuffed animal; a trophy; a piece of jewelry, etc.)
- Another "Show and Tell" game: Visit *places* that have special meaning to you.

931 Grab some books on astrology and see what the stars have to say about your and your partner's personalities. My favorite is *Star Signs,* by Linda Goodman. The fun thing about this book is that it describes every possible pairing of the twelve signs of the zodiac.

Bonus Questions

"Getting to Know You" Questions:
- Do you believe in love at first sight?
- What three adjectives best describe you?
- How did you know you two were in love?
- Which comic book character would you be?
- What animal would you be?

- How are you just like your mother? Father?
- What was your favorite childhood game?
- Are you a lucky person?
- When do you feel most creative?
- What would you do if you won the lottery?
- Do you dream in color?

Staying in Touch

932 Real communication between lovers is one part talking and nine parts listening. Listen, for a change. You'll learn a lot about your partner.

- Listen for the feelings behind the words. We don't always say what we mean, but the emotional content is still there if we tune in to it.
- Listen without interrupting. (Quite a challenge—especially if you've been together for many years!)

933 Respond with love, *regardless* of what your partner says or does. Why? Because behaviors such as complaining, worrying, shouting, and nagging are all *disguised calls for love.* (When a child exhibits these kinds of behaviors we instinctively understand that it comes from fear, and has nothing to do with us personally. Unfortunately, we rarely grant adults this courtesy.) Try to respond to what's *really* going on, not simply to what's on the surface.

934 Give your partner more reassurance. Reinforce her good qualities. Compliment his talents and abilities. Reinforce all the good qualities *that attracted you to your partner in the first place.*

- Tell him what you really appreciate about him.
- Remind her that you really *do* adore her.
- Concentrate on the *positive* when talking to him.
- Focus on who she *really is,* instead of on your unrealistic fantasy of "The Perfect Partner."

Hearing and *listening* are very, very different! Hearing is automatic (you even hear things in your sleep!)—while listening requires conscious choice. Listening is a gift of love you give to your partner.

Messages

935 Make a "Just Married" sign. Tape it to the back windshield of your car before taking a Sunday afternoon drive. People will honk and wave. Pretend you're newlyweds!
(Maybe even stay in the bridal suite of a local hotel!)

936 XOXOXOXOXO
XOXOXOXOXOXOXOXOX
OXOXOXOXOXOXOXOX
OXOXOXOXOXOXOXOX
OXOXOXOXOXOXOXOX
OXOXOXOXOXOXOXOX
OXOXOXOXOXOXOXOX
OXOXOXOXOXOXOXOX
OXyXOXOXOXOXOXOXO

> While most people *sign* their letters with X's and O's, one man wrote a *whole letter* with X's and O's—with a secret message embedded among the kisses and hugs!

XOXOXOXOXOXOXOXOXOXOXOXOXOXOXOXOXOXOXOXOXOX
OXOXOXOXOXOXOXOXOXOXOXOoXOXOXOXOXOXOXOXOX
OXOXOXOXOXOXOXOXOXOXOXOXOXOXOXOXOXOXOXuX
OXOXOXOXOXOXOXOXOXOXOXOaOXOXOXOXOXOXOXOX
OXOXrXOXOXOXOXOXOXOXOXOXOXOXOeOXOXOXOX
OXOXOXOXmXOXOXOXOXOXOXOXyXOXOXOXOXOXoX
OXOXOXOXOXOXOXOXOXnXOXOXXOXOXOXeXOXOXO
XOXOXaXOXOXOXOXOXOXOXOXOXOXOXnXOXOXOXO
XOXOXOXOXOXOXOdOXOXOXOXOXOXOXOXOXOXOX
OXOXOXOXOXOXOXOXOXOXOXOXOXOXOXOXOX
OXoXOXOXOXOXOXOXOXOXO XOXOXOXO
XOXOXOXOXOXOXOXOXOnOXOXOXOX
OXOXOXOXOlOXOXOXOXOXOXOXOX
OXOXOXOXOyOXOXOXOXOXOXOXOXO
XOXOX

937 Write a personal message *some-where* on your body (with washable ink)—and let him discover it.

Chapter Theme Song:
"A Message," Coldplay

Massages

938 Before you leave on a trip, leave a bottle of scented massage oil on the nightstand, along with a note saying, "I'm going to use this on you as soon as I return."

939 Massages come in two varieties: Sensual and sexual. Learn the subtle—but important—differences. A *sensual* massage is soothing, healing, and relaxing. It often lulls your partner to sleep. A *sexual* massage is stimulating and arousing. It often leads to lovemaking. True romantics know when each type of massage is appropriate.

Touch is healing.

940 Some recommended books on massage:
- *The Tao of Sexual Massage,* by Stephen Russell
- *The Art of Sensual Massage,* Gordon Inkeles
- *Lovers' Massage: Soothing Touch for Two,* by Darrin Zeer
- *The Complete Guide to Massage,* by Susan Mumford
- *The Complete Idiot's Guide to Sensual Massage,* by Patti Britton & Helen Hodgson
- *Sensual Massage for Couples,* by Gordon Inkeles & Greg Peterson

ABC

941

A is for Attitude, Available, Accept, Ardor, Accolades, Admire, Aphrodisiacs, Á la Mode, Anniversary, Ambrosia, Ardent, Athens, Australia

Chapter
Theme Song:
"ABC,"
The Jackson Five

B is for Boudoir, Bed & Breakfast, Buttercups, Beaches, Blue, Books, Boston, Balloons, Bicycling, Broadway, Brandy, Bubble baths, Bahamas

C is for Champagne, Creativity, Candlelight, Candy, Chocolate, Convertibles, Casablanca, Cognac, Caviar, Chivalry, Crabtree & Evelyn

D is for Diamonds, Dancing, Daffodils, Dating, Dolls, Dirty Dancing, Dinner, Divine, Dearest

E is for Enthusiasm, Energy, Excitement, Emeralds, Earrings, Elvis, Erotic, Exotic, Expensive, Escapes

F is for Flirting, Fantasies, Feminine, Faithful, France, Flowers, Fruits, French kissing, Foreplay

G is for Garters, Gardenias, Godiva, Get-Aways, Gifts, Glenn Miller, Gourmet, Greece, Gondolas

H is for Hearts, Humor, Hugs, Hideaways, Horses, Honeymoons, Hawaii, Hershey's Kisses, Hyatt, Holidays

I is for Intimacy, Intrigue, Italy, Inns, Islands, Ingenuity, Ice Cream, Ice Skating, Interdependent, Imaginative, Invitation, Incense

J is for Jewelry, Java, Jasmine, Jell-O, Jazz, Journey, Joyful, Jacuzzi

K is for Kissing, Kinky, Kittens, Koala Bears, Kites

L is for Love, Lingerie, Laughing, Love Letters, Lilacs, Lace, Leather, Leo Buscaglia, Lobsters, Lovemaking, Limousines, Love songs, London

M is for Monogamy, Marriage, Masculine, M&M's, Massage, Movies, Mistletoe, Music, Mozart, Moonlight

N is for Negligee, Naughty, Nibble, Nighttime, Nubile, Novelty, Nurture, Nymph, Naples, Nightcap, Nape, Nepal, Necklace

O is for Orgasm, Opera, Orchid, Outrageous, Outdoors

P is for Passion, Perfume, Poppies, Poetry, Persimmons, Paris, Polkas, Panties, Pizza, Photos, Pearls, Picnics, Playfulness, Purple, Parking

Q is for Quiet, Quaint, Quality, Queen, Quebec, Question, QE2, Quiche, Quiver, Quilts

R is for Rendezvous, Roses, Rubies, Red, Reading, Rome, Rituals, Riviera, Restful, Rapture, Rings, Rio, Rainbows

S is for Sex

T is for Tea, Talking, Teasing, Tulips, Titillating, Theater, Tickets, Togetherness, Toasts, Toys, Trains, Trinidad, Travel, Tenderness

U is for Umbrellas, Uxorious, Undress, Undulate, Urges, Unexpected, Union, Under the Spreading Chestnut Tree

V is for Violets, Virgins, Vibrators, Venice, Venus, Valentines, Vegetables, Victoria's Secret

W is for Wine, Wisteria, Walking hand-in-hand, Weddings

X is for X-Rated, Xerographic, Xylophones, Xmas

Y is for Yachts, Yes, Yellow, Yin & Yang, Young-at-heart

Z is for Zany, Zanzibar, Zeal, Zodiac, Zurich

"Do you know your ABCs?" Ask your partner to pick a letter. Then read the list of corresponding words. He or she has twenty-four hours in which to get a romantic gift or perform a romantic gesture based on any one of these key words.

XYZ

942 Always kiss each other hello and goodbye. **B**e there for each other—always. **C**reate an environment of love. **D**o it. **E**scape from the kids. **F**ight fair. **G**ive of your time. **H**andle with care. **I**nspire your partner with your love. **J**udge not. **K**eep your good memories alive. **L**isten to her. **M**ake love with your partner's needs foremost. **N**ever go to bed angry. **O**ffer to handle an unpleasant chore. **P**raise him. **Q**uality Time isn't just for the kids. **R**espect her feelings. **S**ay what you feel when you feel it. **T**ell her you love her every day. Everyday. **U**nderstand your differences. **V**alentine's Day is every day. **W**alk together; talk together. E**X**cite your partner as only you know how. **Y**ou can never say "I love you" too often. **Z**ero in on his little passions.

> Choose a letter. Follow the corresponding piece of advice this week. Choose a different letter next week.

943 Give your partner a "Romantic ABCs Coupon": Write the letters of the alphabet on twenty-six slips of paper. The coupon-holder picks one letter out of a hat. The coupon-giver will create a day of romance with gifts and gestures that all begin with that letter.

FYI

944 The song list from the best cassette tape of romantic music I've ever created:

1. "I Won't Last a Day Without You," by Paul Williams
2. "Coming Around Again," by Carly Simon
3. "Closer to Believing," by Greg Lake/Emerson, Lake & Palmer
4. "Saving My Heart," by Yes
5. "If I Had a Million Dollars," by Barenaked Ladies
6. "I'm Gonna Be (500 Miles)," by The Proclaimers
7. "Symphony No. 35, *Haffner,*" by Wolfgang Amadeus Mozart
8. "In the Mood," by Glenn Miller
9. "Kalena Kai," by Keola Beamer
10. "Crazy," by Patsy Cline

945 There are *three* kinds of people in the world: "Past-Oriented" people, "Now-Oriented" people," and "Future-Oriented" people. Your "romantic style" is often determined by your "time orientation."

- *Past-Oriented* people tend toward the sentimental and nostalgic. They're into scrapbooks and saving things.
- *Now-Oriented* people are spontaneous and often extremely creative. They're into last-minute activities and adventures.
- *Future-Oriented* people are planners and listeners. They're into surprises and grand gestures.

946 It's getting harder and harder to find classic 45 RPM records, and it's almost *impossible* to locate old 78s! Find a local used record shop or call House of Oldies at 212-243-0500, or visit them at 35 Carmine Street in New York City, or visit www.houseofoldies.com.

FYI, romance is habit-forming.

Gift Ideas

947 A *vibrating* massager. Be creative when you use it.

948 Buy her an *entire* outfit. Include: beautiful lingerie, a gorgeous dress, a matching scarf, pin or necklace, and shoes! Spread 'em out on the bed. Wait for her jaw to drop.

949 Satin sheets.

950 Gentlemen: Approach the subject of lingerie *gently.*
- Your *first* lingerie present should *not* be a peek-a-boo bra. (Have a little class,huh?!)
- You might start by giving her a say in the matter: Attach a one-hundred dollar bill to a lingerie catalog along with a note saying "You choose." Or make a custom "Lingerie Coupon."
- How about just paging through some lingerie catalogs together and talking about what each of you likes and dislikes?

Treat her like a queen and she'll treat you like a king.

"When you love someone, all your saved–up wishes start coming out."
—Elizabeth Bowen

Coupon Ideas

951 A basic romantic concept: Love Coupons. Here's a twist: Love Coupons made from the little slips of paper from Hershey's Kisses. Each coupon is redeemable for one kiss.

> ### The Saturday Night Date Coupon
>
> Where? Wherever you want!
> When? You decide.

952 Here are some twists on the concept of "Coupons":

- Coupons made out of your business cards
- Coupons made on restaurant menus
- Coupons made on pillow cases
- Coupons made into bookmarks
- Coupons inserted into computer documents
- Coupons made from magazines

> ### Breakfast in Bed Coupon
>
> Redeemable on any day of your choosing.
> Never expires.

953 Another twist on the Love Coupon idea: "Dollar Bill" coupons: Make a simply sketched "one-dollar bill"; put your picture in the center; make a hundred photocopies; cut them out; make a stack. Then give them to your lover, along with a detailed list of

> ### The Ultimate Bubble Bath Coupon
>
> Complete with scented bath oils, soft music, champagne & candles.

various activities and what they'll cost. For example:

- Dinner out: $5
- An *expensive* dinner out: $15
- A movie out: $3
- A movie in: $1
- I'll cook dinner: $12
- I'll bring dinner home: $1
- One backrub: $4
- Going shopping with you: $20
- Making love: $1
- Making love (*when I don't feel like it!*): $98

> **A Romantic Dinner Coupon**
>
> Gourmet dinner prepared by the coupon issuer. Proper dress required.

How to Understand Each Other

954 There are several systems designed to help you understand yourself and others by utilizing a variety of "personality profile" techniques. Here are some recommended books:

- *The 16 Personality Types: Descriptions for Self-Discovery,* by Linda V. Berens & Dario Nardi
- *Soultypes: Matching Your Personality and Spiritual Path,* by Sandra Krebs Hirsch & Jane A.G. Kise

Also—

The Color Code, by Taylor Hartman
Who Do You Think You Are? by Keith Harary & Eileen Donahue Robinson

• *A Woman's Guide to Personality Types: Enriching Your Family Relationships by Understanding the Four Temperaments,* by Donna Partow

955 Have your handwriting analyzed together. You'll be amazed at what can be "read" in your writing.

956 **Ten Quirky Questions to Help Couples Get Inside Each Other's Heads (and Hearts)**

1. What three *nouns* best describe you?
2. What three *adjectives* best describe you?
3. If you could save time in a bottle, what would you do with it?
4. What do you want to be remembered for?
5. What are your prized possessions?
6. What did you want to be when you grew up?
7. Would you rather be rich or famous?
8. Would you rather live in the far future or the distant past?
9. If you had one more day to live, how would you spend that day?
10. If you were going to write a self-help book, what would you title it?

"He who does not understand your silence will probably not understand your words."
—Elbert Hubbard

"Life is the first gift, love is the second, and understanding the third."
—Marge Piercy

How to Bed & Breakfast

957 It has come to my attention that there are some guys out there who, having made reservations at a romantic bed and breakfast, have arrived there and proceeded to turn on the TV. Or, upon discovering that there is no TV in the room, have called the manager to complain. *No, no, no!*

- Set your TiVo at home before you leave so you won't miss your favorite TV shows.
- Hide your watches in a drawer—go all weekend without bothering with the time.
- A little "afternoon delight."
- Ask your bed and breakfast hosts for suggestions. They always know their communities very well.
- Call ahead and make reservations at several recommended local restaurants.
- Enjoy a bubble bath or Jacuzzi together.
- Bring some inspiring books to read.

> No clocks.
> No schedules.
> No hassles.
> No worries.
> No interruptions.
> No TV.
> No mail.
> No e-mail.
> No phone.
> No stress.
> No kids.
> No pager.
> No computer.
> No diet.

958 And here are some specific Bed and Breakfast resource books for you.

- *Bed & Breakfasts and Country Inns,* by Deborah Edwards Sakach. These B&Bs are visited personally and rated by the American Bed & Breakfast Association.
- *Complete Guide to Bed & Breakfasts, Inns & Guesthouses*—B&B expert Pamela Lanier's comprehensive guide to over 4,000 of the world's inns. Includes favorite recipes from B&Bs worldwide!

- *Recommended Romantic Inns,* by Julianne Belote. Chosen especially for their romantic qualities, these 140 B&Bs are described in detail by the authors, who have visited every site.

> Tip: Make bed and breakfast reservations for Valentine's Day a *year* in advance!

Soundtrack to a Love Affair

959 Those romantic scenes in the movies wouldn't be *nearly* as romantic if they didn't enhance them with *music.* You could take some inspiration from Hollywood and create soundtracks for various romantic activities! I recommend these CDs for these romantic occasions:

For a romantic candlelight dinner:
- *Come Away With Me,* Norah Jones
- *Picture This,* by Jim Brickman
- *Twin Sons of Different Mothers,* by Fogelberg & Weisberg

Make custom CDs of romantic background music. Make CDs of meaningful, romantic songs as gifts for her. Make CDs of songs that were hits while you were dating. Make CDs of your partner's favorite songs.

For lounging by the fireplace:
* *Touch*, by John Klemmer
* *Watermark*, by Enya
* *Past Light*, by William Ackerman

For a drive in the country:
* *Il Bacio*, by Paul Ventimiglia
* *Legends*, by Eric Tingstad & Nancy Rumbel
* *Crossroads*, by Nicholas Gunn

For a Sunday afternoon picnic:
* *Picnic Suite*, by Jean-Pierre Rampal and Claude Bolling
* *No Name Face*, Lifehouse
* *Water Music*, by George Frideric Handel

For lovemaking (romantic & gentle):
* *Canon in D (The Pachelbel Canon)*, by Johann Pachelbel
* *Livin' Inside Your Love*, by George Benson
* *Winter Into Spring*, by George Winston

For lovemaking (hot & sexy):
* *Enigma MCMXC a.D.*, by Enigma
* *Nine-1/2 Weeks* soundtrack
* *Midnight Love*, by Marvin Gaye

Guidelines for a Love Affair

960

The *Friends* of Love
- Faith
- Focus of attention
- Fun-loving attitude
- Stay in touch with your feelings
- Kindness
- Simplicity
- Clarity of your life's priorities
- Sense of adventure
- Creative attitude
- Patience
- Tenderness
- Empathy
- Goodwill
- Attentiveness
- Generosity
- Sense of Humor
- Commitment
- A good therapist/counselor/pastor
- Gifts that touch the heart
- Good role models
- Listening with your heart
- Appreciation for life
- Time—Quantity of time
- Time—Quality time
- Respect for your partner

The *Enemies* of Love
- Emotional withdrawal
- Nagging
- Jealousy
- Complexity of modern life
- Arrogance
- Overly practical attitudes
- Impatience
- Guilt
- Stress
- Selfishness
- Lack of time
- Laziness
- Boredom
- Lack of respect
- Stereotyped attitudes
- Lack of role models
- Stinginess in general
- Stinginess with time
- Stinginess with money
- Rigid attitudes
- Apathy
- Fear
- Grudges
- Resentment
- Immaturity

"It is only with the heart that one can see rightly; what is essential is invisible to the eye."
—Antoine de Saint-Exupery

- Presents that symbolize your love
- Playful attitude
- Eye contact

- Thoughtlessness
- Superior attitude

Have a love affair— *with your spouse!*

Bubble Baths (I)

961a Start simple. Run her a bath. Steaming hot. Full of bubbles.

961b Bath-and-Snack: bubble bath plus grapes, cheese and crackers.

961c Bath-and-Music: bubble bath plus relaxing music. Featuring Enya's CD *Watermark* and George Winston's CD *Autumn.*

961d Bath-and-Bubbly: bubble bath plus champagne, two crystal champagne flutes, and *you!*

961e Bath-and-Book: bubble bath plus a book by her favorite author.

961f Steamy-Bath-and-Steamy-Eroticism: bubble bath plus an erotic book—in which you've highlighted the "steamy" passages. This bath includes a follow-up lovemaking session.

961g Bath-and-Relax: bubble bath for one—plus two hours of peace and quiet (while you take the kids out to McDonald's).

Bubble Baths (II)

961h Bath-for-Two: Watch the movie *Bull Durham.* Watch for the romantic bath scene. Use it for inspiration. (Hint: Candles. Lots and *lots* of candles.)

961i Leaving-Work-Behind: Be waiting for him in the bathtub when he returns from work.

961j Message-in-a-Bottle: Write her a love letter or a poem. Roll it up and stick it in a bottle. Cork it. Float the bottle in the bathtub.

961k Bath-and-Sexual-Gymnastics: Test your agility—make love in the bathtub. If your tub is simply too small, spread towels on the floor and improvise!

961l Bath-and-Products: Explore a wide variety of bath powders, lotions and potions. When you find one that she adores, get *lots* of it.

961m For a touch of class: European soaps and other bath luxuries imported by Katherine March International. Call 800-87-MARCH, or write 9286 S.W. 90th Street, Gainesville, Florida 32608-7246, or visit www.katherinemarch.com.

A Touch of Class

962 Be on the lookout for concepts and gifts that relate to your lover's interests. For example, if your partner loves *Romeo and Juliet*, or Shakespeare, or theater in general, here's an unusual and cool gift idea: "One Page Books" are large, beautifully-designed prints that contain the complete, unabridged text of many Shakespearean plays and sonnets. Each one is a fine art print that measures 32-inches by 45-inches. When framed they are dramatic conversation pieces. These works are currently available:

* *Romeo and Juliet*
* *Macbeth*
* *Hamlet*
* *King Lear*
* *The Tempest*
* *Othello*
* *The Sonnets*
* *A Midsummer Night's Dream*
* *Much Ado About Nothing*
* *Love's Labors Lost*
* *Twelfth Night*
* *The Merchant of Venice*

Visit the One Page Book Company at www.onepagebooks.com.

963 Attend a symphony. Get the program ahead of time, buy CDs of the symphonies to be performed, and listen to each of them *three* times. Even if you're not very familiar with classical music, this will greatly increase your enjoyment of the concert.

You *do* have an elegant fountain pen with which to write love notes and love letters, don't you?! A Mont Blanc pen will add an unparalleled touch of class to your act.

A Touch

964
- Take a massage class together. (Get a catalog from your local adult education center.)
- Give her a custom-made Love Coupon good for a professional massage. (Call local health clubs, chiropractor's offices, hotels, physical therapy clinics, and spas for referrals.)

Chapter Theme Song: "Touch," Amerie

965 Hug. Cuddle. Caress. Touch. Pat. Tap. Brush. Graze. Stroke. Snuggle.

966 Romantics are *sensuous* people. They understand the difference between sensuality and sexuality—and how they enhance one another. Here are fourteen specific ways to enhance the sensuality in your life together:

1. Run your fingers gently through your lover's hair.

2. Focus on one of the five senses at a time.

3. Create a romantic mood at home through soft lighting.

4. Have great music playing in the background all the time at home.

5. Keep three bouquets of fragrant flowers in the house.

6. Focus on touching a different part of your partner's body each day.

7. Prepare an extra-special taste treat for your lover.

8. Include more sensuality in your lovemaking.

9. Slow down, make time, relax.

10. Over the next five weeks, get five small gifts that focus on each of the five senses.

11. Focus on the present moment; appreciate the "now."

12. Buy ten scented candles.

13. Give him a great shoulder massage as he watches TV tonight.

14. Buy a basketful of scented bath oils.

A great resource: *Acupressure for Lovers: Secrets of Touch for Increasing Intimacy*, by Michael Reed Gach, Ph.D.

Ask your lover to tell you the most sensual thing you could do for him or her. *And then do it!*

Work

967 Make sure you find a way to do something romantic *during a time when you're the most busy at work!* A little planning will allow you to be romantic in the midst of your work day.

968 Utilize your partner's secretary and staff as your allies. They can be *invaluable* in helping you spring surprises on him or her. They'll know her schedule; where he's having lunch; and whether he or she has had an especially rough day. All are crucial bits of information you should know.

969 A hot trend in business is TQM—"Total Quality Management." One romantic manager was inspired to create what he also calls TQM—but it stands for "Total Quality Marriage." (Good one!) "Basically, you apply the best business techniques to your marriage," he explains. For example:

- How would you give good customer service to your partner?
- How might you and your partner give each other yearly performance reviews?
- Are each of you being well compensated emotionally?
- Are you using good time management techniques to create more leisure time?

It's *easy* to be romantic when you've got all the time in the world. The challenge is to keep expressing your love even during your busy and difficult times.

970 Create a "Gift & Card Drawer" in your desk at work. At all times your inventory should include: at least ten greeting cards, lots of Love Stamps, several "Trinket Gifts," a couple of *real* gifts, wrapping paper, and bows.

Play

971 View romance as "adult play."

Some people (especially men) tend to view romance as a serious and difficult activity. Nothing could be further from the truth! True romance is easy because it's simply an expression of what's *already inside you:* your feelings of love, caring and passion for your partner.

The concept of *adult play* is a reminder to loosen up, be creative, and remember the fun and passion you had early in your relationship. Adults need to *relearn* how to play—something that came naturally to all of us as children. Many ideas in this book are essentially exercises in *playing*.

> Many couples have confided to me that this single concept has turned their "nice-but-boring" relationship into a fun and passionate love affair.

972 Send a taxi to pick him up after work. Have the taxi driver hand him a sealed envelope. The note inside says, "All work and no play makes you a dull boy—so come and play!" Pre-pay the cab fare (including tip!), and instruct the driver to take him to a local hotel. Have another sealed envelope waiting for him at the front desk. (*You* decide what kind of note to write!) Be waiting for him in the honeymoon suite with chilled champagne and a warm bed.

> "In our play, we reveal what kind of people we are."
> —Ovid

973
- Finger-paint together.
- Finger-paint *each other's bodies!*

974 Use your kids' toys as romantic tools. Crayons are great for writing short notes. Play-Doh is great for sculpting messages and symbols. Legos are great for spelling out messages or leaving a trail through the house from the front door to your bedroom, where you're waiting for a little fun-and-games of your own.

"We don't stop playing because we grow old; we grow old because we stop playing."
—George Bernard Shaw

Sex Tips for Gals

975 More often.

Thousands of men in my Romance Classes have confided or complained that having their ladies wear lingerie more often is the one thing they want intensely that their women tend to resist.

Sex Tips for Guys

976 Make love to her *the way she wants to be made love to.*

> The secret to being a World-Class Lover is contained in one little word, guys: foreplay.

Romanti¢¢¢ Ideas

977 Buy camping equipment instead of going on an expensive vacation. A one-time outlay will assure you of years of inexpensive vacations. (You'll also be prepared for last-minute vacationing opportunities and quickie weekend getaways.)

978 Buy *season tickets* for shows and events that you attend. You'll save money in the long run, you'll get better seats, and you'll go out more! Box seats are great—whether they're at the ballgame or the ballet!

¢¢¢¢¢¢¢¢¢¢¢¢¢¢
¢¢¢¢¢¢¢¢¢¢¢¢¢¢
¢¢¢¢¢!!!!!!!!!!!!!!!!!!!!
!!!!!!!!!!!!!!!!!!!!!!!!!!!!!!!!
!!!!!!!!!!!!!!!!!!!!!!!!!

979 Many symphonies and theaters have discount tickets available on the day or evening of performances. If your partner doesn't mind a little uncertainty, this is a great way to save a few bucks and still enjoy an evening of culture and entertainment.

980 Where to get inexpensive flowers: supermarkets. Street vendors. Meadows. Your own garden. Your neighbor's garden. Outdoor markets. The side of the road.

981 Discover your local community theaters. They're fun, inexpensive, and entertaining. Many small cities and towns have truly *excellent* community theaters. Call them today for a schedule of upcoming shows. Don't forget to call a number of nearby towns, too!

Romantic Idea$$$

982 Under the category of "Spending the Most Money on the Smallest Items," the hands-down winner is...Diamonds!

Under the category of "Extravagance in Times Square," the winner is...

Third row, center orchestra seats to whatever Broadway show is currently most popular. (Unless you have a cousin in the business, you'll need to spring for over-priced—but worth it!—tickets from an exclusive ticket broker.)

$$$$$$$$$$$$
$$$$$$$$$$$$
$$$$$$$$$$$$!
!!!!!!!!!!!!!!!!!!!!!!!!!
!!!!!!!!!!!!!!!!!!!!!!

Under the category of "OH-MY-GOD—I didn't know it was possible," the winner is...

Hiring a big name rock band or comedian to entertain at your private anniversary party. This one will set you back a couple-of-hundred-thousand-dollars (no joke!), but some Very Big Names are available for hire! Some that have performed for private parties include Prince, The Beach Boys, and Robin Williams.

983 Other good ways of spending *lots* of money on your lover:
• Caviar
• A Mont Blanc fountain pen
• A Rolex watch
• A Harley-Davidson Fat Boy FLSTF
• A full-length mink coat
• A Porsche 911 Carrera Cabriolet

984 Dinner at The Wild Boar Restaurant, in Nashville, Tennessee. A wine list that fills a hundred pages and includes three thousand selections, with a total inventory of 15,000 bottles. Eighteen-karat gold table settings. And a $2 million art collection. Oh, and good food, too. Call 615-329-1313.

"The Eskimos have 52 words for snow because it is so special to them; there ought to be as many for love!"
—Margaret Atwood

Lawyers in Love

985 Romance tips for business executives:

- For lawyers in love: Treat your guy or gal like an equal partner in the "firm" of your relationship.
- For salesmen in love: Treat her better than your best customer.
- For VPs in love: Prepare a "Relationship Annual Report" for your mate.
- For advertising execs in love: Create an ad campaign that expresses your love.
- For stockbrokers in love: If there were a "Dow Jones Romance Average," how well are your "relationship stocks" doing?
- For PR execs in love: Create a love-related "PR stunt" for your partner.
- For managers in love: Are you managing your relationship as well as you're managing your career?
- For regional managers: If your partner were in charge of giving bonuses for your "performance" at home, how big would this quarter's bonus be?
- For Junior VPs: Are you practicing your relationship skills as diligently as you're practicing your golf skills?
- For CPAs in love: Conduct a cost-benefit analysis of love in your life.
- For engineers in love: Increase your expression of affection by twenty-three percent.

Chapter Theme Song:
"Lawyers in Love," Jackson Browne

Your career may keep you away from one another for most of the day, but make the time you do have together count.

- For job hunters: Create a Relationship Resume that lists your qualifications.
- For company presidents: Are you providing adequate leadership and inspiration at home?

MBAs in Love

986 More romance tips for business executives:

- For CEOs in love: Are you keeping your most important "shareholder" happy?
- For Big Shot Board Members: Are your daily activities in sync with your "Mission Statement"?
- For CFOs in love: Review your emotional "investment" in your partner.
- For marketing managers: Identify and meet the Strategic Objectives of your relationship.
- For supervisors in love: Delegate more—and get home earlier.
- For manufacturing execs: Do you have your suppliers of romantic gifts lined up?
- For bankers in love: You don't give cheap toasters to your most important customers, do you? *Well?*
- For sales managers in love: Focus 10 percent more effort on your most important customer—and watch your "bonus" increase proportionally.

Chapter Theme Song:
"Back in Business,"
AC/DC

- For computer programmers: Work the "bugs" out of your relationship.
- For quality assurance execs: Ensure the level of "quality time" spent at home.
- For human resources managers in love: Administer to yourself and your mate one of your corporate "Personality Profiles." Then use the results to improve your relationship.
- For entrepreneurs in love: You're creating something new and valuable. Go for it!

For workaholics in all fields: It's a cliché, but it's true: No one, on his deathbed, ever said, "I wish I'd spent more time working."

Hearts (#'s 1-75)

987

1. Make a heart-shaped pizza.
2. Your initials in a heart—in skywriting.
3. Cut the kitchen sponges into heart shapes.
4. While out at a formal dinner, nonchalantly draw a heart on the back of his hand with a pen.
5. Have a heart-shaped pool built.
6. Your initials in a heart—on wet cement in a sidewalk.
7. Trace a heart shape in fogged-up windows.
8. Your initials in a twenty-foot heart in the snow.
9. A quilt with a heart motif.

10. Your initials in a heart—etched on a brick in your patio.
11. Place the pepperoni in the shape of a heart on the pizza.
12. Trace a fifty-foot heart in the sand on a beach.
13. Grill burgers in the shape of a heart.
14. Heart-shaped sandwiches.
15. For math nuts: r = a (1-cosA).
16. Use heart-shaped stickers.
17. Band-Aids with heart designs.
18. Trace a thirty-foot heart on the ice when ice skating.
19. Heart-shaped place mats.
20. A silk tie with hearts on it.
21. A heart-shaped chunk of cheese.
22. A mug with hearts on it.
23. A heart-shaped mug.
24. A heart-shaped door mat.
25. Socks with heart designs on them.
26. Heart-shaped doilies.
27. Heart-shaped eyeglasses.
28. A front-yard flag with hearts on it.
29. Poke holes in a heart-shape in the crust of a freshly baked pie.
30. Make heart-shaped chocolate chip cookies.
31. Heart-shaped confetti.
32. The classic heart-shaped box of chocolates.
33. Heart—shaped chocolate treats.
34. Carve a heart—with your initials in it—in a tree.
35. Get a heart-shaped tattoo with her initials in it.
36. Greeting cards with heart.
37. Fold the dinner napkins into heart shapes.
38. Silk boxer shorts with a heart motif.
39. Draw hearts on the bathroom mirror with lipstick.

Chapter
Theme Song:
"In a Heartbeat,"
Deena Carter

40. Use only Love Stamps with heart shapes on them.
41. Find a wine with a heart motif on the label.
42. Heart-shaped rubber stamps.
43. Heart-shaped cakes.
44. Heart designs in icing on a cake.
45. Heart-shaped candles.
46. Heart-shaped appetizers.
47. Heart-shaped picture frames.
48. Heart-shaped wreaths.
49. Heart-shaped ice cubes.
50. A heart-shaped rug.
51. Find a heart-shaped Jell-O mold.
52. Cut banana slices into heart shapes and put them in Jell-O.
53. Shape pancakes into heart shapes.
54. Cut toast into heart shapes.
55. Cut a heart shape out of toast and fry an egg in the center.
56. Heart-shaped Rice Krispies Treats.
57. Slice strawberries into heart-shapes.
58. A heart-shaped pendant.
59. A heart-shaped pin.
60. Heart-shaped earrings.
61. Heart-shaped pasta.
62. Heart-shaped red balloons.
63. Heart-shaped cookie cutters.
64. Heart-shaped key rings.
65. Heart-shaped candy conversation hearts.
66. Cut the lawn into the shape of a giant heart.
67. Make a heart-shaped kite together.
68. Get a humongous heart-shaped box of Valentine candy.
69. Heart-shaped shrubbery/topiary.
70. A big, heart-shaped ice sculpture.

71. Send an envelope filled with heart-shaped glitter.
72. While tanning, place a small, heart-shaped piece of cardboard on your body.
73. Cut a piece of paper into a heart shape, then write a love letter on it.
74. Scrape the ice off his windshield—in the shape of a heart.
75. Heart-shaped beds (in the Poconos).

Do you remember how to make perfectly symmetrical hearts from grade school? (You fold the paper in half, then draw half a heart against the folded edge. Then cut it out and voilà!)

In My Humble Opinion

988 In my humble opinion, relationships start to go bad at the point when couples stop being romantic. Most couples allow their A+ Relationships to slide into mediocre C-Relationships.

How do you regain your A+ status? By taking creative action based on this wise observation:

"Sometimes progress is going back to where you first went wrong."—C.S. Lewis

> "One word frees us of all the weight and pain of life. That word is love."
> —Sophocles

989 In my humble opinion, every couple should, at some time in their life together: Go skinny-dipping. Take a moonlit stroll on a beach in the Caribbean. Sing silly love songs to one another. Get giddy on champagne. Stay up all night talking and making love and talking and making love and eating and making love and watching old movies and making love and making love. Ride in a Tunnel of Love. Go gambling in Las Vegas. See your favorite singer live in concert. Make a baby. Watch falling stars.

990 In my humble opinion, half of all love advice is erroneous at best, and harmful at worst; three-quarters of all relationship books are simplistic formulas dressed up in psychobabble to impress you.

I am a very positive, optimistic person, *but*—I'm very wary of big promises and simple answers. I don't believe you can turn a D- Relationship into an A+. (People just

> Love without action is not love. At best it is a wish; at worst an imposter.

don't work that way.) You *can* turn a C- into a B+. You an turn a B- into a solid A. And that's *good enough*, don't you think?

My Personal Favorites

991 *The Perpetual Bouquet.* You give your lover one flower a day, placing it in a small vase. Every day you bring one different kind of flower. In a week you'll have a complete bouquet. Keep doing this for three months—every day you remove one wilted flower and replace it with a new one. Your lover will have an ever-changing, always fresh reminder of your love and support for him or her.

992 One of my rituals with Karyn is a changing-of-the-seasons ceremony which uses framed covers from *New Yorker* magazines. We have

My personal favorites...
Song: "I Won't Last a Day Without You," by Paul Williams
Rock group: The Moody Blues
Book: *Stranger in a Strange Land,* by Robert A. Heinlein
Story: "The Artist of the Beautiful," by Nathaniel Hawthorne
TV show: *Babylon 5*
Bed & breakfast: The Victorian Inn, Martha's Vineyard. 508-627-4784, www.thevic.com.
Comic Strip: Calvin and Hobbes
Quote: *"We are each of us angels with only one wing. And we can only fly embracing each other."*—Luciano de Crescenzo
Woman: Karyn Lynn Godek

several covers for each season that hang in our living room. (FYI, we celebrate *five* seasons.)

At the start of each season we go through this little ritual: We set the mood with seasonal music; we fill two brandy snifters with Baileys Irish Cream for the seasonal toast; we bring out the ritual screwdrivers; we open each frame and slide in the new magazine cover; we rehang each frame; then sit back, toast one another, reminisce about the past season, and look forward to the coming season.

Here are our current seasonal musical selections:

- Winter: *Antarctica* by Vangelis
- Spring: *A Winter's Solstice*, a Windham Hill collection
- Summer: *The Sacred Fire* by Nicholas Gunn
- Autumn: *Autumn* by George Winston
- Christmas: *A Charlie Brown Christmas*, by The Vince Guaraldi Trio

Sometimes, depending on our mood, we'll play the appropriate selection from Antonio Vivaldi's *The Four Seasons*.

Best of the Best

993 Best romantic gift: the gift of time

Best romantic present: your own presence

Best romantic car: Triumph Spitfire

Most romantic comic strip: Rose Is Rose

Best romantic TV show ever: *Mad About You*

Most romantic city (in the world): Verona, Italy

Most romantic city (in the USA): San Francisco, California

Best romantic color: Red/PMS #1795 CVU

Most romantic Broadway musical: *Phantom of the Opera*

Best romantic movie: *Casablanca*

Best romantic actress: Greta Garbo

Best romantic actor: Clark Gable

Best romantic hotel: The Grand Hotel, Mackinac Island

Best romantic voice (male): Barry White

Best romantic voice (female): Sade

Best romantic song: "You are So Beautiful (To Me)," by Joe Cocker

Do you agree? Disagree? Voice your opinion at www.1001waystobe romantic.com

Best Brief Advice

994 Gals: You want more *romance*? Give him more *sex*. (Try having sex every night—night after night after night after night—until he *begs* you to stop! Just try it as a little experiment. It just might transform your ho-hum relationship into a raging love affair!)

> No, I'm not joking.

995 Guys: You want more *sex*? Give her more *romance*. (Romance her like Don Juan. Like Romeo. Like Clark Gable. Romance her every day in every way. Romance her using every single idea in this book—and then think up one thousand and one *more* ways to be romantic. And she'll give you all the sex you could ever dream of.)

> Yo, guys, this ain't rocket science!

996 Best way to create more time in your life: Shoot your TV.

997 Use gifts and presents to express love and appreciation. Don't use them to apologize after a fight or make up for some dumb thing you've done. This strategy eventually backfires.

> "Love does not die easily. It is a living thing. It thrives in the face of all life's hazards, save one-neglect."
> —James D. Bryden

998
• The unasked-for gift is most appreciated.
• The surprise gift is most cherished.

Top 10 Reasons to Be Romantic

999a 1. You'll be happier.
2. Your *partner* will be happier.
3. You'll have sex more often.
4. You'll *enjoy* sex more.
5. You'll rise above mediocrity, and create an A+ Relationship.
6. You'll experience the spark of infatuation again.
7. You'll reduce the chance that your partner might cheat on you.
8. You'll increase the probability that you'll stay married.
9. You'll add depth and meaning to your relationship.
10. You will create a safe haven where you can really be yourself.

> You may want to make a scroll of these reasons and present it to your partner.

999b And a few *more* reasons to be romantic:
11. You will be truly heard and deeply understood by one other human being.
12. You'll save money by expressing your love in lots of little, creative ways.
13. Exercising your creativity will benefit you in *other* areas of your life.
14. You'll probably live longer.
15. You'll be better parents.
16. You'll be great role models for your children.
17. You'll be great role models for friends and neighbors.
18. Your children will understand love better than most kids.

> "In dreams and in love there are no impossibilities."
> —Janos Arany

19. Your children will experience what love is really all about.
20. Your children will have a better chance of choosing partners wisely.

Top 45 Reasons to Be Romantic

999c And still *more* reasons to be romantic:

24. You'll come to appreciate your partner's uniqueness.
25. You'll reduce or eliminate therapy bills!
26. You'll get more of what you want out of life.
27. You'll strengthen your self-esteem and self-confidence.
28. You'll never have to write to Annie's Mailbox for love advice.
29. You'll be better able to live your faith (love is central to every religion).
30. You will have the quiet confidence that you've achieved something that few people accomplish.
31. You'll create a truly mature relationship.
32. You'll move beyond treating your partner like a stereotype.
33. You'll have more energy and focus for your career.
34. You'll surprise your skeptical in-laws!
35. You'll deepen your understanding of the opposite sex.
36. You'll reconnect with your creative, impulsive, spontaneous, childlike nature.
37. You'll live up to your true potential in life.
38. You'll never again be panic-stricken on Valen-

Remember: These 45 reasons are only the tip of the iceberg!

tine's Day!

39. You'll never again have to feel guilty for having forgotten a birthday or anniversary.
40. You'll stay young at heart.
41. You'll keep the world spinning. (Love makes the world go 'round.)
42. You'll keep your love alive.
43. Your partner *wants* you to be romantic. What more reason do you need?
44. Why *not??*

#45: Life is simply too short not to be romantic!

The End

1000 Once upon a time...*they lived happily ever after.* The perfect ending to any story, wouldn't you say?

Your story—your personal story, the love story that the two of you are creating together—is somewhere in its middle chapters, I would guess. So how's it going? Is it turning out as you expected? If so, *marvelous!* If not, wrap up the current chapter of your story and create a *new* chapter. An exciting chapter. A fulfilling chapter. A *romantic* chapter.

Imagine that your life is a novel, and you and your lover are its co-authors. You have great artistic license to create a *love* story out of your *life* story. And if you need help in creating some romantic

Chapter Theme Song:
"The End,"
The Beatles
(T.L.Y.T.I.E.
T.T.L.Y.M.)

scenes, please use *1001 Ways To Be Romantic* as a resource. Take these ideas, give them a creative twist and the benefit of your unique personality, and they will truly become *your own*.

> "Love at first sight is easy to understand; it's when two people have been looking at each other for a lifetime that it becomes a miracle."
> —Amy Bloom

The Beginning

1001 In the beginning was the Word. And the word was Love.

Love. It is the single most important word in any language. It is the *defining* experience of what it means to be human. It is virtually the *first* (most welcoming!) word we hear when we are born; it is usually the *last* (most comforting) word we hear before we die; and it is the word we are obsessed with during every year in between.

Even though time passes and every couple creates a history together, love must still be re-created every day. If your yesterdays were great, they help make today even better. If your yesterdays weren't so hot, they help motivate you to make today *different*.

Yes, you *can* turn a C- Relationship into an A+ Relationship. I've helped many couples achieve this goal. *1001 Ways To Be Romantic* can help *you* achieve that goal,

> When it comes to love, the secret is that there is no secret. Simply express love. There are *at least* 1001 ways to do it.

too. This isn't the end—it's just the *beginning* of your life as a happier, more loving, and more loved person.

Love must be made real, brought alive in the world through action, thoughts, and deeds. In a word, *romance*.

"Romance is the fuel that keeps love burning hot."

—Rusty Silvey

Index

50/50 *vs.* 100/100 relationships, 123

A

A+ relationships
balancing thought and action, 139
characteristics of, 14, 164, 174, 261
creating, 132–134
defined, 133
focus of, 134
goals of, 214
learn from, 374–375
recipe for, 376–377
as resources, 195
secrets of, 5, 72
ABC's of romance, 405–408
Above and beyond the call of duty, 5, 6, 41
Acceptance, 38, 58
Acorn Principle, The, 58, 137
Acronyms for romance, 143–144
Actions *vs.* thoughts, 139–141
Adult play, romance as, 100, 314, 424–425
Advertisements, 155, 208
Always, always, always, 70–71
Anniversaries
celebrating, 29, 36, 267, 272, 293
gift list, 360–361
remembering, 44, 80
Anticipating needs, 34
Aphrodisiacs, 24, 250, 321–322, 323
Apologies, 139, 439
Astrology, 113, 181, 290, 336, 400
Attitude adjustment, 368–369
Awareness, raising, 366–367

B

Balancing needs, 297
Balloons, 76, 84, 160
Balloons, hot air, 197
Banners, 8
Bartering, 43
Basics for romantics, 48–49, 361–362
Be prepared, 68–69, 382
Be yourself, 55, 59, 187, 327, 440
Bed and Breakfasts, 92–93, 414–415
Bedrooms, 59–60
Best
of the best, 438
brief advice, 439
date movies, 235–236
kisses in movies and songs, 45–46
love songs, Broadway, 232
love songs, duets, 230–231
love songs of 21st century, 220–223
romantic comedies, 234
romantic couples, 233
romantic movies, 233
song list Greg ever created, 409
Big things to do, 8
Birthdays
cards, 4, 6, 255
cartoon characters, 4, 6, 255
celebrating, 273
gifts, 37
remembering, 43
themes, 253–255
Birthstones, 26–27
Body language, 34
Book lovers, romancing, 344–345
Books, ideas for, 288, 420
Books, lists of recommended, 382, 412–413
Boudoir photography, 387–388
Brainstorming ideas, 362–365
Bridges to understanding, 175–176
Bubble baths, 6, 303, 418–420
Budget friendly ideas, 12, 256, 302, 426–427
Business cards and romance, 341
Business executives, tips for, 429–431
Business of romance, 188–189

C

Candles, 7, 59, 150, 254, 271, 293, 358, 362, 415
Cards, greeting, 6, 8, 76, 124, 182, 188, 255, 276, 296, 313, 343, 363
Carpe diem (seize the day), 314
Cars, ideas for, 283, 369–370, 371
Cash as a gift, 119
CDs (compact discs), 9, 33, 242–243, 415
Celebrations, twists on, 32, 160–161, 340
Champagne, 29
Checklists, romantic, 97–98, 361–362
Chemistry, 14
Child-Sharing Program, 129
Childlike activities, 38, 153–154, 294, 397–398
Children and romance, 340, 347–349
Chocolate, 24–25, 184–185
Choreographing lovemaking, 306–307
Christmas, 269–270
Classic romance, 324, 326–327

Classics and romance, 420
Classy romance, 327–328
Comic strips
  creative uses of, 62, 154
  gift ideas, 238
  parenthood, 129
  pet names, 372
  romantic efforts, 87, 121, 284
  romantically impaired, 3, 16, 139, 147, 273, 342
Commitment, 1, 248–249, 374–375
Common sense in relationships, 137–138
Communication
  importance of, 14, 71, 100, 111
  listening in, 15, 42, 401, 402
  styles, 58, 170–172
  See also Expressing feelings
Concepts for romance, 148, 246–249, 297
Cookies, candies, cakes, 152–153
Cool (unusual) stuff, 155–156, 296
Couple-Thinking, 315
Couple's Day, 164
Coupons
  ABC's of romance, 408
  bookstore, 382
  custom-made, 421
  ideas, 411–412
  lingerie, 31, 90
  love, 83, 349
  musical, 63
  romantic surprise, 82
Creativity
  exercises, 278–280
  increasing, 67–68, 256, 307–308
Cruises, 309, 358–359

D

Dates, important, 188–189
Dating, 261
Deciding to love, 41

Dependence, types of, 214
Diamonds, 13, 26, 191, 289, 336, 427
Differences, dealing with, 99–101, 175
Dining
  in, 4, 31, 60, 285
  out, 13, 61, 286
Do-it-yourself romantic activities, 34, 298
Do's and Don'ts, 37–43, 417–418
Dummies, romance for, 17–18, 19, 39, 201, 239–240, 240

E

E-mail, romancing, 312–313
Electronics and media, 75, 149, 241, 439
Engagement, ideas for, 289–291
Equitable vs. loving relationships, 123
Erotic Fantasy Jar, 250
Erotica, 130–131, 250–252
Escapes, 69, 357–359
  See also Getaways; Vacations; Weekends
Evaluating relationships, 265
Even-Day/Odd-Day Romance, 19
Everyday events, 57
Excuses, lame, 104–107
Expectations, unrealistic, 39
Expensive ideas, 13, 256, 336, 427–428
Expressing feelings and being yourself, 59
  importance of, 100
  modes of, 57–58
  quoting others, 391–392
  by touch, 392
  using poetry, prose, songs, 391–392
  variety in, 71

F

Favorites/preferences, knowing, 178–179, 210–213

Feng shui, 297
Flexibility, 315
Flirting, 56, 111
Flowers
  choosing, 37, 342
  giving, 5, 9, 23–24, 77–78, 109, 301, 331–332
  and notes, 5, 77–78
  standing orders, 19
Food for romance, 319–320, 323
Freshman lessons, 55
Fun, romantic, 70, 100
Fundamentals of romance, 48–49, 361–362
Funny ideas, 154–155, 189–190, 295

G

Games, romantic, 11, 85–86, 164–165, 407
Gardening, 157
Gender
  bigot, 32
  differences/similarities, 58, 170–176, 186
  differences vs. personality, 174
  metaphors, 249
  stereotyping, 1, 14, 40, 134, 140, 168–170, 386–387
Generating ideas, 362–365
Generic romance, 4, 5, 56
Gestures, romantic
  creating, 10–11, 51
  for lovemaking, 183–184
  purpose of, 186
  themes in, 90–91, 96
Getaways, 125, 339
Getting to know you, 178–179, 304–305, 400–401, 413
  See also Understanding, increasing
Gift & Card Drawer, 423
Gift certificates, 120
Gift closet, 68, 201
Gift Day, 113
Gift-of-the-Month Clubs, 148

Gifts
  creative, 9, 10
  custom-made, 299
  do-it-yourself, 276
  expensive, 144–145, 256
  giving for dummies, 239
  hiding, 277–278
  ideas, 410
  kinds of, 73–74
  little things, 391
  money as, 256
  one-of-a-kind, 275
  planning ahead for, 39
  presentation of, 31–33
  purposes of, 95, 439
  shop ahead for, 68
  shopping for, 201–203
  themes and ideas, 90–91,
    96, 237–238
  of time, 263–264
  vs. presents, 94–95, 237
  wrapping, 19, 31, 240
Give-and-take approach, 367
Giving 100 percent, 123
Going out of your way, 5, 6,
  41
Golden Rule, 138
Golden Rules of Romance,
  118–119
Gospel According to Godek,
  The, 186–189
Grading your relationship, 5
Gratification, instant, 112
Greeting cards, 6, 124, 182,
  188, 276, 296, 313, 343,
  363
Greg
  about, 445–446
  best song list created by, 409
  gospel according to, 186–189
  humble opinions of, 435–436
  and Karyn, what they do,
    333–334, 351
  personal favorites of,
    436–437
Guidelines for love, 417–418

H

Habits, romantic, 381

Hands, kissing of, 6
Hanukkah, 271
Hearts, ideas with, 431–434
Help!, 19, 80–82, 147–148
Hide-and-seek, 277–278
Hiking, 157
His and hers, 215–216
Holding hands, 146
Home, ideas for, 150
Honesty, 1
Honeymoons, second, 281
How to use this book, 442–443
How vs. why, 14
How you do it vs. what you do,
  31–33
Humor, 313

I

I love you, ways to say, 52,
  64–67
Ideas jar, romantic, 67
Important vs. urgent, 246
Inexpensive ideas, 12, 256,
  302, 426–427
Infatuation, 4, 14
Initials for romance, 143–144
Inner child, 153–154, 397–398
Inspirational readings, 335
Interests/orientations, 177
Intimacy, 110, 248–249

J

Jewelry, 26–27, 33, 238, 336
Journals, 208, 307, 364
Junior lessons, 57–58

K

Kid-like activities, 38, 153–154,
  294, 397–398
Kisses, 6, 45–46, 122, 398–399

L

Lame Excuses, 104–107
Left-brained, 16–17
Lessons, 14, 55–59
Licenses and romance,
  369–370
LifeChart, 334
Lingerie, 30–31, 89, 90,

130, 131, 410
Listening, 15, 42, 401, 402
Little things, 7, 124
Long-term, thinking, 110
Love
  coupons (See Coupons)
  do's and don'ts, 417–418
  ingredients for, 248–249
  is . . ., 316–318
  letters, 20, 47, 62, 109
  as a process, 49
  romance and, 1–2, 186
  songs and matching movies, 9
  stories, 90–91, 372–374
  vs. romance, 1–2
  the word, 443–444
Love and live, 15, 168, 263,
  282, 362, 369, 410
Lovemaking
  do's and don'ts, 37–38, 310
  improving, 74–75, 200–201,
    250–252
  music for, 306–307
  signals for, 183–184
Loving vs. equitable relationships, 123

M

Mail, romance by, 142–143,
  311–312
Maintenance of relationship,
  148–149
Marching bands, 8
Marrieds, suggestions for,
  111–112, 267–269, 291–292,
  292–293, 369
Martyrdom, 37, 119, 297
Massages, 404, 421
Mathematics and romance,
  123–125
Meanings of names, 396–397
Media and electronics, 149
Mementos, 44
Memories, 99, 358
Memories Box, 44
Memorization musts,
  210–213
Men
  help for, 383–384,

386–387
only for, 108
romantic style and, 21
and women, similarities/differences, 58, 170–176, 186
Messages and romance, 402–403
See also Notes
Metaphors, feminine/masculine, 249
Mˆbius strip, 9–10
Money as gifts, 256
Month of Romance suggestions, 113–118
Most important lessons, 14
Motivating for romance, 365–368
Movie fans, romancing, 355
Movies, 234–236, 354
Music
classical, 101–102, 325
for lovemaking, 306–307
for romantic activities, 415–416
Music fans, romancing, 103
Myths, 168–170

N

Names and romance, 394–397
Naughty ideas, 198–201, 261–262
Negotiation and compromise, 38
Never, never, never, 72
Newspapers, 37
Nice approach, 366
Nonverbal clues, 34
Notes
flowers and, 5, 77–78
funny, 189
love, 7, 9, 52–54, 62–64, 76–77
musical, 103
Numbers and romance, 125–126, 287

O

Obligatory romantic gestures,

6, 55, 343
Oldies but goodies, 352–354
Opportunities, tuning into, 176–179
Opposites, balancing, 99–101
Orientations/interests, 177
Outrageous ideas, 162, 166, 196–198, 356

P

Parenthood, 129
Passion, 14, 163, 248–249
People, kinds of, 216–219, 409
Perfection, 39, 133, 186
Perfume, 27–28
Personal love stories, 90–91
Personality *vs.* gender differences, 174
Pet lovers, romancing, 87–89
Pet names, 395
Photographs, 328–330
Pings, 265
Platinum Rule, 138
Play, ideas for adult, 424–425
Poetry
classic, 204–207
mathematical, 124
presentation of, 11, 12, 76
writing, 47
Postage stamps, 64, 142, 311
Postmarks, 311
Practical jokes, 178
Preparation, 68–69
Prescriptions for romance, 79
Presents *vs.* gifts, 94–95, 237
Presley, Elvis, 102
Principles of love and romance, 186–188
Priorities, 48–49, 119, 151
Proposals, marriage, 289–291
Psychological approach, 366
Public displays of affection (PDA's), 127, 259
Purpose of human beings, 2
Puzzles, 156

Q

Questions to ask, 178–197, 304–305, 400–401, 413
Quests and romance, 398–399
Quotations for romance
ancient, 209–210
characteristics of love, 13, 14, 78, 168, 331, 373, 381, 439, 440
creativity, 276
gender and differences, 22, 175, 384
giving, 240
how to love, 19, 43, 91, 119, 130, 143, 182, 183, 207, 295, 324, 418, 439
kissing, 122, 149, 163
love, the word, 428, 438
love defining who you are, 325, 352, 425
love is, 13, 58, 76, 100, 137, 209, 210, 238, 250, 258, 277, 317–318, 328, 330
marriage, 43, 48, 112, 268, 292, 347, 391, 443
play, 424, 425
romance, 369, 444, 445
time, 263, 352
understanding, 413

R

Radio and romance, 242–243
Rain, ideas for, 122–123
Reasons to be romantic, top, 440–442
Reassurance, 402
Recipe for A+ Relationship, 376–377
Recipes for romance, 319–320, 323
Relationship
concepts, 246
entropy, 247
grading your, 5
Report Card, 135–136
secrets, 7

Remembering important things, 17, 43–44
Reminders, romantic, 34
Repeat, renew, redo, 51
Required romantic gestures, 6, 55, 348
Resources for romance, 80, 190–195, 244–245, 274, 309
Responding with love, 401
Right-brained, 17–18
Rituals of romance, 349–351
Romance
    adult play as, 100, 314, 424–425
    basics of, 361–362
    budget, 12, 256, 302, 426–427
    business of, 188–189
    classic, 4, 324, 326–327
    classy, 327–328
    defined, 55, 100, 314, 316, 393
    for Dummies, 19
    expensive, 13, 256, 336, 427–428
    generic, 4, 5, 56
    little things and, 55
    love and, 1–2, 186
    need for, 392–393
    obligatory vs. optional, 55
    occasional vs. overtime, 248
    purpose of, 2
    quests and, 398–399
    regimen, 381
    resources for, 80
    sex vs., 393
    for Smarties, 20
    as a state of mind/being, 55
    styles of, 21–22
    timing in, 56
    tips for business executives, 429–431
    tips for non-romantics (left-brained), 17–18
    weird and wacky, 86–87
Romance Credit Card, 257
Romantic
    do's and don'ts, 37–43,

    41–43
    top reasons to be, 440–442
Romantics
    characteristics of, 120, 163, 313–315, 388–389
    characteristics of crazy, 390
    defined, 163
    happiness and, 14
Roses, 5, 23, 342
Rules to be broken, 119–120
Ruts, getting out of, 31, 305–306

S
Sacrifices, 37
Science fiction fans, romancing, 337–338
Scrolls, 76, 207, 254, 299
Seduction, 112
Senior lessons, 58–59
Sensuality, 388, 421–422
Sex and sexuality
    books about, 346
    gender differences in, 58
    naughty ideas, 198–201
    tips for gals, 425
    tips for guys, 426
    ways to improve, 74–75, 158, 163, 250–252, 332–333, 439
    for women, 387–388
Sex vs. romance
Sexism and romance, 32
Shakespeare, William, 204–205, 391
Shopping, 19, 69, 108, 201–203
Singles, suggestions for, 110–111, 265–266
Songs, lists of love
    best of 21st century, 220–223
    Broadway's, 232
    duets, 230–231
    to express yourself, 224–229
Songsmith, The, 76, 274
Sophomore lessons, 56
Spirituality, 334–335
Spontaneity, 69, 84, 118, 120, 260, 368

Sports fans, romancing, 109, 284
Stalemate, romantic, 247
Stamps, postage, 64, 142, 311
Stars and moon themes, 180–181, 336–337
Stereotyping, 1, 14, 40, 134, 140, 168–170, 386–387
Stories, love, 90–91, 372–374
Styles of romance, 21, 22
Super Bowl and romance, 108
Supporting your partner, 41
Surprises, romantic, 82, 159, 300
Sweets, 152–153

T
Telephones, 72, 141, 149
Television and romance, 75, 241, 439
Ten commandments for loving couples, 15
Ten Reasons I Love You, 117
Theme gifts, 9
Thesaurus, 308
Thinking as a couple, 315
Thinking long term, 109
Thinking of you, 304
Thoughts vs. actions, 139–141
Time and effort, 118
Time and romance, 50, 263–264, 297
Timing in romance, 56
To Do lists, 34
Togetherness, 213–214
Tokens of love, 78, 156
Touching, 376, 421–422
Trading places, 128
Travel tips, 12, 83–85, 281–282, 359, 377–380
Triad, romantic, 248–249
Trinkets, 86, 213, 423
Trip Survival kit, 84
True romantics, characteristics of, 17–18
Tuning in to opportunities, 176–179

Tuxedos, 108, 130, 327
Two's for couples, 215–216

U

Understanding, increasing
ideas for, 70, 128, 138,
175–176, 400, 412–413
questions for, 304–305,
400–401, 413
See also Getting to know you
Urgent *vs.* important, 246

V

Vacations
in America, 377–378
around the world, 379–380
baths, 303
chocolates, 184–185
escapes, 357–359
exotic, 131–132
second honeymoons,
281–282
spiritual, 334–335
themes, 146, 337–338
timing of, 37
ultimate, 336, 358–359
Valentines Day, 44, 81, 121,
181–182, 342–344, 386

W

Walks, 146
Walls, ideas for, 167–168
Wedding Day, 35
Weddings, 36, 51, 267–268,
292
Weekends, ideas for, 37, 125,
339–340
Weird and wacky romance,
86–87
What you do *vs.* how you do it,
31–33
Why *vs.* how, 14
Women, help for, 109,
384–385, 387–388
Women, suggestions for, 109
Women and romantic style,
22
Women only, 109
Work, ideas for, 151,

189–190, 423
Writing your own, 207–208,
307, 308

Y

Yin and Yang, 99–101
You can/you cannot, 187

Z

Zen Shopping, 202

About the Author

Gregory J.P. Godek is an author and researcher, speaker and performer, husband and father. He was romantic by inclination long before it became an avocation, then preoccupation—and finally—occupation. Greg has been teaching his acclaimed Romance Classes for twenty years.

This book was written at the request of thousands of romantically starved women and romantically impaired men. This book *works*. It's not a deep, theoretical book, and it's not another cute "love" book. It's a practical, inspirational (and occasionally humorous) book.

> "Romantic love. Anything else is a compromise."
> —Gregory Godek

Greg burst upon the national scene with *1001 Ways To Be Romantic* in 1991 and became a national celebrity as his book became an instant classic. No one had ever before combined such a huge number of practical tips with just the right amount of psychology. Greg has since taught romance on Oprah; counseled troubled couples on Donahue; shared tips on Montel; and launched the biggest book signing tour in the history of publishing by unveiling his custom-designed romance bus on *Good Morning America*.

1001 Ways To Be Romantic is a year-round bestseller with more than 1.5 million copies in print; it led to twelve additional books and a CD collection of romantic classical music; and it has been referenced by Jay Leno in his *Tonight Show* monologue. Greg has taught romance to the U.S. Army, to corporate groups, and to audiences around the world. Greg is a teacher and role model, not a therapist or theorist. He does not have a pet theory that he insists you accept. He is highly conscious of the diversity of human experience, of the infinite variability of human personality, of the uniqueness of every individual. Greg believes that romance is about expressing love in thousands of ways that reflect your creativity and your partner's specialness.

Greg has been working on this edition for *years*. Hundreds of new ideas and hundreds of his personal notes are included in this completely revised edition of *1001 Ways To Be Romantic*.

"Godek...is helping transform men and women into modern Romeos and Juliets."
—UPI